Policy Implementation
and PL 99-457

CO-TEACH PRESCHOOL
SCHOOL OF EDUCATION
UNIVERSITY OF MONTANA
MISSOULA, MT 59812

Policy Implementation and PL 99-457

Planning for Young Children with Special Needs

edited by

James J. Gallagher, Ph.D.
Director
Carolina Policy Studies Program
Frank Porter Graham Child Development Center
University of North Carolina at Chapel Hill

Pascal L. Trohanis, Ph.D.
Director
National Early Childhood
Technical Assistance System (NEC*TAS)
Frank Porter Graham Child Development Center
University of North Carolina at Chapel Hill

and

Richard M. Clifford, Ph.D.
Associate Director
Carolina Institute for Child and Family Policy
Frank Porter Graham Child Development Center
University of North Carolina at Chapel Hill

Baltimore • London • Toronto • Sydney

Paul H. Brookes Publishing Co.
P.O. Box 10624
Baltimore, Maryland 21285-0624

Copyright © 1989 by Paul H. Brookes Publishing Co., Inc.
All rights reserved.

Typeset by Brushwood Graphics, Inc., Baltimore, Maryland.
Manufactured in the United States of America by
Thomson-Shore, Inc., Dexter, Michigan.

Library of Congress Cataloging-in-Publication Data
Gallagher, James John, 1926–
  Policy implementation and PL 99-457.

  Bibliography: p.
  Includes index.
  1. Education, Preschool—Law and legislation—United States.
2. Handicapped children—Education—Law and legislation—
United States. 3. Special education—Law and legislation—
United States. 4. Handicapped children—Education (Pre-
school)—United States. 5. Special education—United States.
I. Trohanis, Pascal Louis. II. Clifford, Richard M. III. Title.
KF4197.G35 1989   344.73'0791   88-30324
ISBN 1-55766-013-1   347.304791

Contents

Contributors vii
Preface ix

CHAPTER 1   An Introduction to PL 99-457 and The National Policy Agenda for Serving Young Children with Special Needs and Their Families
       Pascal L. Trohanis 1

CHAPTER 2   Lessons from Implementing PL 94-142
       Edwin W. Martin 19

CHAPTER 3   Implementing The State of The Art and Integration Mandates of PL 94-142
       Margaret C. Wang 33

CHAPTER 4   Strengthening Families of Young Children with Handicapping Conditions: Mapping Backward from The "Street Level"
       Paul R. Dokecki and Craig Anne Heflinger 59

CHAPTER 5   A Parent's Perspective: Implementing PL 99-457
       Martha Ziegler 85

CHAPTER 6   Issues and Directions in Preparing Professionals to Work with Young Handicapped Children and Their Families
       Donald B. Bailey, Jr. 97

CHAPTER 7   Implications of PL 99-457 for Preparation of Preschool Personnel
       Oliver Leon Hurley 133

CHAPTER 8   Leadership and Policy Strategies for Interagency Planning: Meeting The Early Childhood Mandate
       Brian A. McNulty 147

CHAPTER 9   Financing Programs for Young Children with Handicaps
       Harriette B. Fox, Steve A. Freedman, and Brian R. Klepper 169

CHAPTER 10   The Use of Outcome Measures in
             Implementing Policies for Handicapped
             Children
             Duncan MacRae, Jr. 183
CHAPTER 11   The Implementation of Social Policy: A Policy
             Analysis Challenge
             James J. Gallagher 199

Index 217

CONTRIBUTORS

Donald B. Bailey, Jr., Ph.D.
Director of Early Childhood Research
Frank Porter Graham Child Development Center
CB No. 8180
Highway 54, Bypass West
University of North Carolina at Chapel Hill
Chapel Hill, NC 27599

Richard M. Clifford, Ph.D.
Associate Director, Carolina Institute for Child and Family Policy
Frank Porter Graham Child Development Center
CB No. 8040, Suite 500, NCNB Plaza
University of North Carolina at Chapel Hill
Chapel Hill, NC 27599-8040

Paul R. Dokecki, Ph.D.
Professor of Psychology and Special Education
Associate Director, John F. Kennedy Center for Research on Education and Human Development
Box 6, Peabody College
Vanderbilt University
Nashville, TN 37203

Harriette B. Fox, M.S.S.
President, Fox Health Policy Consultants
1140 Connecticut Ave. N.W., Suite 1200
Washington, D.C. 20036

Steve A. Freedman, Ph.D.
Director, Institute for Child Health Policy
5700 S.W. 34th St., Suite 323
Department of Pediatrics, College of Medicine
University of Florida
Gainesville, FL 32608

James J. Gallagher, Ph.D.
William Rand Kenan, Jr. Professor of Education
Director, Carolina Policy Studies Program
Frank Porter Graham Child Development Center
CB No. 8040, Suite 300, NCNB Plaza
University of North Carolina at Chapel Hill
Chapel Hill, NC 27599-8040

Craig Anne Heflinger, M.A.
Research Assistant, John F. Kennedy Center for Research on Education and Human Development
Box 6, Peabody College
Vanderbilt University
Nashville, TN 37203

Oliver Leon Hurley, Ph.D.
Chairman, Department of Special Education
University Plaza
Georgia State University
Atlanta, GA 30303

Brian R. Klepper, Ph.D.
Assistant in Child Health Policy
Institute for Child Health Policy
5700 S.W. 34th St.
State University System of Florida
Gainesville, FL 32608

Duncan MacRae, Jr., Ph.D.
William Rand Kenan, Jr. Professor of
 Political Science and Sociology
Department of Political Science
Hamilton Hall, CB No. 3265
University of North Carolina at
 Chapel Hill
Chapel Hill, NC 27599-3265

Edwin W. Martin, Ph.D.
President and Chief Executive Officer,
 Human Resources Center
I.U. Willets Rd.
Albertson, NY 11507

Brian A. McNulty, Ph.D.
Executive Director, Special Education
 Services Unit
Colorado Department of Education
201 E. Colfax Ave.
Denver, CO 80203

Pascal L. Trohanis, Ph.D.
Associate Professor, School of
 Education
Director, National Early Childhood
 Technical Assistance System
 (NEC*TAS)
Frank Porter Graham Child Development Center
Room 500, NCNB Plaza, CB No. 8040
University of North Carolina at
 Chapel Hill
Chapel Hill, NC 27599

Margaret C. Wang
Director, Center for Research in
 Human Development and
 Education
Ritter Annex, 9th Floor
Temple University
Philadelphia, PA 19122

Martha Ziegler, M.A.
Executive Director, Federation for
 Children with Special Needs
312 Stuart St.
Boston, MA 02116

Preface

THIS VOLUME IS DESIGNED TO PRESENT MANY OF THE SIGNIFICANT ISSUES THAT HAVE come to light that will affect the implementation of an important new federal legislative initiative that focuses on meeting the needs of infants and toddlers with handicapping conditions and their families. Part H of Public Law 99-457, The Education of the Handicapped Act Amendments of 1986, concerns itself with assuring that the needs of infants and toddlers who are developmentally delayed are being met in a comprehensive, multidisciplinary, and coordinated program. In addition, some chapters of this volume discuss ways in which PL 99-457 will affect preschoolers, children ages 3 through 5.

Unlike previous legislation in which the federal government paid a share of the costs of the program that it legislated, funds are provided by the federal government only to cover the states' planning and development money to organize this program, and the states have 4 years to develop their plans to meet this broad directive of serving all eligible children, birth to 3 years of age.

Many of the papers that have become chapters in this volume were originally presented at a 3-day conference meeting in Chapel Hill, North Carolina on Policy Implementation during the spring of 1987. The Bush Foundation of St. Paul, Minnesota, provided major support for that meeting, which was cosponsored by the North Carolina Department of Public Instruction, and The School of Education and The State Technical Assistance Resource Team (START), both at the University of North Carolina at Chapel Hill.

The 11 chapters in this volume are expressive of the extraordinary range and scope of this legislation that attempts to ensure that no children with handicaps will go unattended even from birth, nor will their families be ignored. The first chapter by Pascal L. Trohanis, director of the National Early Childhood Technical Assistance System at the University of North Carolina at Chapel Hill, introduces the reader to an overall portrait of the law and the new national agenda that the law represents. The requirements that are faced by each state that will participate in this implementation are laid out.

Edwin W. Martin, former director of the Bureau for the Education of the Handicapped in the U.S. Department of Education (now the Office of Special Education Programs), reflects on the many tasks that he and his staff faced in trying to implement another major piece of legislation, Public Law 94-142, The Education for All Handicapped Children Act, 1975. An enormous effort in terms of both financial and personnel resources was committed to helping state and local educators meet the many different requirements of that law, and Martin recalls the various barriers he encountered during the implementation process. There are many lessons to be learned from that experience.

Margaret C. Wang, director of the Child Study Center at Temple University, reflects on one particular aspect of the Education for All Handicapped Children Act and that is the requirement that children with handicapping conditions be placed in the *least restrictive environment,* often popularly, and incorrectly, referred to as mainstreaming. As one who has given much time to the integration of children with handicaps into the regular classroom, she talks of the difficulties that such efforts have met and what such experiences may mean for the new legislation.

A major emphasis in the new legislation is placed on the family. The assumption in the law is that the child with a handicap cannot receive maximum benefit from a treatment program unless the family is involved in the development and execution of that program. Paul R. Dokecki and Craig Anne Heflinger discuss the applications of policies that would be designed to strengthen families. In particular, they present a strategy of beginning at the level of the individual family and working up to state and national policy (backward mapping) instead of the more customary approach of starting from abstract policy and trying then to apply it to individual families.

Martha Ziegler, who has long been an activist for the rights of individuals with handicaps, talks about what the new policy may mean, or should mean, to the parents and how they might view these new opportunities. Parents have become much more significant partners in planning and carrying out these programs, and the perspective of parents is both novel and important.

Donald B. Bailey, Jr. discusses the implications of the new law for the preparation of professionals who will play a somewhat new multidisciplinary role, in addition to focusing on their own specialties. Since eight to ten professions are anticipated to play a part in this program, requirements and standards are complex, and Bailey presents an effective set of new approaches to meet the changed requirements.

Oliver Leon Hurley also focuses on the problem of preparing professional personnel for service delivery to young children with handicaps, but his focus is on special education personnel and what changes and modifications in traditional special education training programs are going to be required in order to prepare personnel for this special challenge of working with children and with families.

As Executive Director of the Special Education Services Unit for the state of Colorado, Brian A. McNulty is faced firsthand with the problems and challenges of implementing federal policy on a state level. His insightful chapter focuses on the requirement of extensive interagency planning for the coordinated program that is expected and provides some useful suggestions on how to accomplish the tasks involved.

There is probably no more significant problem to be faced in the implementation of this legislation than how it is going to be financed. The contribution of the federal government is currently restricted to planning and development money for the states. This means that the increased service requirements must be paid for by the states from whatever combination of funds they are able to bring together. Harriette B. Fox, Steve A. Freedman, and Brian A. Klepper, as economists, outline the issues related to finance, which involve both the amount of money needed and the flow of money from these various sources.

Duncan MacRae, Jr. looks at the implementation of the law through the eyes of a policy analyst and, consequently, focuses on the need for strong outcome measures so that it will be possible to provide some answers to the question of whether or not the goals of the program are being met and to establish means by which we can determine the costs to carry out this law. Costs in this instance can mean more than the financing and involve identifying the various risks and benefits that will accompany this implementation process.

Finally, James J. Gallagher, also a policy analyst, presents a policy analytic model by which it will be possible to track the process of policy implementation for this law. In particular, he focuses on the various anticipated barriers that could interfere with the effective transformation of legislative ideas into actions. These barriers can be institutional, psychological, sociological, economic, political, or geographic, and Gallagher describes the most easily anticipated barriers and some strategies for overcoming them.

It is our hope that this collection of papers will stimulate consideration and discussion of the wide range of issues that confront practitioners and decision-makers as they try to implement this new and important piece of legislation that is aimed at bringing about a new level of high quality service for children with handicapping conditions and for their families.

Policy Implementation
and PL 99-457

An Introduction to PL 99-457 and The National Policy Agenda for Serving Young Children with Special Needs and Their Families

1

Pascal L. Trohanis

DURING HOUSE OF REPRESENTATIVES DEBATE ON THE BILL THAT WOULD BEcome Public Law 99-457 (the Education of the Handicapped Act Amendments of 1986), Representative Steven Bartlett (R.–TX) noted: "This bill establishes a national policy on early intervention which recognizes its benefits, provides assistance to states to build systems of service delivery, and recognizes the unique role of families in the development of their handicapped children" (*Congressional Record,* 22 September 1986, p. H 7904).

These amendments to PL 91-230, the Education of the Handicapped Act (EHA), which was passed April 13, 1970, did far more than merely extend and reauthorize existing programs for children with special needs, ages 3–21 years; they charted new policies, particularly for society's youngest and most vulnerable citizens. This new national agenda was fueled by the needs of young children and by the documented benefits of early intervention and preschool services for children, families, and society. Furthermore, the new law recognizes that families play a vital role in the development of their handicapped children, and that implementation of a new policy must build upon "the best of the past" through a partnership of citizens who will provide the leadership for change, and for the betterment of children and families.

PL 99-457 contains a variety of programs. Some are designed to build a base of knowledge and support through research, training, educational technology, demonstration and outreach projects, and technical assistance. Others call for evaluative activities, such as a joint federal study of early intervention to be conducted by the United States Departments of Education and of Health and Human Services. However, two major portions of the law are particularly critical to the systematic expansion and improvement of comprehensive services to infants, toddlers, and preschoolers: Title I—Program for Infants and Toddlers with Handicaps (birth through age 2 years), and Title II—Preschool Grants Program (ages 3 through 5 years).

Descriptions of these two programs provide the core of this chapter. Following these sections is an overview of Titles III and IV, Discretionary and Miscellaneous Programs, and their relevance for early childhood concerns. The chapter closes with a discussion of some of the issues and challenges facing federal, state, and local policymakers and professionals as they work to implement PL 99-457.

DESCRIPTION OF TITLE I: HANDICAPPED INFANTS AND TODDLERS

Title I, or Part H, of the law is an entirely new section of the Education of the Handicapped Act. It creates a discretionary program to assist states in planning, developing, and implementing a statewide system of comprehensive, coordinated, multidisciplinary, interagency programs for all young handicapped children, from birth up to 3 years of age.

In the legislation, Congress declared its finding that "there is an urgent and substantial need" to develop statewide systems in order

> to enhance the development of handicapped infants and toddlers and minimize their potential for developmental delay, to reduce the educational costs to our society . . . by minimizing the need for special education and related services after handicapped infants and toddlers reach school age, to minimize likelihood of institutionalization . . . , to enhance the capacity of families to

meet the special needs of their infants and toddlers with handicaps (*Education of the Handicapped Act Amendments of 1986*, Sec. 671[a]).

Therefore, it became federal policy to provide financial help to states for the following activities:

Planning, developing, and implementing a statewide comprehensive, coordinated, multidisciplinary, interagency program of early intervention services
Facilitating the coordination of payments from public and private sources
Enhancing the capacity of states to provide quality early intervention services and to expand and improve existing services

The statewide comprehensive systems under PL 99-457 are intended to address the needs of infants and toddlers who are experiencing developmental delays or a diagnosed physical or mental condition with a high probability of an associated developmental delay in one or more of the following areas: cognitive development, physical development, language/speech development, psychosocial development, and self-help skills. In addition, states may opt to define and serve "at-risk" children. Children who meet these criteria are eligible to receive early intervention services that are developmental in nature and satisfy the following conditions:

Services must be provided under public supervision.
Services must be provided at no cost, except where federal or state laws allow.
Services must be designated to meet the developmental needs of youngsters across all five delay areas.
Services must meet state standards, as well as new federal standards.
Services include, but are not limited to, family training and counseling, special instruction, speech pathology, occupational therapy, physical therapy, case management, medical evaluation and diagnosis, and screening.
Services are provided by qualified personnel.
Services are delivered in conformity with the Individualized Family Service Plan (IFSP).

The IFSP contains a minimum of seven components to further guide planning and implementation of comprehensive services to youngsters and their families:

1. Multidisciplinary assessment and identification of appropriate services

2. Written IFSP by a multidisciplinary team and with parent or guardian
3. Early intervention services, considering frequency, intensity, and method of delivery
4. Expected major outcomes for child and family
5. Projected dates for services
6. Naming of the case manager from the most immediately relevant profession
7. Transition to Part B services (special education and related services beginning at age 3 years)

Early intervention services provided by these statewide systems must be individualized to meet children's needs and must fit the needs and characteristics of the particular state or governing entity (including the Bureau of Indian Affairs [BIA]). Minimum system components include the fourteen areas shown in Table 1. These components span community, regional, and/or statewide activities.

A state Interagency Coordinating Council (ICC), appointed by the governor, will advise and assist the state's lead agency in planning and operating the comprehensive system. The Council will hold open meetings at least four times a year and report to the governor.

The United States Department of Education will award grants to states and their lead agencies for systems planning and for policy development and implementation for handicapped and at-risk infants and toddlers. (See Table 2 for a list of lead agencies by state.) Through an annual application process with necessary assurances, these grant monies also may be used to pay for direct services to children not otherwise provided for from public and private sources. Furthermore, the monies may be used for expansion and improvement of services already available.

State appropriations for Part H services are based on a census formula. Congress appropriated $50,000,000 for 1987–1988, the first year of the 5-year initiative, and $67,000,018 for 1988–1989 (see Table 3). In order to receive these monies and participate in the Title I Program, a state must meet these general assurances over the following time frame:

First 2 years	–The governor must designate a lead agency. –The governor must establish an Interagency Coordinating Council.
Third year	–The state must demonstrate an adopted public policy for a statewide system.
Fourth year	–The state must demonstrate that its system is in place.

Fifth year and forward — The state must make the services available to all eligible infants and toddlers.

The law places certain conditions on the use of Part H funds. First, these funds may not be used for services that otherwise would have been paid for from another public or private source. Second, since Part H does not supersede other services, the state should not reduce medical or other assistance available, nor alter eligibility under Maternal and Child Health (MCH) or Medicaid for handicapped infants and toddlers.

DESCRIPTION OF TITLE II: HANDICAPPED PRESCHOOLERS

Title II amends Section 619, the Preschool Incentive Grants, of the EHA to create enhanced incentives for states to provide a free, appropriate, public

Table 1. Minimum components of a statewide comprehensive system for the provision of appropriate early intervention services to infants and toddlers with special needs

1. Definition of developmentally delayed
2. Timetable for serving all in need in the state
3. Comprehensive multidisciplinary evaluation of needs of children and families
4. Individualized family service plan and case management services
5. Child find and referral system
6. Public awareness
7. Central directory of services, resources, experts, research and demonstration projects
8. Comprehensive system of personnel development
9. Single line of authority in a lead agency designated or established by the governor for implementation of:
    a. general administration and supervision
    b. identification and coordination of all available resources
    c. assignment of financial responsibility to the appropriate agency
    d. procedures to ensure the provision of services and to resolve intra- and interagency disputes
    e. entry into formal interagency agreements
10. Policy pertaining to contracting or making arrangements with local service providers
11. Procedure for timely reimbursement of funds
12. Procedural safeguards
13. Policies and procedures for personnel standards
14. System for compiling data on the early intervention programs

Table 2. Part H lead agencies

State	Lead agency
1. Alabama	Education
2. Alaska	Health and Social Services
3. American Samoa	Health
4. Arizona	Economic Security/Developmental Disabilities (DD)
5. Arkansas	Human Services
6. California	Developmental Services
7. Colorado	Education
8. Commonwealth of Northern Mariana Islands	Education
9. Connecticut	Education
10. Delaware	Education
11. District of Columbia	Human Services
12. Florida	Education
13. Georgia	Human Resources/Mental Health, Mental Retardation, Substance Abuse Services (MH-MR-SA)
14. Guam	Education
15. Hawaii	Health
16. Idaho	Health and Welfare/DD
17. Illinois	Education
18. Indiana	Mental Health
19. Iowa	Education
20. Kansas	Health and Environment
21. Kentucky	Human Resources
22. Louisiana	Education
23. Maine	Interdepartmental Council
24. Maryland	Education
25. Massachusetts	Public Health
26. Michigan	Education
27. Minnesota	Education
28. Mississippi	Health
29. Missouri	Education
30. Montana	DD
31. Nebraska	Education
32. Nevada	Human Resources
33. New Hampshire	Education
34. New Jersey	Education
35. New Mexico	Health and Environment
36. New York	Health
37. North Carolina	Human Resources/MH-MR-SA
38. North Dakota	Human Services
39. Ohio	Health
40. Oklahoma	Education
41. Oregon	Mental Health (MH)

(continued)

Table 2. *(continued)*

State	Lead agency
42. Palau	Education
43. Pennsylvania	Public Welfare
44. Puerto Rico	Health
45. Rhode Island	Interagency Coordinating Council
46. Secretary of the Interior (BIA)	Education
47. South Carolina	Health and Environmental Control
48. South Dakota	Education
49. Tennessee	Education
50. Texas	Interagency Council
51. Utah	Health
52. Vermont	Education
53. Virgin Islands	Health
54. Virginia	MH-MR-SA
55. Washington	Social and Health Services
56. West Virginia	Health
57. Wisconsin	Health
58. Wyoming	Health

Note: Federated States of Micronesia and Republic of Marshall Islands are not eligible for this program.

education to all eligible handicapped children who will be between 3 and 6 years of age by school year 1990–1991 (or 1991–1992, depending on the availability of federal funding). Congressional data disclosed that there are approximately 330,000 handicapped children, ages 3–5 years, in this country. Of this total, 260,000 currently are being served by states, leaving an estimated 70,000 unserved.

During the summer and fall of 1987, the United States Department of Education made the first grants under the new law to state educational agencies (SEAs) to implement the preschool initiative. These funds were disbursed by SEAs through local educational agencies (LEAs), intermediate educational units (IEUs), and other contracted service agencies. Under guidelines established by Congress during the 1987–1988 school year, at least 70% of these funds went to the LEAs or IEUs, up to 25% could be set aside for SEA planning and related activities, and not more than 5% could be reserved for administrative expenses. For 1988–1989 and thereafter, at least 75% of the funds will flow to LEAs, up to 20% may be set aside, and 5% will be reserved for administration.

Congress appropriated $180 million for school year 1987–1988 and $201 million for school year 1988–1989, with state awards under Title II based on two related formulas or grants. For school year 1987–1988, each state received a basic grant consisting of $300 per "counted" child (those

Table 3. Estimated amounts available for Part H state grants—1987–88, 1988–89

State or outlying area	1987–88 appropriation	1988–89 appropriation
Alabama	767,835	1,017,633
Alaska	244,444	327,644
Arizona	698,032	953,688
Arkansas	453,721	598,950
California	5,558,081	7,687,492
Colorado	706,758	930,408
Connecticut	527,887	721,066
Delaware	244,444	327,644
Florida	1,923,951	2,669,107
Georgia	1,160,478	1,599,138
Hawaii	244,444	327,644
Idaho	248,674	327,644
Illinois	2,312,231	3,041,270
Indiana	1,501,411	1,372,351
Iowa	562,789	721,066
Kansas	527,887	680,361
Kentucky	711,120	918,777
Louisiana	1,064,499	1,395,611
Maine	244,444	327,644
Maryland	811,462	1,116,489
Massachusetts	981,608	1,331,646
Michigan	1,705,816	2,291,129
Minnesota	868,178	1,133,934
Mississippi	567,151	755,956
Missouri	985,970	1,290,940
Montana	244,444	327,644
Nebraska	344,653	441,944
Nevada	244,444	327,644
New Hampshire	244,444	327,644
New Jersey	1,286,997	1,727,069
New Mexico	357,742	471,019
New York	3,154,233	4,285,690
North Carolina	1,081,950	1,482,837
North Dakota	244,444	327,644
Ohio	2,050,469	2,709,812
Oklahoma	741,659	936,223
Oregon	523,524	674,545
Pennsylvania	2,037,381	2,698,182
Rhode Island	244,444	327,644
South Carolina	650,043	878,072
South Dakota	244,444	327,644
Tennessee	837,639	1,128,119

(continued)

Table 3. (continued)

State or outlying area	1987–88 appropriation	1988–89 appropriation
Texas	3,817,363	5,163,762
Utah	510,436	662,915
Vermont	244,444	327,644
Virginia	1,047,048	1,407,241
Washington	898,717	1,180,455
West Virginia	335,928	424,498
Wisconsin	937,981	1,238,605
Wyoming	244,444	327,644
District of Columbia	244,444	327,644
Puerto Rico	901,814	1,203,715
American Samoa	74,028	101,691
Northern Mariana Islands	38,556	67,794
Guam	203,787	271,177
Virgin Islands	163,983	203,383
Republic of Palau	19,647	26,135
Secretary of the Interior (BIA)	611,111	819,109
Republic of the Marshall Islands	-0-	-0-
Federated States of Micronesia	-0-	-0-
TOTAL	$50,000,000	$67,018,000

Source: U.S. Department of Education.

currently receiving a "free appropriate public education" [FAPE]). Additionally, each state was eligible for a bonus grant consisting of up to $3,800 per "estimated" child (those not presently receiving FAPE, but whom the state plans to serve the following year). For school year 1987–1988, the bonus grant was calculated at $3,270 per estimated child. (See Table 4 for preschool grant allocations.) For school year 1988–1989, each state may receive a basic grant of $400 per counted child; the bonus grant was determined to be $2,788 per child.

In order to participate in this grant program, SEAs must have an approved Part B State Plan and provide special education and related services to some children. Additionally, for the 1990–1991 school year, SEAs must amend their Part B State Plans to include policies and procedures that ensure the availability, under state law and practice, of a free appropriate public education for all handicapped children ages 3 through 5 years. Provisions of FAPE include the individualized education program (IEP), due process, confidentiality, and least restrictive environment.

Community services to provide FAPE to youngsters can be imple-

Table 4. 1987–88 estimated allocations to states under Section 619

State or territory	Dec. 1, 1986 3–5 count	Basic grant (in thousands)	1987–88 estimated 3–5 increase	Bonus grant (in thousands)	Total allocation (in thousands)
Alabama	2,666	$ 800	2,553	$ 8,348	$ 9,147
Alaska	768	230	235	768	999
Arizona	2,623	787	202	660	1,447
Arkansas	2,505	752	125	409	1,160
California	23,700	7,110	6,500	21,253	28,363
Colorado	1,489	447	750	2,452	2,899
Connecticut	4,506	1,352	0	0	1,352
Delaware	709	213	20	65	278
District of Columbia	370	111	17	56	167
Florida	8,947	2,684	1,592	5,205	7,889
Georgia	4,442	1,333	400	1,308	2,640
Hawaii	581	174	24	78	253
Idaho	1,270	381	127	415	796
Illinois	22,076	6,623	1,524	4,983	11,606
Indiana	5,099	1,530	9	29	1,559
Iowa	4,929	1,479	0	0	1,479
Kansas	2,801	840	506	1,654	2,495
Kentucky	4,343	1,303	2,652	8,671	9,974
Louisiana	5,130	1,540	10	33	1,572
Maine	2,148	644	250	817	1,462
Maryland	5,971	1,791	0	0	1,791
Massachusetts	8,041	2,412	900	2,943	5,355
Michigan	12,517	3,755	1,422	4,650	8,405
Minnesota	8,731	2,619	210	687	3,306

Mississippi	2,841	852	1,326	4,336	5,188
Missouri	5,297	1,589	200	654	2,243
Montana	1,404	421	65	213	634
Nebraska	2,750	825	62	203	1,028
Nevada	844	253	84	275	528
New Hampshire	1,105	332	77	252	583
New Jersey	12,506	3,752	0	0	3,752
New Mexico	1,249	375	252	824	1,199
New York	5,410	1,623	0	0	1,623
North Carolina	5,541	1,662	2,495	8,158	9,820
North Dakota	1,008	302	0	0	302
Ohio	7,205	2,162	13	43	2,204
Oklahoma	5,635	1,691	0	0	1,691
Oregon	1,177	353	423	1,383	1,736
Pennsylvania	7,134	2,140	2,183	7,138	9,278
Rhode Island	1,200	360	150	490	850
South Carolina	5,671	1,701	1,102	3,603	5,305
South Dakota	1,813	544	0	0	544
Tennessee	6,746	2,024	249	814	2,838
Texas	20,137	6,041	201	657	6,698
Utah	2,093	628	21	69	697
Vermont	487	146	79	258	404
Virginia	8,944	2,683	0	0	2,683
Washington	6,562	1,969	500	1,635	3,603
West Virginia	2,813	844	60	196	1,040
Wisconsin	8,934	2,680	169	553	3,233
Wyoming	301	90	424	1,386	1,477
Puerto Rico	2,279	684	200	654	1,338
American Samoa	4	1	10	33	34

(continued)

Table 4. (continued)

State or territory	Dec. 1, 1986 3–5 count	Basic grant (in thousands)	1987–88 estimated 3–5 increase	Bonus grant (in thousands)	Total allocation (in thousands)
Northern Marianas	26	8	121	396	403
Guam	63	19	63	206	225
Virgin Islands	14	4	36	118	122
Marshall Islands[a]	76	23	24	78	101
Micronesia[a]	76	23	24	78	101
Palau[a]	76	23	24	78	101
National totals	265,783	$79,735	30,665	$100,265	$180,000

Note: Some totals may not add up because of rounding.
[a]Estimates of actual numbers to be submitted.
Source: U.S. Education Department.

mented in a number of different ways. The SEA/LEA may administer home or center-based programs directly or indirectly through contracts with other qualified service agencies. Variations in the length of the service day and type of program are acceptable. Finally, the family is recognized as having an important role in preschool programs, and family services, such as training and counseling, are to be made available.

Two other provisions of Title II are noteworthy. Under the new law, there are provisions on sharing the costs of FAPE among appropriate state agencies:

1. Providing or paying for some or all costs of FAPE (not limited to educational agencies)
2. Supplementing and not supplanting the funds
3. Developing and implementing interagency agreements
4. Permitting no reduction in medical and other assistance available or altering eligibility under MCH/Medicaid
5. Defining financial responsibility of each agency for providing FAPE
6. Resolving disputes over payment

Additionally, the new law builds in some penalties for states that do not achieve a full mandate for FAPE covering 3- through 5-year-olds by the 1990–1991 school year. Failure to comply will result in loss of the new preschool grant money, as well as funds generated under Part B of the State Plan formula for this population group, as well as designated EHA discretionary grants, including those for research, training, and demonstration activities.

OVERVIEW OF TITLES III AND IV: DISCRETIONARY AND MISCELLANEOUS PROGRAMS

Title III reauthorizes a number of diverse discretionary programs that provide support to state policy and program development and implementation. Each program affords opportunities for the conceptualization, trial implementation, and evaluation of ideas and systems.

To implement Title III initiatives, the United States Department of Education may award contracts, grants, or cooperative agreements to designated agencies. A list of some potentially eligible programs that emphasize improved services to young children and their families is presented below.

1. Preservice and inservice personnel training for careers in preschool and early intervention services; each state educational agency also

may establish special programs to prepare appropriate personnel; training and information will be provided to parents of handicapped children and to persons who work with parents
2. General research and demonstration projects to help develop new and improved techniques and devices for serving young children; this includes the design of new curricula, application of new technologies, dissemination of research findings, and development of new tests and scales
3. Demonstration, experimental, outreach, research, and technical assistance projects in early education for children with handicaps
4. Programs to advance the use of newer technologies, media, and materials in the provision of early intervention services

Title IV addresses a number of miscellaneous areas. Some sections are germane to early childhood:

1. Indian children, served by the United States Department of the Interior, shall receive an aggregate amount for each fiscal year to ensure FAPE for all handicapped children starting at age 3.
2. Standards shall be established consistent with credentialing (e.g., certification, licensing, registration) or other applicable requirements for a specific discipline or profession.
3. Evaluation studies shall be implemented to provide data that document the number of children served and existing services, the amount of funds expended, the number and types of personnel employed, as well as a description of services.
4. Children ages 3–5 who are served need not be reported to the United States Department of Education by disability category.

Titles III and IV of the EHA, then, propose to enhance support to young children with special needs and their families by improving the direct services provided by states and communities, and enhancing the capacity of service planners, providers, and parents to meet child and family needs.

SOME ISSUES AND CHALLENGES FOR POLICY IMPLEMENTATION

The process of planning, implementing, monitoring, and evaluating PL 99-457 already is underway, with participation on public and private levels. Congressional intent has been amplified by a published report that accompanied the legislation, and Congress will assess the implementation of the legislation through oversight hearings. Proposed regulations, drafted by the United States Department of Education, provide guidelines for states during the implementation process. Additional assistance is available through information and training materials prepared by advocacy groups and professional organizations.

Translating policy into action will require cooperation across all levels of government, and between public and private sectors. Among the issues to be addressed in improving and expanding services for children with special needs and their families are the following.

1. Coordinating the substance of the separate but related Titles I and II of PL 99-457 must be done in a responsive and coherent manner. Philosophically, these two sections are intended to be interrelated, not treated as separate, independent programs within the state.
2. General plans (visions), responsibilities, and activities, including other federal and state early childhood initiatives (e.g., child care, early education, adolescent pregnancy, child abuse, mental health, Head Start, maternal and child health, Even Start) and the best of current and past practices must be aligned and coordinated.
3. Eligibility requirements, including definition of developmental delay and at-risk conditions, as well as special needs of minority, migrant, rural, native, and Pacific-Basin Americans must be addressed.
4. A comprehensive and community-based early intervention and preschool service mix, including FAPE, IFSP, child identification and placement, case management, developmental evaluation and family assessment, parent training, medical/health-related services, and procedural safeguards must be instituted.
5. The effective transition of children and families through various points of the comprehensive and community service system must be coordinated. Transitions include those from neonatal intensive care units (NICU) to early intervention to preschool programs to kindergarten.
6. Funds, involving formulas, reimbursement costs, payor of last resort, supplanting, and maintenance of effort must be handled appropriately.
7. A comprehensive system of personnel development that addresses such issues as qualification, preservice and inservice training, and licensure/certification must be created.
8. Leadership, coordination, and support among various support activities (TA, research, demonstration, public awareness, etc.) must be provided.

9. Rules, regulations, standards, and guidelines to ensure quality controls must be developed.
10. A data base that provides evidence of both short- and long-term benefits/outcomes must be designed.
11. The "general supervision" concept must be operationalized.
12. Parents must be integrated into the planning, development, and implementation process within communities and on the state level through Interagency Coordinating Councils.
13. All of the above must be monitored and enforced.

These challenges encompass "change for the better" at their core and must be confronted in order to maximize the impact of new national policy goals. MacRae and Wilde (1985) remind policy shapers that it is not enough that problems of implementing the policy be anticipated. The policy must be placed on the agendas of multiple decision makers; it must be in a form that is congruent with legislative intent; and it must be referred to the right organizations for implementation. Thus, if the 13 challenges above are addressed in a bold and visionary manner, America's children and families, and society can realize the concrete benefits of comprehensive systems integrated into communities through the implementation of PL 99-457.

SUMMARY

Through the enactment of PL 99-457, Congress has established a new national agenda: the expansion of opportunities for all eligible young children and their families in the United States to receive the benefits of universal early intervention and preschool services. Specifically, the intent of Congress is to promote child and family development, to minimize the likelihood of institutionalization, and to be supportive of families who have children with special needs. Furthermore, Congress made the realistic assumption that no one agency, advocacy group, parent organization, or discipline could accommodate all the needs of America's children with special needs and their families. To build comprehensive service systems on the best of the past and to incorporate new technologies, all citizens must work together to enhance the abilities and functioning of these children and their families. Representative Pat Williams (D.-MT) aptly described this new legislation:

> [PL 99-457] is the most important thing that this Congress will do for handicapped children up to the age of 5 in this decade and perhaps for the remainder of this century. This legislation will require commitment, effort,

expertise, long hours, and, yes, money. But what great effort in American history has not required all of those things? What great problem in American history has been resolved without the enormous effort from out citizenry and without a fairly high cost attached to it? (*Congressional Record*, 22 September 1986, p. H 7905)

Indeed, PL 99-457 is but another vital step in addressing the requirements of young children with special needs and their families. As Weiner and Koppelman (1987) have observed, "PL 99-457 can be the springboard to reform. The choice—and the responsibility—is left to the states" (p. 109).

REFERENCES

Education of the Handicapped Act Amendments of 1986, PL 99-457, 1986.
Education of the Handicapped Act Amendments of 1986. (22 September 1986). *Congressional Record, 132*(125), H 7893-7912.
MacRae, D., & Wilde, J. (1985). *Policy analysis for public decisions*. Lanham, MD: University Press of America.
Weiner, R., & Koppelman, J. (1987). *From birth to 5: Serving the youngest handicapped children*. Alexandria, VA: Capitol Publications, Inc.

LESSONS FROM IMPLEMENTING PL 94-142

2

Edwin W. Martin

CONGRESS STUDIED SENATE BILL 6 AND A SIMILAR HOUSE BILL FOR APPROXimately 4 years before approving the bill that became Public Law 94-142, the Education for All Handicapped Children Act of 1975. During that time, a number of us worked on the legislation—planning it, drafting it, revising it, arguing among ourselves, compromising, convincing, building support for it among constituencies, doing all the many and varied activities that go on when a major piece of legislation is being shaped and considered.

When the resistance of the executive branch finally was overcome and the law was passed by Congress and signed in 1976, President Gerald Ford presented what was essentially a veto message that had been prepared for him by the Department of Health, Education, and Welfare. But, facing the reality that the Congress had passed the legislation with only seven dissenting votes in each house of Congress, he reluctantly signed it. At this point, there was a tendency among the law's advocates to feel that the battle was over. In truth, a new battle was just beginning.

The processes of implementing PL 94-142 and the new early childhood legislation, included in PL 99-457, the Education of the Handicapped Act Amendments of 1986, will have many similarities. There are at least six major dimensions to the implementation process:

1. Understanding the intent of the legislation
2. Developing regulations that reflect and, it is to be hoped, clarify that intent
3. Communicating with the affected constituencies in the development of the regulations and implementation of the legislation
4. Securing the support of the governed
5. Monitoring the implementation
6. Continuing to affirm the purpose of the act and its continued development as long as necessary and appropriate

UNDERSTANDING THE INTENT OF THE ACT

As the person who was charged with the major responsibility for implementing PL 94-142, I had the advantage of working closely with the congressional staff and other advocates during the 3–4 years that the act was in development. Many of its dimensions were very familiar to me. I had helped to develop some; I had played a role in discussing and revising others; I had heard about still others as they were worked out by the staff members, members of Congress, and so forth. Inevitably, a number of people play a part in developing legislation, as the key staff persons work with a variety of people to develop the final draft. No one person is really a final authority on all dimensions, although the key staff persons in the House and Senate come close.

It is not always possible for staff members of the executive branch to play as close a role in the development of legislation as we did with PL 94-142, so sometimes the people charged with administering the program are not as knowledgeable about the legislation as we were. When that happens, the best thing to do is to review carefully the hearings that led to the development of the legislation and the reports that were developed by the House and Senate committees that studied the legislation. The Senate Report No. 99-315 and the House Report No. 99-860 were specifically developed by the staff of these committees to explain PL 99-457 and to provide information about what each house of Congress intended in its version of the act.

When the House and Senate develop the compromise legislation that is eventually passed, parts of an act generally are changed, so the earlier reports are not completely accurate. Most acts have a conference report that ties together the final developed version. In the new PL 99-457 legislation, a Senate report and a House report are available, but a final conference report is not, because the act was considered near the end of the last congressional session, when there was great time pressure. To permit agreement before the session ended, the Senate accepted most House provisions, and no final conference report was submitted. However, without a conference report, certain ambiguities will be inevitable.

The legislative history that exists in addition to the history written in the reports is heard on the floor of the House and Senate when the bill is considered for its final passage. This results in discussion that also becomes a very important part of the record of Congress in developing the legislation and clarifying its intent. This legislative history will continue to have importance as the process of implementation takes place. The regulations should reflect it, and, if there are court cases under the act, the court will look to the legislative history for guidance as to what Congress's intention was in passing the legislation.

During the process of studying the legislative history and developing regulations under the law, we frequently see expressions of what I might call the arrogance of the executive branch at this juncture. The executive branch frequently attempts to express its ideas and philosophies, whether or not Congress accepted them at the time the legislation was considered. The regulations become the vehicle for this expression. Regulations drawn by the executive branch are supposed to reflect and elaborate on the intention of Congress, but sometimes they subtly change it. This usually leads to a battle between the legislative and congressional supporters and the executive branch before the final regulations are approved. A classic example of this was the attempt by the Reagan administration, in its early years, to change the Education of the Handicapped Act by revising the regulations to weaken and eliminate some of its features. While it is literally illegal to follow this course of action, the burden of proving that the regulations are not a legal reflection of the act falls on someone else, who must file an elaborate court suit. Therefore, administrations frequently are able to have a good bit of leeway during the regulatory process.

DEVELOPING REGULATIONS

The process of developing regulations under PL 94-142 was historic in that we made a decision to deliberately open up the process to include as many participants as possible. During the development of regulations, a great deal of secrecy between program officials and the Department of Health, Education, and Welfare's (HEW) General Counsel's Office was more typical. Sometimes this was justified, in part, to prevent various parties from gaining unfair knowledge of the regulations where it would have been advantageous (e.g., in a competition for funds). In the case of

PL 94-142, however, it seemed unlikely that anyone would be harmed by our process of openness, and I felt that there was a great deal to be gained by involving many sectors of the education community and the public in the process. Although PL 94-142 makes many strong demands on the states and requires states to sign a state plan agreeing to these many requirements, we knew from the beginning that it would be necessary to have the willing concurrence and support of state and local school officials and teachers if the act were really to work. Assurances on paper are different from putting effective programs in place, as shown in this old story from my government days: Two warring bureaucrats were called in by their boss and criticized for not working together. He said cooperation was essential. One finally agreed, "Okay, I'll cooperate, but that's all I'll do!"

The process of developing regulations for PL 94-142 began with gathering several hundred people from across the country and dividing them into discussion groups to talk about major features of the law, such as due process, least restrictive environment (LRE), nondiscriminatory testing, and Child Find (the responsibility for the education agencies to seek out and identify children with disabilities). These discussion groups included special educators, education administrators, advocates, parents, and others, so that a cross section of opinions was obtained. From these discussions, concept papers were developed that attempted to include the major features of different areas and the major practical and philosophic approaches to regulating them. After the concept papers were completed, a set of regulations was developed and circulated for comment. Changes were made in the regulations and specific responses to the comments were made in writing and circulated. In all, more than 1,000 people from across the country participated by providing input into the development of the regulations and by making comments on the first draft of those regulations.

It is my feeling that, as a result, later attempts to change the regulations ran into resistance, not only from the parents and advocates, but also from state and local education officials, representatives of teacher unions, and others, because they had been part of the initial regulatory process and they felt as if the regulations did, in fact, fairly follow the law and its intent. Had the regulations been developed without input from, for example, state and local education officials, and been "rammed down their throats," I am sure that these officials would have had a different attitude toward changing the regulations. Instead, even when there were provisions of the regulations that were troublesome for state officials, they understood that the regulations were not arbitrary wishes on the part of the federal government but, in fact, reflected the spirit of the law.

It may come as a surprise to you that the Congress does not spell out most of the specifics of the legislation, but instead allows the executive branch to perform that function by promulgating regulations that, once they are adopted, have essentially the power of law.

Let me give you an example of why such regulations are necessary. One of the most important features of PL 91-230, the Education of the Handicapped Act, 1970, is the due process procedures, whereby parents are entitled to an impartial due process hearing if they feel that the proposed educational program is inappropriate for their child. The act calls for the state to have a procedure for such due process hearings, and the state education agency must establish and maintain procedures to guarantee procedural safeguards. The act is quite detailed, saying that the parents must be allowed to examine all relevant records, requiring prior written notice to the parents, informing them in their native language, and other features. What it does not spell out, however, is how long this is supposed to take. How long does the school agency have to agree to the hearing? How long does it have to conduct the hearing? How long does it have to provide a report of the hearing? If the parent or the school district decides to appeal the outcome to the state agency, how long do they have to do so? Those matters had to be determined by the Bureau of Education of the Handicapped and developed into regulations. There is a great deal of difference between saying that a decision has to be made in 30 days and saying that it has to be made in 6 months. These matters generally are left to the discretion of the administering agency, and frequently they become matters of great confrontation between the state and local agencies and the federal government as to their appropriateness.

Let me give you an example of a regulatory issue of a different kind. Under the definition of what type of related services must be provided as part of special education, Section 602a (17) includes "medical services," saying that related services also include speech pathology and audiology services, psychology services, physical and occupational therapy services, transportation, and so forth. In the inclusion of medical services, however, there is a proviso, "except that such medical services shall be for diagnostic and evaluation purposes only." Now here it seems clear that, although disabled children in some instances require medical services such as surgery and long-term medical treatment, the Congress did not intend for these to be paid for under the Education of the Handicapped Act.

From this proviso a question arose, one that required quite an elaborate regulation to be written later to resolve it and that eventually went to the Supreme Court. That question was: if a youngster with a physical disability, for example, a child with spina bifida, who is unable to control bladder function, were to be able to go to school, who would have to help catheterize that child? Sure enough, a school district decided that such a service was not its responsibility under the law and that the parents would have to come to the school to catheterize their child, or the child would have to stay home. The school district argued that catheterization was a medical service and therefore not required to be paid for under PL 94-142.

We developed a regulation stating that catheterization was not a medical service, that it was, in fact, frequently provided by aides in medical departments and by practical nurses, and that some children, as they got older, learned to catheterize themselves. Parents also performed this function. We felt that it was possible to see this service as part of the general health services that schools offer through the nurse's office and not as a specific medical service. This may seem like drawing a fine line, but at stake was the rejection of a child from the basic protections of education for all children under the Education of the Handicapped Act. That regulation was studied very carefully by the Secretary of Education at the time, Shirley Hufstedtler, who was herself a Federal Appeals judge before she became secretary. We felt we had an argument that would withstand the scrutiny of the courts and, in fact, the Supreme Court later upheld the principle.

When we wrote regulations of this kind, ones that we knew would be controversial and would cause difficulties, we again attempted to gain as much input as possible, including input from people who opposed them. We struggled with trying to do the right thing under the law and for the child, and at the same time understanding the problems that regulations might cause for the local service providers. It is important to understand that regulations that seem arbitrary and unfair can cause tremendous backlash against the desired program itself. The local officials can undermine the entire program it they feel strongly enough about regulation provisions that they perceive as arbitrary. You can have a classic case of winning a battle and losing the war.

COMMUNICATING WITH AFFECTED CONSTITUENCIES

It should be clear from our discussion so far that we maintained a very close communication, in the development of regulations and in the implementation of the law, with a variety of constituencies: parents, state and local special education communities, the regular education communities, the Council for Exceptional Children (CEC), various organizations serving disabled people, and so forth. We included the chief state school officers, teachers' organizations, and others who had an important part to play in the implementation of the law, although they were not special educators per se. We did this by developing materials for circulation to these groups and by having technical assistance and training programs. In some cases, we made grants to these organizations to conduct training sessions on the act. We did this frequently with organizations in which we sensed that there was some resistance and, rather than have a third party come in to talk to or lecture their members, we gave them grants to develop their own programs. In some cases, this brought them onto our team, as opposed to creating antagonism. Communication with the constituencies continued, not just during the regulation process, but through the period of state plan approval and implementation. Friendly organizations, such as the Council for Exceptional Children, developed information packages that were very useful.

Approving the state plans, which are comprehensive documents, and monitoring the progress of the implementation during the first few years of the act really constitute one continuous process. In each of the first few reviews of the state plans and procedures, major changes were required to bring them into compliance with the law. This frequently required changes in state regulations and even in state law. In fact, most states had to have amendments to their state laws in order to comply with PL 94-142, and legislators frequently resented it.

Democracies work through the willing consent of the governed. PL 94-142 affected not only the state education agency and local education agencies, but other agencies as well, including those operating state programs for people who are retarded or mentally ill and programs involved in supplying Medicaid services. There was a need to reach out to a variety of agencies. One provision of PL 94-142 that was particularly controversial required that the official responsible for education of handicapped children in each state be the official responsible for the general education program. This would include child programs run by other agencies. Both the state education officers and other state agency officials sometimes resisted this arrangement. Education officials were concerned about being held responsible for other agencies, because they did not feel that they could influence the other agencies. The law did provide that they had approval over the transfer of PL 94-142 and related funds, but, in many instances, the political problems to be faced in controlling funds or program standards were intense. That may well be the case again with the new early childhood legislation, where it is necessary to bring numbers of state agencies together in offering comprehensive programs of services for young handicapped children.

SECURING THE CONSENT OF THE GOVERNED

Not every state entered willingly into the contract called for by the Education for the Handicapped Act, that is, the state plan and its various requirements. In fact, there were a number of states that expressed extreme reluctance to participation in the act. We heard, from a number of states, predictions that their legislatures would not change state provisions, particularly with regard to due process and similar dimensions of the act. I remember the Commissioner of Education from Texas saying to me, "Ed, the state board will eat my lunch if I agree to this." New Mexico decided not to submit a state plan and therefore did not receive funds under the Education of the Handicapped Act, so the state was not bound by its requirements. At the time New Mexico announced its intention not to participate, a number of other states in the mountain area (Colorado, Wyoming, Montana, and the Dakotas) had not sent in their state plans either, so there was a chance that we might have had a revolution. With that kind of resistance against the bill, Congress might have decided to make weakening amendments or postpone its effective date.

We had anticipated the possibility that some states might choose this course of action. However, Section 504 of the Rehabilitation Act of 1973 prohibited discrimination against otherwise qualified people in federally assisted programs, including those for elementary and secondary education. During the development of regulations by the Office of Civil Rights for the provisions of Section 504, we defined discrimination in elementary and secondary education so that the definition paralleled the requirements of PL 94-142. As it turned out, parents in New Mexico went into federal district court and sued New Mexico for failing to provide appropriate education for their children and thereby discriminating against them under Section 504. The court ruled in favor of the parents and ordered New Mexico to comply with Section 504, which essentially made them do what they would have had to do under PL 94-142 and for which they would have received federal funds.

Concerns were raised by school board members in Colorado on a number of issues, so I traveled to Colorado to meet with the state commissioner and the local school board associations in their annual conference. There were some board members who misunderstood the law and felt there was an immediate requirement to begin preschool programs, even though the option was with the state for the delivery of those services. My assurances there helped calm some concerns at that point. Another school board member was troubled by individualized education program (IEP) requirements and the concept that schools would have to provide the services that were called for in an IEP. This was particularly significant for many states as they faced the challenge of delivering services such as physical therapy and occupational therapy, which had not been provided previously. This board member, however, was concerned about the fact that some IEP team might decide that a child needed a "snowmobile for therapy," or make some equally ridiculous request. My answer to him was that the people to develop the IEP would be employees of his local school system, the people that he and his board and superintendent had trusted with the children in that district. Such an IEP team would be composed of an administrator from that district, a special education teacher, a regular teacher, and perhaps a school psychologist or a guidance counselor. In addition to the protections that the districts would have through the impartial hearing examiner process, their selection of these professionals in the first place and their continuing supervision of them would make unlikely any kind of frivolous IEP requirement. So it went, as we attempted, step-by-step, to answer questions and relieve fears, not all of which were reasonable by any stretch of the imagination. Many meetings with state officials, including legislators, board members, and executives were necessary to bring about state participation in PL 94-142 and to establish good communication and reduce fears. I might add here that we made compromises as well, and not always with great confidence that our judgments were correct.

There was also a great deal of concern expressed among regular classroom teachers. I used to call this phenomenon the "the-sky-is-falling" phenomenon. The situation was always one in which hordes of special education children, particularly young people with behavioral troubles who were "acting out," were going to inundate the classes of regular teachers, leaving them and other students helpless. Usually, this was happening someplace else and not in the school of the person raising the question. Again, we talked about the concepts of a placement team working to develop an education program that was "appropriate," and that "appropriate" naturally would not be denoted by uncontrollable behavior or inappropriate referral to a regular classroom.

I would not be surprised if there were some stirrings of opposition from groups that felt that the family structure was being weakened by the new early childhood legislation. Back in the days when the Congress first considered making early child care available on a wide-scale basis, numbers of people who were identified with conservative political philosophies opposed it on the basis that it was "communizing" the children of America. Their opposition was strong enough to actually deter the Congress from moving ahead at the time, although there were other factors, such as costs, that presented barriers as well. However, it was a surprisingly strong resistance and was demonstrated only 10–15 years ago. I would be surprised if it did not show up in some form again.

We did make strong efforts to develop cooperative relationships with the federal agencies that were responsible for offering services to youngsters with disabilities—for example, the Crippled Children's Services that operates in various states and the people who administer the Medicaid program. We began by having meetings at the federal level in Washington, D.C. I assigned a person on my staff to a full-time job of trying to develop cooperative relationships between these various organizations at the federal agency level, relationships that might carry over to state and local activities. We also attempted to identify states that were willing to cooperate and local areas where we might identify exemplary practices. Each of those strategies had some limited success, but clearly the principle that underlies the implementation of PL 94-142, and that is relevant today, is that one must secure the support of all the key players, and one must continue to do so over the course of the program. This is important, not only when the bill is being developed so there will be support, but also when the act is being implemented.

One thing I learned from PL 94-142 was the need to continue to "sell" or demonstrate its importance. It was important to teach people why the act was developed, why it was important, and why is was necessary. I remember a conversation that I had with Francis Keppel, now on the faculty of the Harvard Education School, who had served as the United States Commissioner of Education under Presidents Lyndon Johnson and John Kennedy. He was responsible for helping to develop the Elementary and Secondary Education Act, which brought so much help to low-income and disadvantaged children. Francis Keppel told me that he felt that one of the things those responsible for implementation did not do was to continue "selling" Title I after it was passed. He thought that we were on the right track in attempting to do that for PL 94-142. Although we were doing it intuitively, I had not thought about it clearly until that conversation, but I have since, and it seems to me that this is important for PL 99-457 as well. Not everyone will understand why the Congress passed this legislation. People need to know why it is important, even after it is implemented and when the virtually unavoidable backlash sets in as the pains of implementation are felt. There need to be continuing meetings with the public, and continuing efforts with the press and public officials to rally support for the new programs and to demonstrate their value and effectiveness.

We have always been fortunate in that parents have felt that PL 94-142 has fulfilled their purposes reasonably well. When organizations outside the government or government audit agencies have sampled parents' feelings of satisfaction, usually the response has been quite positive. That is not to say that every program is as satisfactory as it should be or that the parents think it is, but they see this act as intended to help and, for the most part, believe that it provides them with positive results. It is important to include parents and to respect their feelings. Too often, educators and professionals push parents aside as being too much trouble, or even as being the opposition.

MONITORING IMPLEMENTATION

The fifth major aspect of implementing a new law is monitoring the implementation. We set up a series of visits to the states that included visits to some of the local education agencies and state schools. During those visits, we sampled compliance with the law: Were their programs in place as promised under the law? Were their IEPs in place? What evidence was there that the parents were participating in the IEP process? What complaints, if any, had been registered and how were those complaints handled? Our samples were much too small and couldn't go deeply enough into ensuring the quality of programs; also, we could not visit enough local school districts or states as frequently as necessary. However, we did have a plan to visit every state at least once every 3 years and to do follow-up conversations and visits, depending on the seriousness of the situation, when our reports indicated deficits. As a result of those visits, we prepared detailed reports and asked the states to describe in writing the corrective actions that they had taken, and we felt that each of those visits resulted in some progress. Sometimes critics felt as if the verbal promises were as far as the changes went, and I am sure that this was a legitimate criticism in some instances. We did have a serious and dedicated staff, however, and we were committed to bringing about these changes. Our observations showed that, step-by-step over the first few years, we made incremental gains in compliance with the law.

For example, when we first began to visit, even though it was after the deadline for services, we found IEPs lacking in many areas. We also found that Child Find services were not in place. These problems were systematically corrected. I have been very disappointed that over the first 4 or 5 years of the Reagan administration, there was almost no compliance monitoring at all. I testified before the U.S. Senate Subcommittee on the Handicapped, May 16, 1985, that on a visit to California earlier that year, I discovered that no one had attempted to monitor PL 94-142 in that state since 1980.

There is evidence now that the procedures for monitoring have been revised and renewed and the states have been notified that monitoring processes are going to go forward. I think that this is good news, not because the role of the federal government should be one of enforcing the law with a police mentality, but because there is a need both for positive and constructive monitoring and for technical assistance to help states learn how to do the things the law intends. Compliance monitoring must make sure that the various requirements of the law are in place.

In my discussions with teachers I listened to their complaints about IEP requirements. I asked them what the minimum components of an IEP should be. They mentioned a current appraisal, goals, and evaluation. I then showed them the law, which called only for those three components—all other requirements had been added at state and local levels. During the time I headed the federal programs, we once were criticized by some people in what might be called the legal rights movement. These people felt that we were not harsh and strict enough in our compliance activities and that we had failed to cut off funds to certain states. After those issues were raised, however, I found that the advocacy community within special education, the parents of handicapped children, the Council for Exceptional Children, and the people who really were responsible for passing the law did not share those critical feelings. They felt that we were striking a reasonable balance in monitoring programs, bringing about changes, and at the same time securing the support of the governed.

AFFIRMING THE PURPOSE OF THE ACT

In conclusion, it is my feeling that the federal laws with which I have worked, for the most part, have been effective. As I think back over the early federal programs supporting teacher training and research, I see that they have led to the development of cadres of professionals who are now staffing our colleges and universities across the country. They have helped us move to a program which, although still far short of our hopes and aspirations as professionals and parents, nevertheless is, based on my observations of a number of countries, clearly the world's leading program in terms of commitment and services to children with disabilities.

I have seen the Handicapped Children's Early Education Assistance Act, PL 90-538 (1968, as amended), which supported models of early childhood programming, grow and develop into the basis for a major professional arm of our field. A whole new literature, a new research system, professional training programs and, of course, massive child services, have been established. This has set the stage for the legislation we talk about today. In bringing this progress about, the work of the University of North Carolina's Frank Porter Graham Center and of James Gallagher, who helped draft that early legislation, is well known.

Programs like PL 94-142 and 89-313 (1966), the State Operated and Supported Schools Program, which provides education funds for state-operated schools for children and state-supported schools (e.g., schools for people who are deaf and for people who are mentally retarded), have worked best, I think, in terms of their broad philosophies and goals, or as I have put it, the broad brush strokes, rather than minute detail. There may be problems with how a school or a district provides a service or develops an IEP, but the basic right to education is established.

The magnificence of the Education of the Handicapped Act, PL 91-230, is that it expresses a moral commitment on the part of this nation to children with disabilities. It is a matter of establishing that people with disabilities share the same constitutional rights as nondisabled people. Having done that, it has changed forever the status of children with disabilities and the status of their parents. That is not to say that school districts are using IEPs as well as they should, or that low-income parents are taking advantage of due process, or that the quality of special education in the United States is what it should be. Clearly, we have not yet achieved the desired results in those areas.

I think it would be unrealistic to assume that the new programs for 3- to 5-year-olds and for youngsters from birth to 2 years will soon achieve full, high-quality service success either. On the contrary, I think what we have to expect is that we have achieved a victory in principle with the passage of the act and that we now begin a long, frustrating process of evolution toward the kinds of quality programs that are necessary. In order to bring about success, we are going to have to be sure that the people who administer the law and the people who are responsible for implementing it understand the intent of the legislation and what their responsibilities are: we must open communication links between people who are responsible for serving the children and people who are responsible for administering the programs. People who are on the firing-line level must feel committed to the programs and see themselves as part of the team, rather than the enemy. The government must use a carrot as well as the occasional threat of a stick to demand compliance when necessary, in its efforts to help people fulfill the purposes of the act.

Finally, as we continue to implement the act and monitor the implementation, we must affirm its purposes and its significance in the lives of children and in the development of the character of the United States. The work that we do is what makes this nation strong—not its military might, not only technological abilities, but commitment to one another, our caring about each other, and our belief in the intrinsic worth of each individual.

REFERENCES

Levine, E.L., & Wexler, E.M. (1981). PL 94-142, An act of Congress. Macmillan: New York.
PL 94-142, *Education for All Handicapped Children Act, 1975.*
PL 91-230, *Education of the Handicapped Act, 1970.*
PL 99-457, *Education of the Handicapped Act Amendments, 1986.*

IMPLEMENTING THE STATE OF THE ART AND INTEGRATION MANDATES OF PL 94-142

3

Margaret C. Wang

TWO IMPLEMENTATION STANDARDS IN SPECIAL EDUCATION HAVE BECOME increasingly clear since passage of the Education for All Handicapped Children Act (Public Law 94-142, 1975). First, exceptional children are entitled to a free, appropriate, public education that is equal in quality to the education available to all other children. Second, special education services for exceptional children should be carried out in regular classrooms and schools, to the fullest extent possible. These interrelated standards for *appropriate* education in the *least restrictive environment (LRE)* may be referred to as the state of the art and the integration mandates of PL 94-142.

Educators, policymakers, and advocates have made significant prog-

---

Support for the preparation of this chapter was provided in part by the Temple University Center for Research in Human Development and Education and in part by the Bush Institute for Child and Family Policy, University of North Carolina at Chapel Hill. The views expressed are those of the author and do not necessarily reflect the positions or policies of the supporting agencies; no official endorsement should be inferred. The author would like to acknowledge especially the substantial editorial assistance of Rita Catalano and Joan Nikelsky in the final editing of this manuscript.

ress nationwide in ensuring the rights of all children—including those with greater-than-usual educational and related service needs—to be provided with instruction that effectively and efficiently meets their individual learning needs and to be educated in integrated settings. A 1985 report to Congress noted that, during 1982–1983, 68% of all the children across the nation who were identified as disabled attended classes with their nondisabled peers for at least part of the time (U.S. Department of Education, 1985).

Although such statistics are impressive and can be celebrated, we have yet to achieve fully the promise and the intent of the state of the art and integration mandates of PL 94-142. Many students continue to be segregated in a variety of disjointed programs; inconsistent and scientifically questionable systems for classifying and placing students in special education programs still are widely in use. Several comprehensive reviews of research and practice in special education in recent years have pointed uniformly to these two continuing patterns as major barriers to implementing appropriate (state-of-the-art) education for all students in the least restrictive (integrated) environment (Heller, Holtzman, & Messick, 1982; Hobbs, 1975, 1980; Wang, Reynolds, & Walberg, 1987–1988).

The twofold purpose of this chapter is to review briefly the major developments and implementation efforts related to the state of the art and integration mandates, and to discuss some of the implications this history would have for reform and future implementation. The discussion is guided by an interest in the central question of why, more than 10 years after the enactment of PL 94-142, the legally required and practically feasible delivery of special education as an integral part of general education programs still is not a widespread reality in the nation's schools.

First, the legal basis for the delivery of special education in regular classrooms is reviewed. Next, the historical evolutions of separate special education systems and the mainstreaming movement are traced briefly. That discussion is followed by an analysis of extant practice and of the current barriers to fulfilling the state of the art and integration mandates of PL 94-142. Finally, prospects for providing more effective and inclusive schooling for all children, including those with special learning needs, are discussed.

THE LEGAL BASIS FOR THE DELIVERY OF SPECIAL EDUCATION IN REGULAR CLASSROOMS

The integration of exceptional children into the regular school environment—commonly referred to as mainstreaming—has long been a major focus of efforts in special education to improve the quality of schooling for students with special learning needs. Serious attempts to integrate these students into the mainstream of the physical, social, and intellectual life of schools have intensified as a result of the wave of legislation and court rulings concerning children's rights to an appropriate education in the least restrictive environment. The legislation and judicial pronouncements in this area are exemplified by PL 94-142, which was passed by the 94th Congress and still is in effect, and by the landmark case of *Brown v. The Board of Education* (1954) and the more recent case of *PARC (Pennsylvania Association for Retarded Children) v. Pennsylvania* (1972).

States and school districts that accept funds from the federal government to help support special education services do so with the understanding that they are subject to the legislative intent of relevant federal laws and congressional acts. With the passage of PL 94-142 in 1975, Congress endorsed a new public policy for state and local educational agencies—namely, the provision of appropriate education in the least restrictive environment. Implementation of this policy calls for moving special education away from the educational apartheid that previously had prevailed, and toward integration into the total educational system. It requires two specific forms of action. One involves "bringing the children back," a sequence of step-by-step plans for the reentry of students presently enrolled in segregated special education programs. The second action involves "keeping the children in." This action emphasizes accommodating and supporting students with special learning needs in general education settings to the maximum extent possible and bringing in special education services as needed. Effective implementation of these actions dictates using the best current know-how to provide effective special and general education services.

Prior to PL 94-142, states had provided standards and financial support for teaching students with special needs, on the condition that these children be separated from regular classrooms for part or all of the school day. A policy of keeping the children in, however, clearly calls for an extension of special education services to include teaching students with special needs in regular classrooms. It is clear from both the legislative history and the actual language of PL 94-142 that Congress intended to mandate special education support for exceptional children while they are in regular class settings.

In the law, the essence of special education is defined as specially designed, individualized instruction that meets the unique needs of a handicapped child (PL 94-142, 34 C.F.R. Part 300.14 [A]). Specific setting, specific kind of teacher, category, and being in the company of similar or dissimilar children for instruction are not part of the definition. Furthermore, the least restrictive environment principle of PL 94-142 places the burden on local educational agencies to justify the removal of students with special needs from regular classrooms. The Congress intended to provide a solid legal basis for maintaining special education delivery as part of general education through the use of state-of-the-art supplementary aids and services to the extent possible, before resorting to partial or fully segregated special education placements.

HISTORICAL PERSPECTIVE ON SPECIAL EDUCATION AND THE MAINSTREAMING MOVEMENT

Implementation of the state of the art and integration mandates of PL 94-142 must be understood in the context of the evolution of special education in this country. Beginning as long ago as the 1890s and early 1900s, the commitment to free and equal educational opportunities for all students has been a staple of educational reform in the United States. Indeed, it has continued to be a major force in establishing and maintaining special education as a component of the nation's public education system. Yet efforts to achieve free and equal educational opportunities have taken two very different, but simultaneous paths. One has been the development of special education as a separate educational system; the other has been a movement to accommodate students with special learning needs in the mainstream.

Development of Special Education as a Separate Educational System

It is not always possible to teach every student effectively in the mainstream. This was strikingly evident in the early 1900s when mass instruction predominated. All students were expected to learn at the same pace and in the same way. The mainstream, or the regular class environment, was narrow and tightly circumscribed. Individual differences in background, motivation, and capability were neither well understood nor tolerated. Under these conditions, many students did not benefit; they left school either uneducated or undereducated.

By the early 1920s, educators and allied human services personnel had begun calling attention to the need to provide special education for students who were essentially denied an education because they did not fit into the limited range of acceptance within the schools. The concern for such children led to the development of a special education system that was administratively and instructionally separate from general education.

Although many educators in the 1920s and 1930s argued that schools should become more open, flexible, and individualized in curriculum and teaching, special educators followed an easier and seemingly more realistic path. They considered their chief task the prompt delivery of education to the "outcasts." The separation of these students from regular classes had several tangible and immediately gratifying effects. It made students with special needs highly visible; it moved philanthropy in the direction of special education; and it deterred confrontation with the general education system. Indeed, the separation drew plaudits from many general educators. The result was a rapid growth in special classes and special schools.

During those years, growing numbers of teachers were trained and classes and schools were designed specifically to serve students identified as blind, partially visually impaired, deaf, hard-of-hearing, ambulation impaired, health impaired, speech impaired, socially maladjusted, emotionally disturbed, brain injured, mentally retarded, slow learners, or mentally gifted. States began to designate separate funds for particular types of special education, over and above the support for general schooling, if certain standards were met. The state standards encouraged full or partial separation of students with special needs from the mainstream of education.

As noted by Reynolds and Lakin (1987), it was not a mere coincidence that Binet's work on intelligence testing, begun in France at the turn of the 20th century, was quickly adapted for use in the United States to predict which students were likely to perform poorly in general education programs. This focus on testing led to the strategy of setting aside students with poor prognoses for academic success, not because of evidence that they would achieve better in special education programs, but simply because they were expected to do less well than their peers in general education classes.

Through the 1940s and 1950s, special education based on the separation model grew in terms of size, professional endorsement, and public acceptance. The dual pattern of general and special education continued to expand and flourish through the 1970s. Several generations of Americans became acculturated to it. For years, general and special education maintained and developed distinct structures and styles while coexisting in a relationship that seemed to be mutually beneficial.

The Mainstreaming Movement

In the 1920s and 1930s, when special education was starting to develop separately, general educators were beginning to respond to the burgeoning knowledge base in psychology regarding human learning and personality development. Drawing from this knowledge base, many elementary and secondary schools opened up and expanded their curricula; they began to personalize instruction and the educational decision-making process for individual students (Wang & Lindvall, 1984). However, by the time the influence for this trend in general education could be felt, the structure of separate special education for exceptional children had solidified.

Nevertheless, beginning in the late 1920s, many professionals did not agree that the delivery of high quality special education was incompatible with student life in the mainstream. These educators experimented with various means of providing the greater-than-usual instruction and services required by exceptional children—while these students attended the same neighborhood elementary and secondary schools as their sisters, brothers, and friends on the block.

The delivery of special education and related services while the recipients attended general education classes included physical, social, and instructional integration. Trial efforts to teach exceptional children of all kinds (i.e., deaf, blind, retarded, ambulation impaired children) in regular schools were often successful. These efforts interacted with the sweeping national public policy changes that spanned the 1950s, 1960s, and 1970s to accelerate a realignment of relationships between special and general education. This realignment involved major changes in the pattern of separate educational systems that had long predominated.

In the early 1950s, the landmark Supreme Court decision on racial integration (*Brown v. The Board of Education*, 1954) released a tide of personal sentiment and civil rights actions that continues to have an impact on the nation's educational, social, economic, and political systems. Hundreds of laws and regulations that discriminated on the basis of race, sex, age, handicap, religion, or national origin have been rewritten or dropped altogether. It was probably the public policy changes on the national scene that tipped the scales in the direction of those special and general educators who earlier had argued on rational and professional grounds that special education, because of its increased sophistication and portability, could be delivered effectively in the context of general education. They maintained that it was no longer necessary to separate students with special learning needs, except in extreme cases or for occasional short, intense periods of instruction. Particularly since the late 1970s, evidence for this view has grown and has demonstrated that the mainstream is not just for general education students; it also can accommodate a full range of exceptional children, providing them with appropriate and adequate support (cf. Heller et al., 1982; Wang et al., 1987–1988).

EXTANT PRACTICE AND IMPLEMENTATION BARRIERS

To date, there has been only limited compliance with the public policy that calls for educating exceptional students together with all other children to the greatest extent feasible. Although a growing percentage of students with special learning needs are being served in regular school environments for at least part of the time (U.S. Department of Education, 1985), pervasive implementation problems remain. Built-in funding disincentives and current special education classification systems frequently are cited as major barriers. They have resulted in excessive proceduralism, which is propagated by, and in turn reinforces, the belief that the most fiscally expedient and pedagogically appropriate approach to providing special education for students who require greater-than-usual instructional and related service support is to organize the special services separately from general education programs and students. In a recent article titled "Disabling Help: Special Education at the Crossroads," Gartner (1986) notes the following:

> This belief produces a set of practices that shunts too many students inappropriately—too quickly and without good reason—into special education, serving them poorly there, and (in part as a result of this poor service) doing little to return these students to general education. The problem lies not with PL 94-142. It lies in the actions of state education departments (legislatively and administratively), in local districts (organizationally and operationally), and within the general and special education communities. (p. 72)

In addition to excessive proceduralism, the narrowness of current classification categories has produced disjointed bureaucratic structures for funding and monitoring the plethora of special programs. The inefficient processes by which these various school programs are partitioned for management have made the positions of school principals very difficult. Likewise, the profession of school psychology has been compromised, insofar as psychologists are the ones who are expected to actually make classification decisions based on narrow categories of exceptionality. Bureaucratic rules and regulations often are not tempered by professional considerations, which leads to increasing intellectual and moral frustration over what is perceived to be an expanding "nonsystem" of education.

Funding Disincentives and The "Catch 22" in Special Education Reform

Current special education funding policies produce major complications for implementing the state of the art and integration mandates of PL 94-142. Policies that govern who pays for what, and under what conditions, frequently have been singled out as one of the most serious deterrents to the institutionalization of mainstreaming programs in local schools. Wang and Reynolds (1985) have described a recent case that illustrates the nature and effects of these obstacles. They briefly trace the successful implementation of special education services as an integrated component of the general education program in regular classrooms, followed by the discontinuation of this demonstrably effective approach because of funding disincentives.

The case described by Wang and Reynolds (1985) involved the implementation of the Adaptive Learning Environments Model (ALEM) (Wang, 1980, 1981; Wang, Gennari, & Waxman, 1985) in five schools of the New York City school system. The ALEM was introduced in these schools in 1982–1983 as an alternative intervention for mainstreaming students classified as mildly handicapped (i.e., learning disabled, mildly behaviorally disordered, and educable mentally retarded students) into regular classes on a full-time basis. The mainstreamed students enrolled in the ALEM classes formerly had been placed in self-contained, full-time, special education classes.

Data collected throughout the 1982–1983 school year suggest that the ALEM was implemented effectively at all five schools, and that the program produced a variety of positive outcomes. Both the general education students and the mainstreamed special education students in the ALEM classes made significant achievement gains, greater than expected, in reading and math. The mainstreamed special education students made average gains of a little more than 1 year in reading and math (compared with the national norm of a 1-year expected gain). By contrast, an average gain of 6 months was obtained by students with special education classifications similar to those of the mainstreamed ALEM students but placed in self-contained, special education programs. Positive changes in classroom processes was another outcome in the ALEM classes. For example, there were significant increases in the instruction-related interactions between teachers and students and in the constructive interactions among students. Overall, there were essentially no differences in the classroom behaviors of the general education students and the mainstreamed special education students.

As a result of the positive outcomes for the mainstreamed special education students in the ALEM classes, about 30% of these students were recommended by teachers and principals for decertification (removal of the handicap classification) at the end of the school year. This contrasts sharply with the average decertification rate of less than 3% for students in the New York City school system with similar classifications enrolled in self-contained, special education classes. Another indicator of the feasibility and effective implementation of the ALEM as a full-time mainstreaming program was a strong recommendation by parents, instructional staff, local school officials, and central district administrators to continue and extend the program at the end of the first year of implementation.

Despite the evidence of the ALEM's effectiveness and the endorsement of its feasibility by all major stakeholder groups, the school board decided to discontinue the program's implementation after the successful first year. This decision was based on a state regulation that excludes the full-time mainstreaming of special education students as a special education service eligible for state funding support. In accordance with this regulation, the Office of Special Education of the New York Department of Education ruled that reimbursements could not be allowed for providing special education support to identified special education students who are mainstreamed full-time. Thus, rather than forfeit the reimbursements that ordinarily would be made to their local schools, the school board ordered that all special education students mainstreamed in ALEM classes that year be returned to self-contained, special education classes, or to "pull-out" resource room arrangements for the following academic year. (For thorough reports of this case, see Wang & Reynolds, 1985; and Wang, Rubenstein, & Reynolds, 1985.)

The "Catch-22" aspect of this case is summarized by Wang and Reynolds (1985) as follows:

> Given: Special education funding should be used to provide the best possible education for handicapped students in the "least restrictive environment."
>
> Finding: Provision of effective instruction for handicapped students in regular classes is feasible.
>
> The "Catch": Provision of educational services that are tailored to the learning needs of handicapped students in regular classes cannot be supported by special education funds under current policy guidelines.
>
> Consequence: In order to maintain levels of special education funding support provided by state departments of education to local education agencies for meeting the instructional and related service needs of handicapped students, mainstreamed handicapped students have been returned to self-contained special education classes and special education resource room programs where they are being educated in more restrictive environments. (p. 501)

The incompatibility between state funding policies and efforts to fully implement PL 94-142 is due, in part, to what Gallagher (1981) has called "policy interpretation" by the agencies in charge of translating the law. In the mid-1970s, when PL 94-142 was enacted, there were no well-recognized, thoroughly tested systems for providing greater-than-usual instructional support for students with special learning needs in regular classes, even though there was widespread acceptance of the concept of mainstreaming and a federal policy that "separate is not equal." The part-time integration of general education and special education students, based on the resource room model, had become an accepted pattern. In this model, special education is provided outside of the general education program on a part-time basis, thereby allowing students who are judged ready for mainstreaming to be integrated into regular classrooms for part of the school day. Students judged ready are usually those classified in the mild handicap categories such as learning disabled, mildly behaviorally disordered, or educable mentally retarded. During the first decade after passage of PL 94-142, this part-time, pull-out approach expanded in many variations to become the predominant practice in special education.

The establishment of resource rooms for the provision of special education and related services has formed the basis for, as well as the barrier to, full compliance with the integration mandate of PL 94-142. It is now common for states to issue regulations or standards that specify the makeup of settings like resource rooms, special classes, and itinerant instructional arrangements. In addition, states have regulations and standards for entry into and exit from such approved special education settings, as well as formulas for determining the amount and conditions of the funding that may be given to local educational agencies to help meet the costs of special education. The funding formulas of most states are weighted to reward separateness rather than to encourage the provision of special education and related services in the least restrictive environment, as part of the general education program. A school receives *more*, rather than *less*, funding when it places a greater number of students in more restrictive settings. Thus, the rhetoric in educational programming and funding policy may embrace the goals of PL 94-142, but separateness prevails in the reality of current practice.

It is not surprising that state funding systems continue to reward separateness and that the states have not set standards and regulations for the delivery of special education in regular classes, even though that is the most desirable model according to federal law and court decisions. Until recently, there was no urgent need for states to change their practices in this area. There were few systematic attempts to implement the integration mandate of PL 94-142 by providing special education in regular classes, and there was no strong evidence of the practicability and efficacy of this approach.

In the 1980s, however, several research-based models have been shown effective in providing special education in regular classrooms.

Many of these models are considered to be exemplary special education practices, and they have been recognized in several recent major reviews by study groups and commissions (cf. Heller et al., 1982; Mayor's Commission on Special Education, 1985; Wang et al., 1987–1988). Furthermore, the general trend nationwide has been to become more inclusive by gradually assimilating larger and more diverse populations of children into regular schools (U.S. Department of Education, 1985). This is reflected in efforts within regular classes and schools to accommodate increasingly greater numbers of handicapped, minority, migrant, bilingual, and other children who are considered to be out of the mainstream. Thus, the time is ripe for serious examination of current funding policies and regulations in light of the programming and attitudinal trends toward bringing the children back to, and keeping them in, regular classrooms.

The Research Base on Extant Classification Systems

Researchers and practitioners consistently have singled out current classification practices as a critical obstacle to the implementation of appropriate education in the least restrictive environment (cf. Heller et al., 1982; Hobbs, 1975; Wang et al., 1987–1988). Based on findings from his landmark work focusing on issues in this area, Hobbs (1975, 1980) concluded that the approaches used in schools to classify and place students in special education programs were "a major barrier to the efficient and effective delivery of services to them and their families" (Hobbs, 1980, p. 274). A similar conclusion was drawn by the National Academy of Sciences (NAS) panel that investigated the disproportional rates of placement of minority and male children in special education programs. The NAS panel pointed out that current classification systems for identifying students who require special education have been shown in many cases to be educationally ineffective while also burdening schools with excessive administrative and financial costs (Heller et al., 1982).

Findings and conclusions from a recently completed synthesis of research, policy, and practice in special education (Wang et al., 1987–1988) corroborate those of Hobbs and the NAS panel. This work comprises 45 chapters organized around nine major topic areas: 1) education of deaf children and youth, 2) education of visually handicapped children and youth, 3) handicapped infants, 4) mild mental retardation, 5) behavioral disorders, 6) learning disabilities, 7) learning characteristics of handicapped students, 8) effectiveness of differential programming in serving handicapped students, and 9) noncategorical programming for serving handicapped students. In the reviews across all nine topics, the authors cite the lack of consistency in defining categories of children as a major problem in classification and in structuring educational programs. These problems are particularly serious for students with mild and moderate handicap labels.

Differences in state eligibility criteria have resulted in large disparities in the percentages of students classified as educable mentally retarded (from 0.49% in Alaska to 4.14% in Alabama); learning disabled (from 0.83% in New York to 5.20% in Maryland); and emotionally disturbed (from 0.04% in Mississippi to 3.09% in Utah) (Morsink, Thomas, & Smith-Davis, 1987). Gerber (1987) notes that "efforts to install practical, instructional, or programming guidance from research are severely hampered [by] . . . persistent variability in characteristics of school-identified samples of students classified under the various categories of mild handicap" (p. 38). Moreover, as noted by Keogh (1988) in her review of research and practice in the education of children with learning disabilities, classification often is influenced by multiple factors other than children's instruction-related needs. These factors include the availability of physical space and professional staff; the competition among programs and services; and the guidelines and pressures of federal, state, and local agencies and policies (Keogh, 1988).

Services for learning disabled students have shown the largest growth of all categories in recent years, and this area now presents a great challenge to classification and service delivery in special education. Keogh (1988) cites Edgar and Hayden's (1984–1985) finding that the number of individuals for all handicap conditions has increased 16% since 1976–1977, while the number for learning disabilities (LD) has increased 119%. The LD category is probably the least well-defined of all special education categories, and yet it has grown so rapidly. Ysseldyke (1987) reports that "more than 80% of normal students could be classified as learning disabled by one or more definitions now in use." Even within the same state, the LD category can present major difficulties, as indicated in the following example, a summary statement by Smith, Wood, and Grimes (1988):

> More than 45% of the students enrolled in Colorado's LD programs did not meet the state criteria for placement (Shepard & Smith, 1981). This result is in agreement with Algozzine and Ysseldyke's (1981) finding that 51% of the LD students in their study did not meet placement criteria. Further, Ysseldyke, Algozzine, Shinn, and McGue (1982) found no significant difference between low achievers and identified LD students. . . . [These studies] suggest the lack of consistency in decisions made by special education MDTs [multidisciplinary teams]. (p. 110)

The emotional disturbance category is similarly problematic. Lakin (1983) analyzed the results from randomly selected studies of emotionally disturbed children that were published over a 10-year period up to 1978. He found that "over 80% of the studies reviewed selected subjects by presence in a setting . . . or by soliciting and accepting nominations of subjects without any attempts to substantiate, quantify, or qualify the cases of those nominations" (Lakin, 1983, pp. 130–131). Likewise, Nelson and Rutherford (1988) observe that "who is or is not labeled behaviorally disordered for a given educational program or research investigation is likely to depend as much on political and subjective factors as on objective behavioral criteria." (p. 125)

Furthermore, research suggests that most educational plans currently designed for students with special learning needs are unrelated to screening and diagnostic classifications. In addition, categorical, compensatory, and remedial programs often are concerned more with administrative procedures than with the substantive goals of education (Reschly, 1987). Consequently, techniques that have been identified as highly productive for both general and special education (cf. U.S. Department of Education, 1986; Wang et al., 1987–1988; Wittrock 1986) tend to be overlooked as alternative interventions for helping students with special learning needs remain in regular classrooms. Examples of such identified techniques are mastery learning, cooperative learning, adaptive instruction, and school-based home enrichment.

Admittedly, administrative concerns must be addressed—the questions of who requires what special services, and who should provide them. But these concerns should no longer be the focal point of effort to comply with the legal mandates of PL 94-142. After more than 10 years of this approach, it is time to take stock of what has been learned from research and practical experience. Now we need to do some critical rethinking and restructuring that will take us beyond the service delivery mode to a quality of services mode for monitoring the efficiency and effectiveness of special education.

In his analysis of school reform efforts, including compliance with PL 94-142, Seeley (1984) notes that the continuing preoccupation with the who and what questions is a fundamental conceptual flaw. When certain children are not learning, or are not learning enough, the first reaction typically is to find ways to improve or expand their school's instructional and/or related services. However, according to Seeley, the problem in many schools is not with the instructional services themselves but with the relationship between the services and student learning. Improved or expanded services, which often are provided at great effort and expense, increase the instructional resources available, but they do not necessarily increase and improve student learning. The illusion of improvement may be created through the addition of more or better-trained teachers, smaller classes, more advanced equipment, and newer curriculum materials. However, unless these resources and accompanying services demonstrably improve student learning, we simply have provided different, and often more expensive, services that actually may be ineffective.

Many of the issues surrounding classification and eligibility for services, including the questions of who should receive and who should provide what services, will be resolved when improved student learning becomes the primary focus of special education efforts. These efforts then will focus on the efficient and effective implementation of special education to maximize learning for students who require greater-than-usual instructional and related service support.

THE PROSPECTS FOR DEMONSTRABLY EFFECTIVE IMPLEMENTATION

Full compliance with the state of the art and integration mandates of PL 94-142 to develop fully each student's talents will be possible only when educational productivity is increased for *all* students. Research on what makes learning more productive has been compiled, synthesized, and critically analyzed in recent years. This research suggests ways of delivering instruction that are substantially superior to traditional, widespread practices (Wang & Walberg, 1986). Many alternative interventions have been tested, and a variety of traditional practices and innovative techniques in both general and special education have been found effective in learning. Even though the state of the art of educational research is ahead of the state of actual practice in schools, many improvements are feasible and could be implemented to benefit general education students and students with special learning needs alike.

Figure 1 presents a general overview of the knowledge base derived from an integrative analysis of findings in the recent literature on effective teaching and school effectiveness research (Walberg, 1984; Wang, Reynolds, & Walberg, 1986; Wittrock, 1986). The first column of Figure 1 lists features of effective classroom learning environments. The corresponding expected outcomes are grouped into four categories: development of positive attitudes toward learning, acquisition of a variety of learning skills, mastery of subject matter content, and development of positive self-perceptions. The Xs indicate that findings from research studies suggest relationships between the implementation of specific features and the achievement of particular student outcomes. For example, programs that include frequent, systematic evaluation of progress and feedback are associated with at least seven expected student outcomes: motivation for continuing to learn, ability to study and learn independently, ability to plan and monitor learning activities, ability to obtain assistance from others, mastery of content and skills for effective functioning, mastery of content and skills for further learning, and confidence in one's ability as a learner. The information shown in Figure 1 suggests that a substantial knowledge base can be applied to the improvement of current practice in general and special education.

The list of effective practices in special education is not very different from the findings summarized in Figure 1. Among these practices are teachers working together in teams; frequent evaluation of, and feedback on, each student's performance; use of a diagnostic-prescriptive process to plan and monitor students' learning progress; and close school-home cooperation. Research suggests that many of the same practices are used by both effective special education teachers and general education teachers who successfully serve mainstreamed students in regular classrooms (Brophy, 1986; Brophy & Good, 1986; Wang et al., 1987–1988). Such findings give substantive reasons for the belief that, with help provided by special needs professionals, general education teachers can accommodate the needs of special education students. The overall similarities in the research bases on effective special and general education suggest the feasibility of restructuring the two systems so that a continuum of services can be provided and the vision of educational excellence for *all* students, including those with special needs, can be realized in regular class settings.

DISCUSSION AND RECOMMENDATIONS

In summary, the present approach to providing instructional and related support for students with special needs clearly is not meeting the standards prescribed by PL 94-142. The practices currently used to determine eligibility for special services are exceedingly costly and educationally ineffective. They do not ensure the kind of accountability that is desired by child advocates and educators. Neither do they have the potential to adequately accommodate the demographic realities of the coming decade.

Demographic Changes and Challenges

As we look to the future, the inefficiencies in current educational practice can be expected to pose increasing problems. Every indicator shows that the number and the proportion of children with special needs are rising

Features of effective classroom learning environments	Expected student outcomes — Development of positive attitudes toward learning			
	Enjoyment in taking part in learning activities	Viewing help-giving and help-receiving as positive experiences	Special interest in certain learning areas	Motivation for continuing to learn
Instructional content that is:				
Essential to further learning			X	
Useful for effective functioning in school and society			X	X
Clearly specified				
Organized to facilitate efficient learning				X
Assessment and diagnosis that:				
Provide appropriate placement in the curricula				X
Provide frequent and systematic evaluation of progress and feedback				X
Learning experiences in which:				
Ample time and instructional support are provided for each student to acquire essential content	X		X	X
Disruptiveness is minimized	X			X
Students use effective learning strategies/study skills				X
Each student is expected to succeed, and actually succeeds, in achieving mastery of curriculum content, and accomplishments are reinforced	X		X	X
Alternative instructional strategies, student assignments, and activities are used	X			X
Management of instruction that:				
Permits students to master many lessons through independent study				X
Permits students to plan their own learning activities	X			X
Provides for students' self-monitoring of their progress with most lessons	X		X	X
Permits students to play a part in selecting some learning goals and activities	X		X	X
Collaboration among students that:				
Enables students to obtain necessary help from peers	X	X		
Encourages students to provide help	X	X	X	
Provides for collaboration in group activities	X	X	X	

FIGURE 1. Examples of features of classroom learning environments and expected student outcomes. The X indicates that extant findings from studies on effective teaching and learning suggest relationships between the implementation of specific features and the achievement of particular student outcomes. (Source: Wang, M.C., Reynolds, M.C.,

Acquisition of a variety of learning skills			Mastery of subject matter content		Development of positive self-perceptions			
Ability to study and learn independently	Ability to plan and monitor learning activities	Ability to obtain assistance from others	Mastery of content and skills for effective functioning	Mastery of content and skills for further learning	Confidence in one's ability as a learner	Confidence in oneself as a contributing member of the school/community	Confidence in one's ability to take self-responsibility for learning and behavior	Perceptions of internal locus of control
			X	X	X			
			X	X				
X	X		X	X	X		X	
X	X		X	X	X		X	
X			X	X	X			
X	X	X	X	X	X			
			X	X	X			X
X	X		X	X			X	
X	X	X	X	X	X		X	
			X	X	X	X	X	
X	X		X	X	X			
X	X		X	X	X			X
X	X		X	X	X			X
X	X		X	X	X		X	X
X	X		X	X	X		X	X
	X	X	X	X	X		X	X
		X	X	X		X		X
	X	X	X	X	X	X	X	X

Walberg, H.J. [1986]. Rethinking special education. *Educational Leadership*, 44, 28–29. Reprinted with permission of the Association for Supervision and Curriculum Development and Margaret C. Wang. Copyright © 1986 by the Association For Supervision and Curriculum Development. All rights reserved.)

and will continue to rise in the coming years. Demographic data show that the number and percentage of children living in poverty have increased steadily in recent years. This trend will be sustained because of higher fertility rates for women at low income levels, compared to those for women at average or higher income levels. The significance of growing numbers of poor children is that poverty correlates with a greatly increased need for remedial educational services. The rates at which children are judged by teachers to need remedial or special education are much higher for children in poverty than for children from families with greater economic resources (Wang, 1987).

Another reason for continuing growth in the number of children with special needs is the dramatic increase in infant survival rates. Currently in the United States more than 1 infant in 20 is placed in an intensive neonatal care unit at birth or soon after, with low birth weight being a frequent factor in such placements. The survival rate of these children has improved greatly, but the disability rate also has increased. Data from the Collaborative Perinatal Study (Broman, Nicholas, & Kennedy, 1975) and other major studies (Wiener, 1968) suggest that special education services are required as much as 2.5 times more frequently for low birth weight children than for normal birth weight children (Scott & Carran, 1988).

Still another important demographic factor is a general increase predicted for the school-age population. From 1975 to 1985, the school-age population decreased from 51 to 44 million, but, in a reversal of that trend, the number is expected to approximate 50 million by the year 2000 (Reynolds & Lakin, 1987). The overall increase in the number of school-age children, including greater proportions of students with special needs, is likely to contribute to the negative climate in which general education has been forced to compete for funds to support special programs.

Seeking Solutions through Early Intervention

The statistics on increasing numbers of students with special needs have particular implications for the design of improved education programs for children from birth through age 5. There are considerable findings to support the contention that early intervention can have substantial and immediate positive effects for young children with special needs (White & Casto, 1985). These include gains in physical, cognitive, language-speech, and psychosocial development (U.S. House of Representatives Committee on Education and Labor, 1986). Of equal importance is the growing evidence that the need for special education placements in later school years is reduced significantly for children who receive early intervention services (Lazar & Darlington, 1982; Schweinhart & Weickart, 1981; U.S. House of Representatives Committee on Education and Labor, 1986).

Since the late 1960s, there have been several major federally supported vehicles for delivering educational and related services to mildly handicapped and at-risk preschool children—the Handicapped Children's Early Education Program, Head Start, Follow Through, and the Preschool Incentive Grants issued under PL 94-142. Studies of these and other programmatic efforts have yielded an important knowledge base for the features of effective early intervention. These features include services for family involvement and parent training; instruction in survival skills, with a focus on developmental and pre-academic skills expected of entering students; and use of instructional strategies and classroom structures like those in kindergarten or first grade (e.g., Gallagher & Bristol, 1988; Vincent et al., 1980; Zeitlin, 1981). The intent of the second and third design features is to prepare young children for effective integration into regular school and classroom environments.

Early intervention programs for mildly handicapped children could be highly compatible settings for experimenting with noncategorical approaches to the design and delivery of educational services (Nevin & Thousand, 1987). Distinctions in cognitive, behavioral, and social skills among children categorized as learning disabled and mildly mentally retarded often are difficult to determine during the preschool years. In fact, many parents and educators fear that the imposition of mild handicap labels at such an early age can become a self-fulfilling prophecy (Lerner, 1985; Mercer, 1983).

Recent efforts to improve the structure and delivery of early intervention programs have built upon the accumulated knowledge base and practical experience in ways that help ensure full compliance with the state of the art and integration mandates. The Education of the Handicapped Act Amendments of 1986 (PL 99-457, 1986) have validated and expanded the potential of early intervention for improving services to young children with special needs. Consequently, the amendments reduce the number of students who will be placed in special elementary and secondary school programs. PL 99-457 mandates each state to begin providing free and appropriate preschool interventions for all handicapped children ages 3 through 5 by fiscal year 1991. It also provides funding for the development and implementation of statewide, multidisciplinary, interagency programs for handicapped infants and toddlers. This initiative addresses the long-standing need for broad-based, systematic practices in handicapped infant screening, family services, follow-up, and program evaluation (Hart, 1988).

Several of the stated objectives of PL 99-457 reflect a commitment to apply the lessons learned from the history of separateness in special and general education. Among these objectives are greater interagency cooperation and the use of multidisciplinary evaluation to diagnose the specific learning needs of individual children. The amendments also encourage experimentation, including the development, demonstration, and dissemination of "program models and exemplary practices in the areas of special education and early intervention" (§ 641[a][4]). In addition, the amendments respond to the need to link training efforts in special and general education: Special grants are endorsed for the development and demonstration of pre-service training programs "for regular educators . . . and for the inservice training of special education personnel, including classroom personnel who serve handicapped children and personnel providing early intervention services" (§ 308). Thus, PL 99-457 and the programmatic and administrative developments being implemented as a result, may be viewed as important precursors of system-wide improvement in the provision of state-of-the-art, integrated education for children of all ages.

In its report on the Education of the Handicapped Amendments of 1986, the United States House of Representatives Committee on Education and Labor (U.S. House) endorsed early intervention programs that focus on the quality of instruction rather than the administrative encumbrances of special labels, categories, and funding sources (U.S. House, 1986). The report notes, "It is the Committee's understanding that a child's special educational needs are the determining factors in designing an appropriate program; not the availability of certain services or administrative conveniences" (p. 40). The Committee's report encourages research and demonstration projects to improve the coordination of services in general and special education, particularly in avoiding the use of "different and sometimes conflicting methods of instruction" for handicapped children (p. 32).

The report also mandates that state and local educational agencies should focus their evaluations of early intervention programs on age groups rather than categories of disability. The Committee notes that this amendment "will enable States to identify and serve young handicapped children and infants and toddlers without having to categorically label these children by disability category because of the existence of the data collection requirements" (p. 39). PL 99-457 further stipulates that national evaluations of programs for handicapped children should include reports of "the number of handicapped children and youth in each state who are participating in regular educational programs. . . . "(§ 406).

Directions for System-Wide Improvement

To achieve nationwide improvement in the provision of appropriate education in the least restrictive environment for students from preschool through high school, progress is needed on three fronts: policy, administration, and programming.

On the policy front, the first move toward a productive collaboration between general and special education should be to eliminate the inherent disincentives in current funding policies that have thwarted attempts by local districts and schools to comply with the state of the art and integration mandates of PL 94-142. Special education funding must be linked to a full continuum of services that can be delivered in regular classes, including supportive aids and preventive services.

Administratively, productive linkages must be established among classroom instructional staff and school-based and district-based special education support staff. A variety of changes in functions and roles needs to occur. General education teachers at all school levels and in all curriculum areas should become more knowledgeable and competent to teach exceptional students of all kinds. They will not replace special education teachers or other specialized professionals; rather, the two groups will work closely together, along with parents, to identify, plan for, guide, instruct, and evaluate the progress of individual students with special needs. As more schools build up strong support systems, including consultation, teaching assistance, staff development programs, and a variety of curriculum materials and instructional approaches, general education teachers will be better able to instruct students with special needs in regular class settings.

Programmatically, special education must be understood in terms of the whole educational enterprise. The effective integration of special needs students in regular classes requires an educationally powerful mainstreaming system, including a special education program that is an integral part of a unified, school-wide approach. In such an approach, as much of the special education program as possible is provided in regular classes; specialized settings are used only when essential and for limited periods of time. As noted by Reynolds and Birch (1982), training should be emphasized as a function of special educators, school psychologists, speech clinicians, school social workers, and other specialized staff, all of whom should work to share their competencies with general education teachers and other staff members. In this context, general education teachers have the option and, indeed, the responsibility, to call in specialists to help with students' learning and related service problems at the time of need, when the students can benefit most, rather than waiting for children to "greatly" fail before they can be taken out of general education programs to receive special education services.

A revered Chinese educator once said, "A journey of a thousand miles must begin with a single step." PL 94-142 represents an important first step. Educators, researchers, and policymakers can prolong the journey by continuing the debate over who should receive, and who should deliver, special education services, or they can accept the challenge to guide and reshape the field of special education in the long journey to realizing the full promise of PL 94-142. We must take stock of our more than 10 years of experience and build upon the advances made on behalf of students requiring greater-than-usual education and related service support, as we move forward to accept the challenge of restructuring current delivery systems in ways that more effectively and efficiently meet the requirements of the Education for All Handicapped Children Act of 1975—both the spirit and the letter of the law.

REFERENCES

Algozzine, B., & Ysseldyke, J.E. (1981). Special education services for normal children: Better safe than sorry? *Exceptional Children, 48*, 238–243.

Broman, S.H., Nicholas, P.L., & Kennedy, W.A. (1975). *Preschool IQ: Prenatal and early development correlates.* New York: John Wiley & Sons.

Brophy, J.B. (1986). Research linking teacher behavior to student achievement: Potential implications for instruction of Chapter 1 students. In B.I. Williams, P.A. Richmond, & B.J. Mason (Eds.), *Designs for compensatory education: Conference proceedings and papers* (Vol. 4, pp. 121–179). Washington, DC: Research and Evaluation Associates, Inc.

Brophy, J., & Good, T.L. (1986). Teacher behavior and student achievement. In M.C. Wittrock (Ed.), *Handbook of research on teaching* (3rd ed., pp. 328–375). Washington, DC: American Educational Research Association.

Brown v. The Board of Education, 347 U.S. 483 (1954).

Edgar, E., & Hayden, A.H. (1984–1985). Who are the children special education should serve and how many children are there? *The Journal of Special Education, 18*(4), 523–539.

Gallagher, J.J. (1981). Models for policy analysis: Child and family policy. In J.J. Gallagher, & F. Haskins (Eds.), *Models for analysis of social policy: An introduction* (pp. 37–77). Norwood, NJ: Ablex Publishing Co.

Gallagher, J.J., & Bristol, M. (1988). Families of young handicapped children. In M.C. Wang, M.C. Reynolds, & H.J. Walberg (Eds.), *Handbook of special education: Research and practice: Vol. 3, Low incidence conditions.* Oxford, England: Pergamon.

Gartner, A. (1986). Disabling help: Special education at the crossroads. *Exceptional Children, 53*(1), 72–76.

Gerber, M. (1987). Application of cognitive-behavioral training methods to teaching basic skills to mildly handicapped elementary school students. In M.C. Wang, M.C. Reynolds, & H.J. Walberg (Eds.), *Handbook of special education: Research and practice: Vol. 1. Learner characteristics and adaptive education* (pp. 167–186). Oxford, England: Pergamon.

Hart, V. (1988). Handicapped infants introduction. In M.C. Wang, M.C. Reynolds, & H.J. Walberg (Eds.), *Handbook of special education: Research and practice: Vol. 3. Low incidence conditions.* Oxford, England: Pergamon.

Heller, K.A., Holtzman, W., & Messick, S. (Eds.). (1982). *Placing children in special education: A strategy for equity.* Washington, DC: National Academy of Sciences Press.

Hobbs, N. (1975). *The futures of children.* San Francisco, CA: Jossey-Bass.

Hobbs, N. (1980). An ecologically oriented service-based system for the classification of handicapped children. In S. Salzinger, J. Antrobus, & J. Glick (Eds.), *The ecosystem of the "sick" child* (pp. 271–290). New York: Academic Press.

Keogh, B.K. (1988). Learning disability: Diversity in search of order. In M.C. Wang, M.C. Reynolds, & H.J. Walberg (Eds.), *Handbook of special education: Research and practice: Vol. 2. Mildly handicapped conditions* (pp. 225–251). Oxford, England: Pergamon.

Lakin, K.C. (1983). Research-based knowledge and professional practices in special education for emotionally disturbed students. *Behavioral Disorders, 8,* 128–137.

Lazar, I., & Darlington, R. (1982). Lasting effects of early education: A report from the consortium for longitudinal studies. *Monographs of the Society for Research in Child Development, 47*(2–3, Serial No. 195).

Lerner, J.W. (1985). *Learning disabilities: Theories, diagnosis, and teaching strategies* (3rd ed.). Boston: Houghton Mifflin.

Mayor's Commission on Special Education. (1985). *Special education: A call for quality.* New York: Author.

Mercer, C.D. (1983). *Students with learning disabilities* (2nd ed.). Columbus, OH: Charles E. Merrill.

Morsink, C.V., Thomas, C.C., & Smith-Davis, J. (1987). Noncategorical special education programs: Process and outcomes. In M.C. Wang, M.C. Reynolds, & H.J. Walberg (Eds.), *Handbook of special education: Research and practice: Vol. 1. Learner characteristics and adaptive education* (pp. 287–311). Oxford, England: Pergamon.

Nelson, C.M., & Rutherford, R.B., Jr. (1988). Behavioral interventions with behaviorally disordered students. In M.C. Wang, M.C. Reynolds, & H.J. Walberg (Eds.), *Handbook of special education: Research and practice: Vol. 2. Mildly handicapped conditions* (pp. 125–153). Oxford, England: Pergamon.

Nevin, A., & Thousand, J. (1987). Avoiding/limiting special education referrals: Changes and challenges. In M.C. Wang, M.C. Reynolds, & H.J. Walberg (Eds.), *Handbook of special education: Research and practice: Vol. 1. Learner characteristics and adaptive education* (pp. 273–286). Oxford, England: Pergamon.

PARC (Pennsylvania Association for Retarded Children) v. Pennsylvania, 343 F Supp. 279 (E.D. Pa. 1972).

PL 94-142. (1975). *The Education for All Handicapped Children Act.* Washington, DC.

PL 99-457. (1986). *Education of the Handicapped Act Amendments of 1986.* Washington, DC.

Reschly, D.J. (1987). Learning characteristics of mildly handicapped students: Implications for classification, placement and programming. In M.C. Wang, M.C. Reynolds, & H.J. Walberg (Eds.), *Handbook of special education: Research and practice: Vol. 1. Learner characteristics and adaptive education* (pp. 35–58). Oxford, England: Pergamon.

Reynolds, M.C., & Birch, J.W. (1982). *Teaching exceptional children in all America's schools* (2nd ed.). Reston, VA: Council for Exceptional Children.

Reynolds, M.C., & Lakin, K.C. (1987). Noncategorical special education: Models for research and practice. In M.C. Wang, M.C. Reynolds, & H.J. Walberg (Eds.), *Handbook of special education: Research and practice: Vol. 1. Learner characteristics and adaptive education* (pp. 331–356). Oxford, England: Pergamon.

Schweinhart, L.J., & Weikart, D.P. (1981). Effects of the Perry Preschool Program on youths through age 15. *Journal of the Division for Early Childhood, 4,* 29–39.

Scott, K.G., & Carran, D.T. (1988). Identification and referral of handicapped infants. In M.C. Wang, M.C. Reynolds, & H.J. Walberg (Eds.), *Handbook of special education: Research and practice: Vol. 3. Low incidence conditions.* Oxford, England: Pergamon.

Seeley, D.S. (1984). Educational partnership and the dilemma of school reform. *Phi Delta Kappan, 65*(6), 383–388.

Shepard, L.A., & Smith, M.L. (1981). *The identification, assessment, placement, and remediation of perceptual and communicative disordered children in Colorado.* Boulder: Laboratory of Education Research, University of Colorado.

Smith, C.R., Wood, F.H., & Grimes, J. (1988). Issues on the identification and placement of behaviorally disordered students. In M.C. Wang, M.C. Reynolds, & H.J. Walberg (Eds.), *Handbook of special education: Research and practice: Vol. 2. Mildly handicapped conditions* (pp. 95–123). Oxford, England: Pergamon.

U.S. Department of Education. (1985). *Seventh annual report to Congress on the implementation of Public Law 94-142: The Education for All Handicapped Children Act.* Washington, DC: Author.

U.S. Department of Education. (1986). *What works: Research about teaching and learning.* Washington, DC: Author.

U.S. House of Representatives, Committee on Education and Labor. (1986). *Report on the Education of the Handicapped Act Amendments of 1986.* Washington, DC: Author.

Vincent, L., Salisbury, C., Walter, G., Brown, P., Gruenewald, L., & Powers, M. (1980). Program evaluation and curriculum development in early childhood/special education: Criteria of the next environment. In W. Sailor, B. Wilcox, & L. Brown (Eds.), *Methods of instruction for severely handicapped students* (pp. 259–301). Baltimore: Paul H. Brookes Publishing Co.

Walberg, H.J. (1984). Improving the productivity of America's schools. *Educational Leadership, 41*(8), 19–30.

Wang, M.C. (1980). Adaptive instruction: Building on diversity. *Theory Into Practice, 19*(2), 122–127.

Wang, M.C. (1981). Mainstreaming exceptional children: Some instructional design considerations. *The Elementary School Journal, 81*(4), 195–221.
Wang, M.C. (1987, May). *Gearing up to meet the challenge of providing for the schooling needs of children and youth in a large urban setting in the 1990s.* Commentary presented at the Brown II Seminar Series Commemorative Program, Philadelphia School Board, Philadelphia, PA.
Wang, M.C., Gennari, P., & Waxman, H.C. (1985). The Adaptive Learning Environments Model: Design implementation, and effects. In M.C. Wang & H.J. Walberg (Eds.), *Adapting instruction to individual differences* (pp. 191–235). Berkeley, CA: McCutchan Publishing Corp.
Wang, M.C., & Lindvall, C.M. (1984). Individual differences and school learning environments. In E.W. Gordon (Ed.), *Review of research in education* (Vol. 11, pp. 161–225). Washington, DC: American Educational Research Association.
Wang, M.C., & Reynolds, M.C. (1985). Avoiding the "Catch 22" in special education reform. *Exceptional Children, 51*(6), 497–502.
Wang, M.C., Reynolds, M.C., & Walberg, H.J. (1986). Rethinking special education. *Educational Leadership, 44*(1), 26–31.
Wang, M.C., Reynolds, M.C., & Walberg, M.J. (Eds.) (1987–1988). *Handbook of special education: Research and practice* (3 vols.). Oxford, England: Pergamon.
Wang, M.C., Rubenstein, J.L., & Reynolds, M.C. (1985). Clearing the road to success for students with special needs. *Educational Leadership, 43*(1), 62–67.
Wang, M.C., & Walberg, H.J. (1986). Classroom climate as mediator of educational inputs and outputs. In B.J. Fraser (Ed.), *The study of learning environments 1985* (pp. 47–58). Salem, OR: Assessment Research.
White, K., & Casto, G. (1985). An integrative review of early intervention efficacy studies with at-risk children: Implications for the handicapped. *Analysis and Intervention in Developmental Disabilities, 5*, 177–201.
Wiener, G. (1968). *Long-term study of prematures: Summary of published findings.* Washington, DC: Office of Education, Department of Health, Education, and Welfare. (ERIC Document Reproduction Service No. ED 043389, PS003651.)
Wittrock, M.C. (Ed.). (1986). *Handbook of research on teaching* (3rd ed.). (A Project of the American Educational Research Association.) New York: Macmillan.
Ysseldyke, J.E. (1987). Classification of handicapped students. In M.C. Wang, M.C. Reynolds, & H.J. Walberg (Eds.), *Handbook of special education: Research and practice: Vol. 1. Learner characteristics and adaptive education* (pp. 253–271). Oxford, England: Pergamon.
Ysseldyke, J.E., Algozzine, B., Shinn, M., & McGue, A. (1982). Similarities and differences between low achievers and students classified learning disabled. *Journal of Special Education, 16*, 73–85.
Zeitlin, S. (1981). Learning through coping: An effective preschool program. *Journal of the Division for Early Education, 4*, 53–61.

STRENGTHENING FAMILIES OF YOUNG CHILDREN WITH HANDICAPPING CONDITIONS
MAPPING BACKWARD FROM THE "STREET LEVEL"

4

*Paul R. Dokecki
and Craig Anne Heflinger*

THERE HAVE BEEN PRECIOUS FEW WATERSHED EVENTS IN THE SOCIAL ECOLogy of families of children with handicapping conditions. Public Law 94-142, the Education for All Handicapped Children Act of 1975, surely was one. Many of us hope and expect that PL 99-457, the Education of the Handicapped Act Amendments of 1986, is another, especially for young children. Indeed, the law and the expressed intentions of major national policy actors present a new public policy, one that reflects insights gained from research, practice, and analysis—a policy that lays out truly significant goals and objectives to be achieved on behalf of young children with handicapping conditions and their families. But as Hargrove (1975) has reminded us, sandwiched between the analysis of a policy and the evaluation of its eventual achievement of goals and objectives, there is the crucial "missing link" of implementation.

A glimpse of the analysis that led to the enactment of PL 99-457 is given in Title I, Part H, Section 671. (a) Findings:

> The Congress finds that there is an urgent and substantial need—
> 1) to enhance the development of handicapped infants and toddlers and to minimize their potential for developmental delay,
> 2) to reduce the educational costs to our society, including the Nation's schools, by minimizing the need for special education and related services after handicapped infants and toddlers reach school age,
> 3) to minimize the likelihood of institutionalization of handicapped individuals and maximize the potential of their independent living in society, and
> 4) to enhance the capacity of families to meet the special needs of their infants and toddlers with handicaps.

These are words to warm the hearts of those concerned with America's families and children. The rationale so many of us in the research, advocacy, and service communities have been developing and articulating over the years now appears as the rationale of a major piece of federal legislation.

Policy goals and objectives for handicapped infants and toddlers and their families are specified in Section 671. (b) Policy:

> It is therefore the policy of the United States to provide financial assistance to States—
> 1) to develop and implement a statewide comprehensive, coordinated, multidisciplinary, interagency program of early intervention services for handicapped infants and toddlers and their families,
> 2) to facilitate the coordination of payment for early intervention services from Federal, State, local, and private services (including public and private insurance coverage), and
> 3) to enhance their capacity to provide quality early intervention services and expand and improve existing intervention services being provided to handicapped infants, toddlers, and their families.

Truly, the day of early intervention for young handicapped children and their families seems to have arrived.

Taken together, the analysis of need and the specification of policy goals and objectives presented in Part H of PL 99-457 suggest an implicit theory of the social ecology of young children with handicapping conditions. Mapping forward from the uppermost levels of the policy system, this theory seemingly can be summarized in a six-component argument: 1) In order to reduce educational costs, prevent institutionalization, and maximize citizens' capacity for independent living, 2) financial assistance provided by the federal government to the states 3) enables the development of statewide early intervention systems in order to 4) help marshall early intervention programs throughout the service system from state to local levels and involving both the public and private sectors and, thereby, to 5) enhance young handicapped children's development and help prevent developmental delay. 6) The strengthening of families helps to bring about these positive developmental outcomes. This telegraphic statement of the presumed theory of PL 99-457 is breathtaking. We encounter bold conjectures, as with any good theory, and are exposed to death-defying leaps over organizational chasms. (See chapters 10 and 11 in this volume for a discussion of public policy as hypothesis.)

There are many organizations potentially involved in the implementation of PL 99-457, organizations from the federal to the local level, both public and private, and with different professional orientations. Indeed, there are so many organizations that we should worry about authority, accountability, decision making, the ability to veto decisions, the availability of resources, whether or not adequate incentives and capacities exist throughout the involved organizations, the likelihood of advocacy and constituent group support, and the depth of community awareness and support. Moreover, the many organizations participating in the implementation of PL 99-457 are not neatly and hierarchically arranged, but rather they are what political scientists call "loosely coupled," and it is never easy to get loosely coupled organizations to coordinate efficiently and effectively. The underlying theory, however, seems reasonable, and the law's goals and objectives are important and laudatory. Can we get there from here? The key to success is effective implementation.

In this chapter, we attempt to help forge Hargrove's (1975) "missing link" of implementation from one particular perspective, that of the social ecology of families and children. Typically, the analysis of implementation is from the top down, that is, by the forward mapping just used to present the implicit theory of PL 99-457. There is another approach, however, characterized by Elmore (1979–1980) as backward mapping. The approach in backward mapping is to decide what a policy is supposed to achieve at the ground level, at what Lipsky (Lipsky, 1980; Weatherley & Lipsky 1977) calls the "street level," the level where the rubber hits the road. Having carefully specified these street-level policy outcomes, the implementation analytic task is to map backward from the loosely coupled organizations involved in the policy system to determine what must be in place or occur at successively higher levels of the system. It is as if we turn the policy telescope around and look through the lens at the other end. The resulting vista is unusual, but important.

Thus, we choose to begin our implementation analysis by viewing the social ecology of families at the street level, with our lens focused on the task of elaborating on or unpacking what PL 99-457 seems to seek to achieve in strengthening the families of infants, toddlers, and preschoolers with handicapping conditions. In that regard, we focus on Title I—Handicapped Infants and Toddlers, an amendment of PL 94-142 by the addition of Part H. We touch on Title II—Handicapped Children Aged 3 to 5—only as it relates to Part H. We have chosen this focus because Part H is what makes PL 99-457 a watershed piece of legislation.

Our approach in mapping backward from the street level pursuant to effective implementation of PL 99-457 is an extension of research done by our group at Vanderbilt. One strand of that work culminated in the publication of *Strengthening Families* (Hobbs et al., 1984). Another strand is the dissertation of William C. Donovan, Jr. (under Dokecki's supervision), which entailed an implementation estimate of Senator John Chafee's (R.-RI) Community and Family Living Amendments of 1985 (S 873). We also draw on the work of our Vanderbilt colleague, Erwin Hargrove (Hargrove et al., 1981, 1983) concerning the implementation of PL 94-142, and on the work of Robert Moroney (Moroney, 1986; Moroney & Dokecki, 1984), who collaborated with us at Vanderbilt, served on the faculty at the University of North Carolina at Chapel Hill and in the Bush Institute, and is currently at Arizona State University.

STRENGTHENING FAMILIES

The backward mapping approach to implementation analysis requires that we clarify and elaborate on what PL 99-457 intends at the street level for families of infants, toddlers, and preschoolers with handicapping conditions. We include preschoolers at this point because of our conviction that the developmental needs of children under 6 within the family should be seen as whole cloth. Moreover, PL 99-457 also is concerned with the role of families in providing services to the 3–5 age group. In addition to the need identified in Part H to "enhance the capacity of families to meet the special needs of their infants and toddlers with handicaps," the House Committee Report (U.S. House, 1986, p. 6) asserts, regarding Section 619, that "the Committee received overwhelming testimony affirming the family as the primary learning environment for children under six years of age and pointing out the critical need for parents and professionals to function in a collaborative fashion" (p. 20).

In our implementation analysis, we assume that a major goal of PL 99-457 is strengthening families as a means of promoting the human development of young children with handicapping conditions. Given that assumption, our intent is to elaborate on what this concept of strengthening families might mean pursuant to effective implementation. In that regard, Hobbs et al. (1984) observed:

> Human development, properly understood, focuses not only on individuals and their personal developmental potentials but also on the *contexts* in which individual development occurs. The most influential of these is the family, and the family, of course, is set within its own developmental context, the community. If we fail to take account of these pervasive influences on the course of human development, we fail to understand human development itself. We believe that the strengthening of families within supportive and caring communities is a desirable goal in and of itself (see Moroney, 1986). More importantly, however, we believe that competent families and supportive communities are indispensable elements of any effort to realize the full potential of human development in our society. (p. 2)

This quotation is foundational to understanding the social-ecological approach to the families of young children with handicapping conditions.

Dokecki and Heflinger (1988) have pointed out that to emphasize the social ecology of families is to take on a commitment to promoting community and human development values, especially at the street level, where families live their everyday lives. This value commitment can be expressed in two interrelated ways:

1. The aim of intervention should be to enhance community, so that individuals and their families may develop to their potential. Individuals and families have a legitimate claim on community resources and support in the performance of their developmental tasks.
2. The aim of intervention should be to enhance human development, so that individuals and their families may be effective participants in the community. The community can legitimately expect individuals and families to master their developmental tasks. (Dokecki, 1983, pp. 115–116)

The pursuit of these values relative to young children with handicapping conditions requires that we pose four general questions about program and policy implementation. Does the implementation process: 1) enhance the community of the children and their families, 2) strengthen the families, 3) enable the parents to do their jobs well, and 4) enhance individual development and protect the rights of all the individual members of the families? Brief elaboration is in order.

In assessing the capacity of policy implementation to enhance the community of young children with handicapping conditions and their families, additional specific questions must be posed. Is the implementation process demeaning because it devalues and stigmatizes these children and their families, causing them to lose self-esteem? Is it divisive because it separates them from their community and allows, even encourages, invidious social comparison? Does the implementation process bestow unwarranted advantage that goes beyond what is needed to meet special and socially important needs? On the positive side, does it increase shared heritage, mutual aid, and community building because it brings children with handicapping conditions and their families together with other children and families, highlighting human commonalities and shared values?

The capacity of policy implementation to strengthen families of young children with handicapping conditions can be assessed, first, by inquiry concerning its ability to improve the capacity of these families to master a broad range of developmental tasks. This capacity is built through services that enhance parents' knowledge, skill, and ability to make decisions about their children. Furthermore, does the implementation process improve the liaison or linkage functions that mobilize social resources and supports needed by these families? In this regard, families should be helped both to identify and make use of formal human service agency networks and to look toward more primary kinds of social support, such as family members, kinship groups, neighbors, and voluntary associations. Finally, does the implementation process protect these families from unwarranted intrusion and allow parents choice, by providing a variety of service options and adequate information about these options?

Assessment of the capacity of the implementation process to enable the parents of young children with handicapping conditions to do their jobs well also requires the posing of additional questions: Does the process minimize stress by making available to these parents essential resources, such as time and energy, knowledge, and resources—and consequent positive effect, including feelings of worth—in order that they may better carry out their parental functions? Does the implementation process promote shared responsibility between parents and service providers; in other words, does it operate according to enablement and empowerment principles? Parents are enabled when they are treated as capable adults and helped by professionals to become even more capable. Empowerment occurs when parents are provided with resources and legal rights so they may negotiate effectively with societal institutions.

The final value element—enhancing the individual development and protecting the rights of all the individual members of families with young children with handicapping conditions—entails several questions: Does the implementation process enhance the opportunities for all individual family members to develop competence and achieve self-realization, by providing services that enhance physical, cognitive, affective, and interpersonal development? Does it protect individual members of the family from abuse and severe neglect?

We present this value framework and associated questions at this point to orient those concerned with the implementation of PL 99-457 with the complexities of strengthening families—the outcome that the legislation presumably is trying to achieve at the street level. We use this framework in the next section to structure our analysis. First, however, we must determine what PL 99-457 seems to suggest should occur, as we map backward from the family through the community and then through the loosely coupled service and policy systems. What follows is a tentative outline of the steps and elements, in approximate bottom-to-top order, entailed in the implementation of PL 99-457, using language and concepts explicitly stated in the law:

1. Coordinated early intervention in the least restrictive environment to strengthen families and thereby enhance the development of handicapped children over the 0–5 age span
2. Appropriate involvement of extended family and kin
3. Appropriate use of informal social supports in the community
4. Case management to ensure coordinated services across the 0–5 age span
5. Development of the Individualized Family Service Plan (IFSP)
6. Performance, review, and updating of multidisciplinary evaluation
7. Service agency coordination at the local level
8. Child Find activities to locate eligible children and families
9. Public awareness campaign to alert eligible children and families
10. Development of central directory of available agencies and services
11. Agency coordination at the state level
12. Development of a personnel preparation strategy to ensure the availability of qualified service people
13. Establishment of the Interagency Coordinating Council (ICC)
14. Development of a statewide system to organize and coordinate all elements of the implementation process
15. Use made by the state of existing planning efforts for young handicapped children and their families
16. Selection and activation of the lead agency by the governor
17. Governor's decision-making about participation and the state's general approach
18. Federal agency coordination
19. OSEP (Office of Special Education Programs) implementation of regulations and overall provisions of the law

20. Development of OSEP regulations
21. Report of federal data collection and evaluation to Congress
22. Congressional oversight and reenactment of EHA (the Education for All Handicapped Children Act, PL 94-142, 1975)

In the following section, the questions from the value framework are considered within the context of these tentative PL 99-457 backward-mapping steps. We are trying to identify barriers to implementation and key issues that implementors must consider seriously. In order to identify barriers, however, we must first consult the implementation analysis literature to identify factors that have been shown to influence implementation effectiveness. In that regard, Donovan's (1986) analysis of the implementation of the Community and Family Living Amendments of 1985 is instructive. In work done under Dokecki's supervision, Donovan drew on the work of Allison (1980), Baird and Ashcroft (1984), Chase (1979), Dokecki (1978), Elmore (1978, 1979–1980), Garwood (1984), Hargrove (1975), Hargrove et al. (1981, 1983), Hobbs et al. (1984), Kelman (1984), March and Simon (1958), Mazmanian and Sabatier (1983), Nakamura and Smallwood (1980), Ripley and Franklin (1982), Shadish (1984), Thompson (1967), and Weatherley and Lipsky (1977). Selected questions from Donovan's analysis that might be applied to the implementation of PL 99-457 include:

1. Does PL 99-457 give local implementors necessary authority?
2. Are there more organized constituency groups that support PL 99-457 than oppose it?
3. Does PL 99-457 allow for and provide for ongoing constituency involvement?
4. Does PL 99-457 make adequate provision for the availability of the necessary funding to carry out the policy?
5. Is the goal of PL 99-457 consistent with the goals and purposes of the state agency that would be responsible for its implementation?
6. Does PL 99-457 recognize the importance of the state agency responsible for implementation and allow for state discretion?
7. Do the sanctions described in PL 99-457 prompt state compliance with the policy?
8. Do the contingencies related to funding in PL 99-457 assist with state compliance?
9. Is PL 99-457 consistent with the existing social system and ideologies in which it is to be implemented?
10. Is the funding plan for PL 99-457 realistic?

Donovan used these kinds of questions, focused on the Community and Family Living Amendments, in a survey of directors of state mental retardation programs. In this chapter we adopt the spirit of his analysis in order to backward map from the bottom-up perspective of the street level, from the perspective of strengthening families and the early intervention services that families need in order to meet the developmental needs of their young children with handicapping conditions.

Thus far in this chapter, we have presented three perspectives on the implementation of PL 99-457: 1) an analytic framework emphasizing community and human development values that shows what strengthening families might mean at the street level, 2) a backward-mapping schema of the levels of activity that might be entailed in implementing PL 99-457, and 3) a series of implementation questions reflecting the current state of the policy research literature. With these general perspectives in mind, we can proceed now to our specific implementation analysis.

IMPLEMENTATION ANALYSIS

In this section, we apply the policy value framework developed for *Strengthening Families* (Dokecki, 1983; Hobbs et al., 1984) in order to structure an implementation analysis of PL 99-457, especially Title I, Part H — Handicapped Infants and Toddlers. This analysis is a hybrid of the two typical approaches to implementation analysis: 1) the conduct of an implementation estimate *before* a policy is developed, in order to allow implementation feasibility issues to help structure the development of a policy; and 2) the analysis and evaluation of a policy *after* it has been implemented, in order to derive lessons for future action. Obviously, PL 99-457 has been enacted but regulations have not been drafted, and little, if any, governmental activity has taken place at either the federal or state level. Our analysis, therefore, both probes the intent of the legislation and raises issues and questions about how it may actually come to be implemented. It also should be recalled that we are taking a bottom-up, backward-mapping, street-level approach.

Value Element 1: Does The Implementation Process Enhance Community?

Implementation processes that "promote the coming together of people around shared values and the pursuit of a common cause enhance community at both the local, face-to-face level and the national level, where people also concern themselves with the well-being of citizens who are strangers to them" (Hobbs et al., 1984, p. 46).

A. Is The Implementation Process Demeaning to Any Group? As well intended as Part H of PL 99-457 appears to be, there may be a significant risk of stigmatizing children and their families by singling them out for service. As we have learned from the implementation of PL 94-142, parents of many eligible children choose not to seek services because their interpretation of the "special education" process and being labeled "handicapped" has to do with being mistreated and discriminated against—what Gallagher (1981) referred to as a psychological barrier to implementation.

The implementation of Part H is likely to follow that of PL 94-142 in requiring certification or labeling before the child and family are eligible for services. The definitions of both "developmentally delayed" and "at risk of having substantial developmental delay" are left to the states under Part H, and states may attempt to adapt the previously existing certification categories under PL 94-142 for use with younger children. The assessment and certification procedures under PL 94-142 go hand in hand in this regard, and attempts to standardize assessment and certification under Part H may well be developed to connect with the extant system for older children. The risk involved in such a procedure is twofold: 1) some parents may be deterred by the prospect of having their child, and themselves, so labeled—and parents of infants, toddlers, and preschoolers may be even more sensitive to this labeling process than parents of older children; and 2) the labeling of children as "developmentally delayed" or "at risk" could result in more harm than benefit in certain cases (Gilkerson, Hilliard, Schrag, & Shonkoff, 1987; Hobbs, 1975; Rhodes, 1975). In this regard, noncategorical identification of young children with handicapping conditions has been called for (Smith & Schakel, 1986). Moreover, Hobbs (1975) stressed that services should be needs-based rather than categorically based, and the language of Part H seems to reflect this needs-based focus, drawing from a developmental, instead of a pathological or deficit, approach. Yet the precedent of the status quo, as reflected in the PL 94-142 implementation and the bureaucratic structures and procedures already in place, are powerful factors. This issue has fairly obvious implications for selection of the lead agency, constitution of the Interagency Coordinating Council, and the general issue of governmental and service agency coordination.

B. Is The Implementation Process Divisive? Policies that are socially divisive work against social coherence and solidarity (Dokecki, 1983) and violate the civil rights commitment of the United States. One of the driving forces behind PL 94-142 was the civil rights movement being extended to handicapped citizens in the early 1970s, and the right of free association is one of the basic legal principles of that piece of legislation (Turnbull et al., 1983; Turnbull & Turnbull, 1979). PL 99-457, amending and extending the provisions of PL 94-142, however, raises concerns over the implementation of the "least-restrictive environment" (LRE) principle. First, under Title II, which addresses the needs of 3- to 5-year-olds and their families, there exists great risk of establishing a segregated service system. Universal, publicly supported education or child care services do not exist in most states for children under age 6, so access to an extant system where the LRE principle can be implemented is limited. The LRE debate regarding preschool-age children is already raging (e.g., see *Education of the Handicapped*, 1987, March 18).

The LRE debate becomes even more problematic when Part H comes under scrutiny. There are the questions of just what "special instruction" is (§ 672, 2[E]ii) for infants and toddlers and how this instruction in non-segregated and least restrictive environments is to be provided. Some argue that home-based services are the treatment of choice for this age group, and that segregation problems would not exist if center-based services were not offered. But what of the other early intervention services listed under Section 672? How can any or all of these services be offered in the least restrictive environment? If the needs-based, developmental logic of the legislation is followed, a universal or "generic" system available to and used by all children and their families would be made available, if that system best met the needs of the child and family. Yet such a universal system does not exist for infants and toddlers, any more than it exists for preschoolers. Furthermore, Part H avoids mention of LRE in the language of the law. How is this to be interpreted by those who must plan and implement the system and those who will participate?

Divisiveness through segregation of children with handicapping conditions and their families may be an inherent facet of Part H. This divisiveness may be justified, however, by referring to the warranted advantage discussed in the next section. If the services needed by children and their families are available only through an "exceptionalistic" approach, perhaps this divisiveness is a "necessary evil" until such time as universal parent education, child care, and related services are fiscally and politically acceptable in the United States. This results in the same dilemma that the labeling issue produces.

C. Does The Implementation Process Bestow Unwarranted Advantage? At first appearance, Part H will provide many services needed and wanted by a sizeable clientele, yet those eligible for services are only a small subset of the young children and their families in the United States. A majority of all children and parents would probably benefit from a coordinated service system, information and referral services for the myriad of community agencies, family training (parent education), help with case management, and possible diagnostic medical services. In this regard, the case for universal parent education and child care has been developed in *Strengthening Families* (Hobbs et al., 1984). Universal availability of such services, however, is both fiscally and politically remote at this time.

It may be argued that Part H provides a warranted advantage to certain children and their families, based upon the principle of vertical equity: that special needs call for special help. We have a legal tradition of allocating benefits to citizens who have been underserved previously, and the case for early intervention services for young children with handicapping conditions is strong. Although we know that exceptionalistic approaches may result in blaming the victim (Dokecki & Strain, 1973; Ryan, 1976), enough children and their families may receive services under the "at-risk" category that we may begin to approach a universalistic system. To return to a cautionary mode, however, history teaches that, in times of limited resources such as the present, services are restricted and eligibility requirements are tightened. Under PL 94-142, we have experienced a shift away from serving mildly handicapped youngsters (e.g., by changing the diagnostic category of mental retardation, we have observed a decertification rate of as much as 75% [Heflinger, Cook, & Thackery, 1987]) to a focus on children with severe handicaps, in both service delivery and research funding. Again, implementation of Part H will have to contend with a strong bureaucratic precedent in order to retain a developmental rather than a deficit approach.

Value Element 2: Does The Implementation Process Strengthen Families?

Central here is the notion that "strong families are the foundation of meaningful community, and they provide the context for the human development of their members. In addition, the family as a system has developmental tasks to master and has responsibilities for relating to other systems within society" (Hobbs et al., 1984, p. 49).

A. *Does The Implementation Process Improve The Capacity of Families to Master a Broad Range of Developmental Tasks?*
The concern here is that implementation be effected so that "parents are enabled to maintain and enhance their capabilities for making intelligent choices and managing resources in the interest of their children" (Hobbs

et al., 1984, p. 31). The language of Part H certainly implies a focus on the enhancement of family functioning. Family needs are specifically mentioned in Section 676(b)3, to be a target of the "timely, comprehensive, multidisciplinary evaluation," and both family strengths and needs relating to enhancing the development of the child with a handicap are to be specified as components of the Individualized Family Service Plan. Moreover, the renaming and reconfiguration of the Individualized Education Program of PL 94-142 to become the Individualized Family Service Plan is potentially significant. Enhancing the knowledge, skill, and decision-making capacities of families is possible, given the stated purposes of the legislation. The question of how to get there from here, however, remains. The IFSP appears to lack the contractual basis of the IEP, potentially leaving it to be viewed as a "wish list" of recommendations, rather than a contract for services to be provided or paid for by the lead agency. Also, we have a public service bureaucracy that typically has focused on children, often to the exclusion of their families, in both health and education. The choice of the lead agency and the nature of the Interagency Coordinating Council certainly will influence the amount of family focus and participation that actually occurs. For example, how capable are state departments of education of operating with a family focus, rather than strictly a child focus? The arguments for and against the public schools serving preschool-age children and their families were explored in depth by our research group, in the context of developing child care and parent education public policy. Many of the same points are germane to the discussion of PL 99-457:

> It can be argued that expansion of programs in the public schools is a natural extension of the already existing framework of nursery school, public preschool, and kindergarten [and, as we are discussing, special education], including, of course, the present focus in many on parent involvement and participation. There are a number of potential advantages of such an expansion: Programs organized through the schools would reduce the fragmentation and duplication of services by concentrating them within one organizational entity; they would build on the strengths of existing organizational arrangements, rather than creating new ones; they would rationalize the allocation of resources; they could well ensure equity by distributing services uniformly and providing open access to services; they could contribute to the continuity of care, parent education, and related services; they could provide a means for improving the capabilities of care givers and parent educators; and they could improve accountability by providing for parent and community participation. There are potential disadvantages to providing child care and parent education [and, in this argument, services to infants and toddlers with handicapping conditions and their families] through the schools. Implementing programs through the schools, it is sometimes ar-

gued, would introduce rigidity into child care and possibly into parent education and would undermine the rich diversity that currently exists; it would overburden the public school system by grafting onto it a new social program; it would stifle innovation and overemphasize narrow academic preparation; it would introduce a system of teacher certification and placement that is sometimes self-serving and has in the past discriminated against minorities; it would exclude parent and community involvement; and it would be unlikely to promote community development goals for poor, disenfranchised, and underserved populations. (Hobbs et al., 1984, pp. 240–241)

B. Does The Implementation Process Improve The Liaison or Linkage Functions of Families as They Relate to The Social Resources and Supports They Need?
The number one goal of Part H of PL 99-457, as stated on the first page of the legislation, underlines the linkage theme: "to develop and implement a statewide, comprehensive, coordinated, multidisciplinary, interagency program of early intervention services for handicapped infants and toddlers and their families" (§ 671(b)(1)). This linkage and coordination theme yields the legislation's requirements for a statewide system, case management, the individualized assessment, and the IFSP. The intent, then, convincingly addresses this section's question. But what of the actual implementation? There are critical issues at the levels of: 1) the individual child and his or her family, and 2) the service delivery system, where there exists the serious possibility for discontinuity, instead of coordination.

At the level of the individual child and family, the case management component listed under Section 672(2)(E) has been heralded as a crucial component for any service system, and particularly for early intervention. In the past, families, especially those with children with severe handicapping conditions, have experienced the service delivery system as both fragmented and dehumanizing (Gorham, DesJardins, Page, Pettis, & Scheiber, 1975). Being "referred around" or "falling between the cracks" (McNett, 1980) often follows their initial attempt to discover what is going on with their child and where appropriate services are available. The case management component is included to avoid these cracks, by building in a linkage function. Just what case management will be in early intervention services, however, is yet to be determined. Many models of case management exist, with varying levels of involvement of professionals and parents. A promising approach is the human development liaison (HDL) model (Hobbs, 1982; Wheeley, 1981a, 1981b). The National Association of Social Workers (NASW) (1984) similarly offers a promising and well-defined model. Users of the liaison or any other case management approach, moreover, must recognize that families exist within formal human service and informal social support networks, and case management must help parents identify and make use of these networks. This is clearly one means of enhancing the capacities of families. Both the HDL and NASW models also stress the importance of linking advocacy and case management, yet advocacy on behalf of young children with handicapping conditions and their families is not mentioned in the wording of the legislation. The model of case management chosen and the disciplinary ties established will importantly shape the implementation of the entire service system.

Beyond these disciplinary issues, the implementation of PL 99-457 poses the threat of discontinuity in meeting needs as a child progresses through the developmental sequence. First, the yet undefined process of case management leaves open the possibility that first one and then another professional person will be assigned as case manager, as the child moves through a variety of service settings. The effectiveness of case management hinges on the ability to maintain an ongoing, supportive relationship with the family, and the likelihood of this happening in the face of case manager changes is greatly diminished. Second, PL 99-457 has a built-in discontinuity in its separation of services for children birth through age 2, the infants and toddlers, from the rest of the service delivery system, since ages 3–5 are dealt with in another section and essentially have been joined with ages 6 and over. What will happen to families and children as they hit the transition from ages 2 to 3? Many problems become evident: 1) the lead agency may be different for the birth–2 and 3–5 groups, yielding bureaucratic discontinuity that may result in gaps or in families being given "the runaround"; 2) the handicapping conditions that are eligible for services change significantly across the two sections of the legislation, possibly resulting in the decertification of many children, making them and their families suddenly ineligible for continued service; and 3) the types of services available to children and their families vary across the two sections of the legislation—the strong family focus in Part H seems to become diminished, case management is no longer mentioned—and current experience provides many examples of services becoming much sparser as children move from already existing early intervention programs to educational jurisdiction under PL 94-142. These discontinuities are potentially harmful to young children with handicapping conditions and their families and must be addressed during the implementation process.

At the level of the service delivery system, the language describing a "statewide, comprehensive, coordinated, multidisciplinary, interagency program of early intervention services" must meet the test of reality at the street level. At this level, a variety of actual and possible services exists, and many well-meaning service providers and administrators intend to implement the policy and reach its goal, yet innumerable barriers loom. The ideal here would be the development of a continuum of care that incorporates medical, educational, developmental, mental health, and related services, ranging from nonrestrictive, primary prevention activities in the community, through early identification and early intervention, to outpatient and day treatment programs, regular and special instruction, and to residential or inpatient services (Hobbs, 1982; Knitzer, 1982, 1984). These services would be defined by the level of need of the individual child and family and set up so that a child could enter the system at the most appropriate level and be able to move, without impediment, "up" and "down" the system as needed. A basic assumption of the continuum-of-care approach is that services are to be provided in the least restrictive setting possible; widespread prevention and early intervention programs are needed in order to decrease the need for any child or family to enter the system at a more restrictive level of care. PL 99-457 provides some authority and incentive for such a continuum to be put together, but the coordination of multiple public and private agencies and the definition of lines of authority will be no easy task.

C. *Does The Implementation Process Protect The Family from Unwarranted Intrusion and Allow Parents Choice?* Part H has been lauded for the focus on family participation, yet what about family protection from unwarranted intrusion? Three key notions here are voluntariness, choice among alternatives, and confidentiality.

In order to avoid the threat of unwarranted intrusion, it seems self-evident that family participation in either assessment or service delivery must remain optional, at the discretion of the family. Although it appears that family participation is in the best interest of the child, the needs of the family in its own right must be respected. The fine line between intervention and interference should be scrutinized carefully by service providers. Minimizing parent stress is related to guarding against intrusion and is discussed under Value Element 3, but here we are raising the question of how to guarantee voluntariness. The service system, be it educational or health or mental health, has traditionally been professionally driven, and it is the direct service providers, the street-level bureaucrats (Lipsky, 1980; Weatherley & Lipsky, 1977), who often make the judgment about the type and amount of family participation. The spirit of PL 99-457, however, emphasizes shared responsibility with parents, and refusal to participate must be one of the options available. Parental choice must be built in on multiple levels, from what services can best benefit their child to how they will participate. Similarly, *real* choice means having a variety of options and avoiding the constraint of merely choosing from what is available, rather than being able to select what is needed. (How to deal with parents' choice to refuse participation if the best interests of the child are judged to be jeopardized by this refusal is discussed under the question of the protection of individual rights.)

Confidentiality is specifically mentioned in the legislation, and a structure to guarantee it already has been put into place by previous federal legislation, including the Privacy Act (PL 93-380, 1974) and the implementation of record keeping under PL 94-142. Many parents, service providers, and administrators are already familiar with procedures like locking file cabinets and securing release-of-information consent forms. Continued and expanded vigilance on this issue is needed, however, since PL 99-457 will entail even more family and personal information than previously has been gathered. Moreover, record keeping is a two-way street, and family access to records should be as respected as the principle of confidentiality. This raises again the theme of shared responsibility, where both service providers and parents jointly plan and make decisions about services. Records should be useful to both parents and service providers—school psychologists and other multidisciplinary team members could well examine their current practices in this regard—and access to records should be more than legalistic. Access is better viewed as an active process of sharing and obtaining feedback on formal documents and other records as part of the case management process.

Before leaving this value element concerning strengthening families, mention must be made of research and measurement issues. There is a clear need for rigorous research efforts to: 1) determine family needs and 2) evaluate program effectiveness in meeting family needs. Key to this effort would be the development of measurement instruments that guide family strengthening intervention efforts and against which such interventions can be evaluated. Furthermore, James Gallagher (personal communication, March 7, 1988) makes the telling point that easy access to such defensible, creditable, and valid instruments on the part of early intervention agents could enhance their willingness and ability to include family matters in their plans.

Value Element 3: Does The Implementation Process Enable Parents to Do Their Jobs Well?

Parent enablement is the primary means within implementation to strengthen families. "Policies that enable parents to make competent decisions for their family strengthen the family and enhance the well-being, developmental status, and rights of all family members" (Hobbs et al.,

1984, p. 50). We already have discussed many of the issues regarding the role of PL 99-457 in strengthening families. There are two additional concerns.

A. Does The Implementation Process Minimize Stress by Making Essential Resources Available to Parents? Stress is endemic to being a parent, and parents of young children with handicapping conditions have been dealt more than their share (Beckman-Bell, 1981). PL 99-457 should, in theory, minimize stress by making available more services and payment for those services. These additional resources and their coordination through case management should help minimize the "cracks" in the service system and deter much of the run around that parents have experienced (McNett, 1980).

The parent participation in the assessment, decision-making, and service delivery promoted by Part H, however, may increase, instead of diminish, parental stress in some circumstances. Turnbull and Turnbull (1982) point out that three assumptions underlying parent participation in PL 94-142, and now PL 99-457—1) that parents can and will want to participate, 2) that parents can function as advocates to ensure the rights of their children, and 3) that parents need and want training and counseling in order to continue the educational process at home—may not reflect the needs, wants, or capabilities of all parents. These authors call for the development of a range of parent involvement choices that recognize the evolving needs of parents and offer flexibility.

B. Does The Implementation Process Promote Shared Responsibility between Parents and Service Providers, Including Professionals? PL 99-457 refers to parent participation in numerous facets of assessing and planning for meeting the needs of the child and family. The opportunity exists for the legislation to be implemented in such a way that parents and service providers work together as equal partners in evaluation, decision-making, and intervention. This partnership, however, has never fully blossomed under the implementation of PL 94-142 (Turnbull & Turnbull, 1982). Despite IEP requirements, parents often have remained passive participants (Brickerhoff & Vincent, 1986; Yoshida, Fenton, Kaufman, & Maxwell, 1978), and the procedural safeguards in the due process mechanism often have served to heighten school-parent conflict, rather than encourage cooperation (Fiedler, 1985). The professionally driven nature of the current service delivery system must be recognized. Instead of promoting parental involvement in the treatment of their children, the service delivery system traditionally has discouraged their participation. Although regulatory mechanisms mandate parental attendance and signature in formal decision-making meetings, parents often are excluded from meaningful participation in the evaluation process or in the pre-meeting conferences held to put together all the information. Professionals typically maintain the expert role, discounting parents' knowledge and ability to care for their handicapped child. This approach fosters the dependence of families instead of contributing to their enablement, empowerment, and independence. Services often are unavailable at less restrictive, more supportive levels and often become available only when they are a "substitute" for family care. Moroney (1986) conducted an extensive review of the literature and found four professional perspectives on families with handicapped members:

1. The family as part of the problem: Family pathology—genetic, social, or both—is viewed as causing the problem and interfering with treatment.
2. The family as a resource to the handicapped person: Families are acknowledged as caregivers, but not as having needs in their own right.
3. The family as team participant: The family is viewed as part of the caregiving team in treatment.
4. The family as needing resources: The focus here shifts from the individual handicapped member to the family as a unit in its own right, a unit that needs support.

Although all four of these perspectives might, and probably will, influence the implementation of PL 99-457, the third and, especially, the fourth are truly in the spirit of strengthening families. As Moroney and Dokecki (1984) have argued:

> In most instances, families caring for handicapped members have demonstrated their abilities to function as primary care givers, with professionals assuming secondary roles by working through the families. The abilities of the families to identify relevant needs and to provide appropriate care are recognized. Moreover, to continue as primary care givers, families require various supportive services in their own right; professionals should shift their current focus on the handicapped persons and accept families as legitimate objects of intervention. Again, it is not a matter of one over the other, but a concern for balance.
>
> There is a need to move away from the pathological model and to create a service delivery system that assumes that family members are capable care givers and that their judgments may be trusted. Such development would, of course, require a major reorientation of professional attitudes and a significant departure in current thinking. To successfully implement such an initiative, professionals would begin by asking the care givers what services or resources would, in their opinion, enable them to continue as care givers, and then provide them. What the professional thinks is beneficial becomes secondary, and requests from family members are not to be translated by the

professional into services that agencies are organized to provide, or services that the professional believes are important.

If professionals were to function in such a way that they supported families, new roles would have to be developed. The "new" expert would need to be sensitive to the family unit, understand what it means for a family to function as care giver, and be knowledgeable about community resources. (p. 234)

Value Element 4. Does The Implementation Process Enhance Individual Development and Protect The Rights of All Individual Members of The Family?

Recognized here is the fact that "all family members—parents and children—have ongoing development tasks to master. Similarly, all family members, including even very young children, have fundamental human rights" (Hobbs et al., 1984, p. 52). PL 99-457 has grown from a legal tradition that emphasizes the rights of the individual, in this case, of the child with a handicapping condition. PL 94-142 guaranteed the right of a free, appropriate public education for *all* handicapped children. Procedural safeguards were included to protect the rights of the individual child and family. For its part in this value element, PL 99-457 gets high marks for intention. Specific concerns arise, however, when we take a closer look at implementation.

A. Does The Implementation Process Enhance The Opportunities for All Individual Family Members to Develop Competence and Achieve Self-Realization?

This legislation was developed specifically to enhance the educational and developmental opportunities for infants, toddlers, and preschoolers with handicapping conditions. The vertical equity principle, discussed above under Value Element 1, supports handicapped children's need for a supplement of public resources in order to realize their full potential. Based on either a human capital or a human development argument (Hobbs et al., 1984), the enhancement of individual development and competence promises to benefit the child, the family, the community, and the United States. PL 99-457 legislates and authorizes funding for such opportunities.

The word "appropriate" in "free appropriate public education" is key to the enhancement of individual opportunities. This legal principle is primary, prior even to that of the right to free association, which promotes mainstreaming (where "appropriate") and the least restrictive environment (Turnbull et al., 1983; Turnbull & Turnbull, 1979). The appropriateness of individual opportunities under PL 99-457 and PL 94-142 is determined by the multidisciplinary assessment and the individualized program (§ 677). We already have discussed the importance of parents as equal partners in the assessment and the IFSP, and in the process of determining just what is appropriate. We have identified problems, discovered from PL 94-142, that may jeopardize this partnership. Similarly, we already have raised the concern that "available" services may take precedence over "appropriate" services. These concerns also are critical in regard to enhancement of individual opportunities. A further threat to enhancement of individual opportunities, already mentioned, is the potential for discontinuity of care over the course of the child's development. Changing service settings, case managers, agencies, and possibly even lead agencies, causes gaps in service and lack of linkage that threaten the continuity of care that enhances both child and family development.

B. Does The Implementation Process Protect All Individual Members of The Family from Abuse and Severe Neglect? When the individual child with handicapping conditions is the focus, two places where abuse may occur in the implementation of PL 99-457 are the service system and the family.

Protection of parents and individual children from potential system abuse is the intent of the procedural safeguards (§ 680). The timely administrative resolution of complaints, confidentiality requirements, record access, surrogate guardianship, and written notice all serve to provide such protection. Inappropriate placement is to be avoided through the multidisciplinary assessment and IFSP process. We already have presented some of the potential pitfalls with each of these safeguards. In this section, we highlight the omission of the LRE principle in Part H as a serious threat to the enhancement of individual opportunities and as a possible source of abuse and severe neglect. The LRE principle was established as a legal principle in serving handicapped children in PL 94-142 and in the lawsuits that preceded that piece of legislation. The LRE principle not only provides the opportunity for children with handicapping conditions and their families to avoid stigmatizing segregation (right of free association), but it also provides protection against unwarranted restrictive placement of children. Institutionalization of persons with handicaps in residential/inpatient settings, unless judged the most appropriate setting by the school district's multidisciplinary team, must be guarded against for infants and toddlers, as well as for the preschoolers (protected under Part B) and school-age children. Segregated programs and classrooms also may run the risk of being unwarranted restrictive settings. Integrating special services into the regular child care service system, where appropriate for individual children and families, appears to be a more desirable option than establishing a parallel, and potentially uncoordinated, system of care.

The strengthening of families and the enablement of parents should, of themselves, diminish the potential for abuse and neglect of family members. Children with handicapping conditions, especially those below school age, have been at higher risk for abuse and neglect than other children (Daley & Wilson, 1984; Schrimshaw, 1984). The family support mechanisms built into this legislation appear to have the potential for providing those needed resources that were lacking in the past and whose absence probably contributed to high levels of family stress and isolation.

A related concern is when and how to intervene when a child is at risk of abuse or severe neglect in the family system. In PL 99-457, as in PL 94-142, this may become an issue when the parent refuses assessment or services to the child although professionals judge these services to be beneficial and necessary for developmental progress. The legislation clearly states what the parents may do if the system refuses appropriate services, but not what the system may do if the parents refuse. Just what services are needed and appropriate cannot be determined without parental participation, but serious consideration must be given to just what is in the best interests of the child. An approach to implementation is needed that recognizes "the importance of parental rights to the maintenance of the family unit but that stops short of allowing these rights to work to the significant detriment of individual family members" (Hobbs et al., 1984, p. 52). The fine line called for here is particularly important for young children, to whom the family is crucial for well being, but who also are especially vulnerable to the negative effects of abuse and neglect.

CONCLUSION

With these considerations of the situation of individual members of families of young children with handicapping conditions, we end our formal implementation analysis. From the perspective of a values-oriented approach to policy analysis, emphasizing community and human development values in pursuit of strengthening families, we have raised questions and identified issues—at the levels of community, family, parent, and individual—that should be addressed in the course of implementing PL 99-457. There surely will be many choice points throughout the policy and service systems, as the goals and objectives of this watershed legislation are operationalized. Our intent was not to prescribe or proscribe specific choices. Rather, we have suggested general directions and principles that might inform debate about implementation.

We hope that we have demonstrated that the value framework, with its attendant questions, is an effective means of elaborating on PL 99-457's stated goals and objectives for young children with handicapping conditions and their families. The real and ultimate success of the legislation should be evaluated against its intentions at the street level of the everyday lives of families and children. Much of the current discussion about implementation of PL 99-457 concerns adequacy of resources, constituency support, organizational incentives and capacities, professional territoriality, lines of authority and accountability, and so forth. It is right that these topics should be identified and debated; they will have significant influence whether or not the law is adequate to its intentions. That great majority of policy actors who operate from the top down and engage in forward mapping should be ever mindful of the bottom-up perspective of families and children and should consider also engaging in backward mapping.

We did not intend to draw "either/or" distinctions between top down and bottom up, forward mapping and backward mapping, the organizational level and the street level. A "both/and" perspective is clearly preferable to either/or, and has been incorporated in this chapter.

Implementation truly is the "missing link" that is being forged at this stage in the history of PL 99-457. In all our top-down concerns with the machinations of the policy and service delivery systems, however, our focus on what is really at stake in PL 99-457 must be kept intact: strengthening families—because they are the most crucial element in the social ecology of young children with handicapping conditions.

REFERENCES

Allison, G.T. (1980). Implementation analysis illustrated by a teaching exercise. In L. Lewin & E. Verdung (Eds.), *Politics as rational action* (pp. 237–260). New York: Reidel Publishing Company.

Baird, S.M., & Ashcroft, S.C. (1984). Education and chronically ill children: A need based policy orientation. *Peabody Journal of Education, 61*(2), 91–129.

Beckman-Bell, P. (1981). Child related stress in families of handicapped children. *Topics in Early Childhood Special Education, 1*(3), 24–54.

Brickerhoff, J.L., & Vincent, L.J. (1986). Increasing parent decision-making at the individualized educational program meeting. *Journal of the Division for Early Childhood, 11*, 46–58.

Chase, G. (1979). Implementing a human services program: How hard will it be? *Public Policy, 27*, 387–435.

Daley, M., & Wilson, M. (1984). Child abuse and other risks of not living with both parents. *Ethology and Sociobiology, 6*, 197–210.

Dokecki, P.R. (1978). Mental retardation: The labeling perspective. In J.P. Das & D. Baine (Eds.), *Mental retardation for special educators* (pp. 247–258). Springfield, IL: Charles C Thomas.

Dokecki, P.R. (1983). The place of values in the world of psychology and public policy. *Peabody Journal of Education, 60*(3), 108–125.

Dokecki, P.R., & Heflinger, C.A. (1988). Families and the developmental needs of dually diagnosed children. In J.A. Starks, F. Menolascino, M. Albarelli, & V. Grey (Eds.), *Mental health in people with mental retardation: Diagnosis, treatment, and service programs* (pp. 435–444). New York: Springer-Verlag.

Dokecki, P.R., & Strain, B. (1973). Intervention 2001: Transactional and developmental perspectives. *Peabody Journal of Education, 50,* 175–183.

Donovan, W.C., Jr. (1986). *Implementation analysis of a public policy on the care and treatment of persons with severe disabilities.* Unpublished doctoral dissertation, Vanderbilt University, Nashville, TN.

Education for All Handicapped Children Act of 1975. PL 94-142.

Education of the Handicapped. (1987, March 18). Alexandria, VA: Capitol Publications, Inc.

Education of the Handicapped Act Amendments of 1986. PL 99-457.

Elmore, R.F. (1978). Organizational models of social program implementation. *Public Policy, 26,* 185–228.

Elmore, R.F. (1979–1980). Backward mapping: Implementation research and policy decisions. *Political Science Quarterly, 94,* 601–616.

Fiedler, C. (1985). *Conflict prevention, containment, and resolution in special education due process disputes: Parents' and school personnel's perceptions of variables associated with the development and escalation of due process conflict.* Unpublished doctoral dissertation, University of Kansas, Lawrence.

Gallagher, J.J. (1981). Models for policy analysis: Child and family policy. In R. Haskins & J.J. Gallagher (Eds.), *Models for analysis of social policy: An introduction* (pp. 37–77). Norwood, NJ: Ablex Publishing Co.

Garwood, S.G. (1984). Social policy and young handicapped children. *Topics in Early Childhood Special Education, 4*(1), 1–8.

Gilkerson, L., Hilliard, A, III, Schrag, E., & Shonkoff, J.P. (1987). Point of view: Commenting on PL 99-457. *Zero to Three, 7*(3), 13–17.

Gorham, K.A., DesJardins, C., Page, R., Pettis, E., & Scheiber, B. (1975). Effect on parents. In N. Hobbs (Ed.), *Issues in the classification of children* (Vol. II, pp. 154–188). San Francisco: Jossey-Bass.

Hargrove, E.C. (1975). *The missing link: The study of the implementation of social policy.* Washington, DC: The Urban Institute Press.

Hargrove, E.C., Abernethy, V., Graham, S.G., Cunningham, S., Ward, L.E., & Baughn, W.K. (1981). School systems and regulatory mandates: A case study of the implementation of the Education for All Handicapped Children Act. In S. Bacharach (Ed.), *Organizational behavior in schools and school districts* (pp. 97–123). New York: Praeger.

Hargrove, E.C., Graham, S.G., Ward, L.E., Abernethy, V., Cunningham, J., & Vaughn, W.K. (1983). Regulation and schools: The implementation of equal education for handicapped children. *Peabody Journal of Education, 60*(4).

Heflinger, C.A., Cook, V.J., & Thackery, M. (1987). Identification of mental retardation by the SOMPA: Nondiscriminatory or nonexistent? *Journal of School Psychology, 25,* 177–183.

Hobbs, N. (1975). *The futures of children.* San Francisco: Jossey-Bass.

Hobbs, N. (1982). *The troubled and troubling child.* San Francisco: Jossey-Bass.

Hobbs, N., Dokecki, P.R., Hoover-Dempsey, K.V. Moroney, R.M. Shayne,

M.W., & Weeks, K.H. (1984). *Strengthening families.* San Francisco: Jossey-Bass.
Kelman, S. (1984). Using implementation research to solve implementation problems: The cause of energy emergency assistance. *The Journal of Policy Analysis and Management, 4*(1), 75–91.
Knitzer, J. (1982). *Unclaimed children: The failure of public responsibility to children and adolescents in need of mental health services.* Washington, DC: Children's Defense Fund.
Knitzer, J. (1984). Mental health services to children and adolescents: A national view of public policies. *American Psychologist, 39,* 905–911.
Lipsky, M. (1980). *Street-level bureaucracy.* New York: Russell Sage.
March, J.G., & Simon, H.A. (1958). *Organizations.* New York: John Wiley & Sons.
Mazmanian, D.A., & Sabatier, P.A. (1983). *Implementation and public policy.* Glenview, IL: Scott Foresman.
McNett, I. (1980). Part II: Mental health services for handicapped fall between agencies. *APA Monitor, 11,* 15.
Moroney, R.M. (1986). *Shared responsibility: Families and social policy.* New York: Aldine.
Moroney, R.M., & Dokecki, P.R. (1984). The family and the professions: Implications for public policy. *Journal of Family Issues, 5,* 224–238.
Nakamura, R.T., & Smallwood, F. (1980). *The politics of policy implementation.* New York: St. Martin's Press.
National Association of Social Workers, Inc. (1984). *NASW standards and guidelines for social work case management for the functionally impaired.* Silver Spring, MD: Author.
Rhodes, W.C. (1975). *A study of child variance: Volume 4: The future.* Ann Arbor: University of Michigan.
Ripley, R.B., & Franklin, G.A. (1982). *Bureaucracy and policy implementation.* Homewood, IL: The Dorsey Press.
Ryan, W. (1976). *Blaming the victim* (rev. ed.). New York: Random House.
Scrimshaw, S.C.M. (1984). Infanticide in human populations: Societal and individual concerns. In G. Hausfater & S. Hardy (Eds.), *Infanticide: comparative and evolutionary perspectives* (pp. 439–462). New York: Aldine.
Shadish, W.R., Jr. (1984). Lessons from the implementation of deinstitutionalization. *American Psychologist, 39,* 725–738.
Smith, B.J., & Schakel, J.A. (1986). Noncategorical identification of preschool handicapped children: Policy issues and options. *Journal of the Division for Early Childhood, 11,* 78–85.
Thompson, J.D. (1967). *Organizations in action.* New York: McGraw-Hill.
Turnbull, A.P., & Turnbull, H.R., III. (1982). Parent involvement in the education of handicapped children: A critique. *Mental Retardation, 20*(3), 115–122.
Turnbull, H.R., III, Brotherson, M.J., Czyzewski, M.J., Esquith, D.S., Otis, A.K., Summers, J.A., Van Reusen, A.R., & DePazza-Conway, M. (1983). A policy analysis of "least restrictive" education of handicapped children. *Rutgers Law Journal, 14,* 489–540.
Turnbull, H.R., III, & Turnbull, A.P. (1979). *Free appropriate public education: Law and implementation.* Denver: Love Publishing Company.
U.S. House of Representatives. (1986). *Education of the Handicapped Act*

Amendments of 1986: Report from the Committee on Education and Labor (Rep. No. 99–860). Washington, DC: Author.

Weatherley, R., & Lipsky, M. (1977). Street-level bureaucrats and institutional innovation: Implementing special education reform. *Harvard Educational Review, 47*(2), 171–197.

Wheeley, B.M. (1981a). The human development liaison specialist: I. Theory, person, and process. *Journal of Community Psychology, 9,* 316–320.

Wheeley, B.M. (1981b). The human development liaison specialist: II. An emerging profession. *Journal of Community Psychology, 9,* 321–330.

Yoshida, R., Fenton, K.S., Kaufman, M.J., & Maxwell, J.P. (1978). Parent involvement in special education planning process. *Exceptional Children, 44,* 531–533.

A Parent's Perspective
IMPLEMENTING PL 99-457

5

Martha Ziegler

BEFORE PUBLIC LAW 94-142 (THE EDUCATION FOR ALL HANDICAPPED CHILdren Act of 1975) became law, parents and their children were the consumers (sometimes the victims) of decisions about the kinds of intervention and services a child received, and rarely the makers of decisions, no matter how intimately those decisions affected their lives. When children could legally be excluded from school because of their handicapping conditions, there were few decisions open to parents. Frequently the only option parents had was to "rubber stamp" recommendations made by others.

Making decisions is responsibility: making effective decisions is power. Empowerment of parents *qua* parents through opportunities for active decision-making has been one of the most exciting by-products of PL 94-142. The framers of the law envisioned an active, fully participatory role for parents of children with handicaps, and they saw this kind of active participation by parents as a crucial protection of the children's rights.

It has not been universally easy for educators and service providers implementing PL 94-142 to work with parents as consumers with guaranteed decision-making powers, and the implementation of the new programs for infants and toddlers under the PL 99-457 (The Education of the Handicapped Act Amendments of 1986) will not be any easier. Educators and service providers will face the added challenge of working with parents at the time when those parents are most vulnerable and are themselves in need of sensitive assistance.

This chapter presents a parent's point of view toward the challenge of ensuring active participation of parents in decision-making as PL 99-457 is implemented. The chapter first addresses the topic of disclosure—the manner in which a child's identified disability is reported to the parents—and the ways in which decisions about immediate medical intervention are handled. Next, the chapter discusses parents' need for a context in which to view the disability, information that will help them make decisions about their child's future and other related family issues, and support from professionals as parents confront these decisions. Finally, the policy implications of the decision-making role of parents under PL 99-457 are addressed.

THE "VIOLENCE OF DISCLOSURE"

With the birth or early identification of a young child with a disability, the parents are in a state of shock, totally vulnerable, and wholly lacking in self-confidence. If the diagnosis is presented in an insensitive manner, it may take years for the family to recover.

Dr. Elizabeth Zucman, a French physician working in pediatric physical medicine and rehabilitation, has written a very insightful monograph titled *Childhood Disability in the Family: Recognizing the Added Handicap* (Zucman, 1982). In reviewing the international literature on the effects of having a child with a disability in the family, Zucman traced attitudinal and behavioral changes in some of the professionals (physicians and other hospital personnel) whose role it is to inform parents of their child's disability. Her review persuaded her that families suffered an added handicap, one brought on, at least in part, by what she refers to as the "violence of disclosure, the insensitive way the disability of an infant or child is revealed by professionals to the parents—and the subsequent feelings of isolation, guilt, and anger which the parents (especially the mother) experience" (p. 5). Becoming aware of this added handicap caused changes in the attitude and behavior of some professionals involved.

Individual parents often report problems caused by the negative manner in which the presence of the disability has been communicated to them. In a recent study, Ann Turnbull reported that several of the parents she had interviewed characterized this communication as "unduly pessimistic" (Turnbull, Blue-Banning, Behr, & Kerns, 1987). One father observed, "When normal children are born, the doctors do not recount for parents all of the problems that could happen to their child, like drug involvement, flunking out of college, sexual promiscuity, or teenage suicide; however, when a child with Down syndrome is born, the doctors only point out the negative" (p. 123–124). Such negative attitudes and behavior on the part of primary caregivers can have devastating effects on crucial decisions that must be made by the parents.

An example is the decision whether or not to withhold lifesaving treatment for newborns with disabilities. In the most extreme cases, fortunately rare, parents have been advised to agree to withholding treatment, only to find that the infant survives but is more seriously handicapped than he or she would have been if treatment had been provided. In other cases, treatment is withheld and the infant does not survive, despite the fact that other people with similar disabilities have gone on to lead productive, satisfying lives.

Some of the negativism perceived by parents of children with disabilities is the result of outmoded, unexamined attitudes, based on information that predates the revolutionary changes in law, philosophy, and educational technology that have occurred during the last 20 years. Recent developments in educational technology—including better understanding of behavior and child development and the use of adaptive devices by children and adults with disabilities—have dramatically improved the expected outcomes for many of these children. Unfortunately, children and families continue to suffer needlessly because of the long time lag between new discoveries and widespread knowledge about them among practitioners.

PARENTS' NEED FOR A CONTEXT

For effective, active decision-making to occur, there must be a context, a framework of shared philosophy and overall goals, that enables parents to work with their professional partners to examine the facts and reach appropriate conclusions that will benefit each individual child.

My experience with my own daughter, Mary Ann, in her early years may help to illustrate some of what I mean by context and overall goals. My daughter, now 24, underwent a comprehensive series of medical and psychological tests during the period between her 30th and 36th months of age and was diagnosed as autistic. Having the most minimal understanding of autism myself, I nevertheless was confronted endlessly by well-meaning social workers with the same frustrating question: "Mrs. Ziegler, what do you see as the long-term prognosis for your daughter?" I never knew what to answer; I still do not know what answer was expected. I do have some idea now, though, why I always found that question irritating: it is a limiting, shutting-down, boxing-in kind of question. It implies that if we can just once and for all establish her limitations, then we will not need to ask any more really penetrating questions.

How much more helpful it would have been if teachers and others had gone about helping my husband and me to frame a context for our planning. They could have helped us pose more meaningful questions, like the following:

What kind of life do we hope our daughter will have?
Where do we want to see her live?
What kind of work do we want to help her plan for?
What skills will she need in order to have friends and a social life?
What should we be doing now to get ready for that life we wish for her?
How can we prepare her for a life of meaningful choices?
How can we help her achieve a maximum amount of control over her own life?
What can we as a family do to promote healthy self-esteem in our daughter as she grows up?

I do not list these questions as a criticism of the people who tried so hard to help our daughter, for much has been learned during the intervening years about planning within the context of the child's whole life. Guidance has come from both the federal government and the research community. The "transition initiative," developed by Assistant Secretary of Education Madeleine Will early in her tenure, called for new ways of planning the bridge between the school years and adult life for young people with disabilities, especially those with severe disabilities. The initiative encouraged parents and educators to look first at outcomes—what the young person can be expected to be doing in adult life—and then work backward to the kind of education and planning that are needed to achieve that goal. For example, if the young person is expected to live within his or her home community, then during school years he or she should be learning and practicing the skills required for such a life. Similarly, educational leaders at research centers such as Syracuse University, the University of Wisconsin, and the University of Oregon emphasize the importance of practicing these skills within the real community, not just rehearsing in a classroom. Professionals and parents now need to utilize that information to improve our planning and our decision-making for our children.

Such questions as those I have listed, posed early on and repeated regularly, can help parents frame a meaningful context for their planning, their decision-making, and their participation in the Individualized Education Program (IEP) and the Individualized Family Service Plan (IFSP).

When I look back, I cannot believe how totally in the dark I was operating! Even in the area of language development, in which a child with autism has the most urgent and most obvious need, I really had a very limited framework. I did not think in terms of communication, only in terms of speech. Not until she was in her late teens, and my daughter and I both were exposed to the work of Dr. William Condon at Boston University Medical School, did I begin to really listen to my daughter, to tune in to what she was trying to communicate, much of the time through her own richly metaphorical language.

A recent example of Mary Ann's metaphorical expression of her deeply felt emotion occurred after the death of her paternal grandparents, 6 months apart. Her grandparents lived in a very small town in central Pennsylvania. Their house was one block from the town square and the town clock, which loudly but benignly strikes the hours. After the second grandparent's funeral, Mary Ann looked out the window of the empty house and said, "There's nothing left but the town clock."

INFORMATION AND SKILLS FOR DECISION-MAKING

In addition to a context, parents obviously need information in order to reach effective decisions about their child's education and other services. The following is a list of some of the kinds of information that parents need:

Information about the disability itself—not only limitations, but also possibilities; treatment choices; preferred methods of education, if relevant; and success stories of people with that particular handicapping condition

Knowledge of relevant laws, including PL 94-142 and PL 99-457, Sec. 504 of the Vocational Rehabilitation Act, and state special education laws

Knowledge about services, such as respite care, that are available to the child and to the family

Exposure to "state-of-the-art" educational programs

Understanding of the importance and implications of various kinds of tests and assessments

Information about sources of financial assistance, such as private insurance, Supplemental Security Income (SSI), and Medicaid

Knowledge about the community in which the family lives—local government, local leadership, and community organizations and services, as well as relevant state agencies

In addition to information, parents also need special skills in order to secure the programs and services to which their child is entitled, and to perform their own participatory, decision-making role effectively. Parents need to have, or to acquire, the following skills:

Basic research skills in locating and evaluating the necessary information, obtaining copies of laws and regulations, and identifying key government and agency persons
Assertiveness and communication skills
Documentation methods: letter writing, telephone logs, and so forth
Advocacy strategies

Needless to say, parents usually do not come equipped with all of this information and the array of skills; most of us have had to learn as we go. Workers in early intervention programs can play a key role in helping parents acquire the information and skills they so badly need. Parents can be referred to such resources as the disability organization that represents their child's needs; the nearest parent training and information center; a local parent support group (if none is available, parents may be encouraged to start one); or the local parent advisory council, now required or encouraged in many states. This kind of assistance now is available to parents in most states.

OTHER AREAS OF PARENTAL DECISION-MAKING

In addition to the variety of decisions that parents must make about educational issues and the development and implementation of the IFSP and the IEP, there are other kinds of issues facing parents. For most of these latter decisions, despite their importance, parents have access to very little help.

First, many prospective parents, especially women age 35 and older, must make a decision whether or not to become pregnant, knowing the statistical probabilities of conceiving a baby with a disability. If they choose to proceed, the parents confront two more decisions: whether or not to have the fetus tested for disabling conditions and whether or not to terminate the pregnancy should a disability be identified through prenatal testing. Physicians often assume the answers to these questions, especially the last one, without realizing that they are imposing their own set of values and ethics upon the patient. Prospective parents need a wealth of accurate information and respectful permission to make their own personal decisions in such matters.

One major set of questions confronts every parent of a child with a disability, questions surrounding brothers and sisters. For families whose firstborn child has a disability, an immediate question is, "Should we have more children?" Except for genetic counseling in cases where the disability has an established genetic basis, it is amazing how little information is available to help families make this basic decision. Following this first question comes a second: "If we decide to have more children, should we have just one, or two, or more?" Parents need information and support in sorting out such issues as financial implications, the psychological well-being of all their children, and their own health, in addition to questions of risk of disability. But this kind of aid has been provided only scarcely to parents. No one can answer these questions for someone else, but especially trained family counselors could provide the kind of information that would facilitate sound, personal choices. If there is research being done in this area, the results are not reaching many families yet. On the basis of my own experience with parents, I know that large numbers of parents would be happy to share their hard-earned knowledge in this area with sensitive researchers.

In those families where the child with a disability does have siblings, whether older or younger, parents confront an additional question: "How do we ensure that our nondisabled children not only receive, but feel that they receive, their fair share of attention and love?" Not only do parents need information and assistance in framing and answering such crucial family questions, but they also need support and encouragement at critical times in the course of parenting their nondisabled children. When problems arise, it is very difficult to sort out the role of the disabled sibling from other, unrelated environmental factors. At such times, honest and open discussion can be very important. Professionals can help parents, not only by encouraging such openness, but, more importantly, by modeling this behavior.

I remember when a counselor in my son's elementary school suggested that I read *The Magic Years* (Fraiberg, 1959), a book that describes young children's flawed, almost superstitious concepts of cause and effect. At the time, I did not really understand what I was reading; at least, I did not make the appropriate connections to my son. For some reason I did not feel comfortable about admitting my bewilderment. It was unfortunate that the counselor did not follow up with discussion; since she was working with my son she could have helped me understand the implications for him. Only many years later, when I read another article that complemented the book, was I able to fit some pieces together and understand what the counselor evidently assumed that I would learn from the book. Eventually, I figured out that when my son and his autistic sister got into fights and she did not respond normally, by hitting back or yelling for help, there was a strong risk that my son was learning a dangerous lesson, namely, that his anger had no external limits and, thus, that the world is a very scary place.

SUPPORT FOR PARENTS, AS PARENTS

One of the ways in which professional caregivers can be most helpful to parents of newborn or newly identified children with disabilities is to encourage and support the parents as parents. Such reinforcement does as much as anything else to build the parent's self-confidence as a parent, as a decision-maker, and as a partner in the care and nurturing of the child. While both parents require such support, it is particularly important for mothers, since they usually serve as primary caregivers for children in the family. Therefore, the remarks of this section emphasize the needs of mothers of children with disabilities.

One way that professionals can help support mothers as mothers is to adopt a policy of always allowing the mother to be present during therapy, testing, or other necessary sessions with the young child. Departure from such a policy should occur only for exceptional reasons. In case of doubt about her presence, the mother should be welcomed. Such a policy conveys a message to the mother that she plays an important role with the child, and that she is a partner who can be expected to contribute valuable input and can be relied upon to carry out any follow-up activities that may be indicated by the session.

The "specialness" of the disability can all too easily overwhelm all other interactions between child and parents. One parent advocate has urged that, in the implementation of the new federal programs for infants and young children, we remember to "mainstream the parents" from the very beginning. Her reminder is a critical one. Especially when the child with the disability is the firstborn, it is all too easy for the mother to be pulled psychologically into a "special" context around the child. Before long, mother and child are set up for a segregated, "specialized" life for the child, a direction that is not really fair to mother or child. Conversely, some mothers, overwhelmed by "specialness," occasionally may need reminders to respond to the same maternal instinct and to apply the same parenting skills with the child who has a disability as with their other children.

Mothers should be encouraged to ensure that their children with disabilities have as much opportunity as possible to play with other infants and young children of the same age in day care, nursery school, Sunday school, and at the local playground. Inclusion in these "normal" settings will benefit both the young child and the mother. The child will forego the stigma and stunted social and emotional growth that inevitably result from segregation from his or her age peers. The mother will be able to interact with and learn from mothers of children the same age as her child, and she, too, will escape some of the stigma and isolation of segregation.

The mother of a young child with a disability will need support in this first effort, or it may backfire. There is a risk that it will only reinforce the "differentness" of her child and of her experience as a mother. This risk can be minimized by bringing whatever specialized resources are needed to the normal setting rather than removing the infant and mother to a segregated setting.

With the coming expansion of early intervention and preschool programs for children with special needs, it is extremely important to keep infants and their mothers within the mainstream, if only for the sake of their own perceptions. Physicians, early intervention workers, teachers, and all other caregivers must help each mother view her young child first as a child, and second as a child with special needs.

POLICY IMPLICATIONS

The needs of parents both as parents and as effective performers of the roles mandated by law have important policy implications, especially in the area of personnel training. Physicians and other health care professionals, early childhood teachers, therapists, and social workers will need training that includes exposure to the large body of experiential knowledge that parents possess. They need this knowledge, in addition to their more formal training, in order to develop the skills necessary for supporting and assisting the parents with whom they will become partners.

In addition to training considerations, policy-makers must address the need for better sharing of information among special educators, early childhood educators, health care professionals, parents, and advocates. All of these people need to know that persons with the severest kinds of disabilities now work and live in the community, and they need to know about new models of support for home care, such as respite care. It cannot be assumed that these busy professionals will exchange information; policy-makers must structure this exchange through meetings, newsletters, and other methods.

Terminology also plays an important role in parent-professional relationships. Policy-makers, trainers, and implementers need to be sensitive to differing perceptions of a particular term or concept. For example, a family may attach to the word "intervention" its negative connotation—that is, "hindrance" or "interference"—while the helping professional sees only the positive meaning of "modification." Parents, too, will need to become aware of these linguistic distinctions as they assume their roles as decision-makers and, sometimes, as negotiators.

Families will need adequate, but not overwhelming, information to facilitate the decision-making process. They will need to learn the appropriate questions to pose each step of the way. They will need to learn a new role: that of case manager in their child's life and their lives. They will benefit from exposure to various models of early intervention and early education. And they will continue to need to understand the history of the laws affecting their children, so that they can understand the reasons for the role they are asked to assume.

These needs have implications for the Parent Training and Information (PTI) projects, the program of national parent-to-parent assistance established by Congress in PL 98-199. Under the new requirements of PL 99-457, the PTI projects will need to expand their services to that group of parents whose children are not yet in school. The parent projects also could offer specialized training and information to parents serving on Interagency Coordinating Councils (ICC) and other similar committees. Like training programs for early intervention and early childhood professionals, these parent projects may need additional resources in order to expand their programs to provide parents of very young children with needed information and support.

Experience with the implementation of the Education for All Handicapped Children Act (PL 94-142) has confirmed the importance of parents as decision-makers and monitors of their children's education. There is every reason to believe that this affirmative role will continue, especially if parents receive the support they need in order to perform effectively their functions as parents and as decision-makers about education and other services for their children with special needs.

REFERENCES

Fraiberg, S.H. (1959). *The magic years.* New York: Scribners.

Turnbull, A.P., Blue-Banning, M., Behr, S., & Kerns, G. (1987). Family research and intervention: A value and ethical examination. In P.R. Dokecki & R.M. Zaner (Eds.), *Ethics of dealing with persons with severe handicaps: Toward a research agenda* (119–140). Baltimore: Paul H. Brookes Publishing Co.

Zucman, E. (1982). *Childhood disability in the family: Recognizing the added handicap.* New York: World Rehabilitation Fund.

APPENDIX

RESOURCES FOR PARENTS

The following selected agencies, operating on a national or regional basis, will respond to inquiries from parents concerning laws, services, support groups, and other information.

National Information Center for Children and Youth with Handicaps (NICHCY)

NICHCY offers information about specific disabilities; state-specific information about state agencies, parent groups, and advocacy organizations; and other topics of interest to parents and professionals. Their address is:
NICHCY
Box 1492
Washington, DC 20013
1 (800) 999–5599 (toll-free)

Parent Training and Information (PTI) Centers

Approximately 50 coalitions of parents of children with disabilities operate PTI centers offering information, support, and training workshops for parents of children with disabilities within a specific state or region. Information about the nearest parent center is available through the TAPP (Technical Assistance for Parent Programs) Project, at the following locations:

TAPP Central Office
Federation for Children with Special Needs
312 Stuart Street
Boston, MA 02116
(617) 482–2915

TAPP Northeast Regional Office
Parent Information Center
P.O. Box 1422
Concord, NH 03301
(603) 224–6299

TAPP Midwest Regional Office
PACER Center, Inc.
4826 Chicago Avenue
Minneapolis, MN 55417
(612) 827–2966

95

TAPP West Regional Office
Washington State PAVE
6316 South 12th Street
Tacoma, WA 98465
(206) 565-2266

TAPP South Regional Office
Parents Educating Parents
Georgia Association for Retarded Citizens (ARC)
1851 Ram Runway, #104
College Park, GA 30337
(404) 761-2745

Issues and Directions in Preparing Professionals to Work with Young Handicapped Children and Their Families

6

Donald B. Bailey, Jr.

EACH YEAR THOUSANDS OF MEN AND WOMEN EMBARK ON A RITUALISTIC journey with a common goal: becoming a professional. Whether the field be medicine, law, nursing, architecture, or education, entry into a profession invariably requires specialized preparatory experiences. Initial preparation usually consists of several years of education in an institution of higher learning, including enrollment in a specific professional school or department. Faculty in those schools are charged with transmitting to

---

Preparation of this manuscript was supported in part by Special Education Programs, Special Education and Rehabilitative Services, United States Department of Education, Grant No. G008401614. The opinions expressed do not necessarily reflect the position or policy of the United States Department of Education, and no official endorsement by the U.S. Department of Education should be inferred. The author expresses appreciation to the following persons, who provided key information essential for Table 2 and who provided feedback on earlier drafts of this chapter: Coral Cochrane, Betsy Crais, Diane Davis, Ruth Humphry, Gail Huntington, Mildred Kaufman, Lynn McDonald, Pat Pearson, Rune Simeonsson, Stuart Teplin, and Pam Winton.

students the accumulated knowledge of their profession, ensuring the attainment of basic competencies necessary for success in the profession, and socializing students to develop a sense of professional identity.

Completion of the professional program generally is marked by two documents, a degree, indicating that the student has met the basic requirements of the institution, and a certificate or license, indicating the student has mastered the basic competencies of the profession. After entry into the chosen field, the professional continues to accumulate practical knowledge through experience. In addition, most professions require some form of continuing education to ensure that professionals keep informed of the latest techniques, issues, or regulations in the field.

The preparation of professionals and, subsequently, professional practice, change when new theories evolve, new knowledge is developed, or when the accumulated experience of clinicians suggests a need to change existing professional practice. Professions also should adapt to the changing needs of clients, pressing societal concerns, and, occasionally, legislative mandates or court decisions. Professions that are sensitive and responsive to such changes and demands will survive and, indeed, flourish. Those that are rigid and inflexible run the risk of being ignored, isolated, or having their responsibilities usurped by other professionals who have the vision to see and respond to important needs for services.

The passage of Public Law 99-457, The Education of the Handicapped Act Amendments of 1986, exemplifies an external force that undoubtedly will increase the need for qualified professionals from several disciplines and influence the way those professionals are prepared at both the preservice and inservice levels. By mandating services for handicapped preschoolers ages 3–5 years, providing strong incentives for infant intervention, and mandating specific intervention components such as family assessment, interdisciplinary planning, an Individualized Family Service Plan (IFSP), and case management, the legislation serves as a stimulus for both quantitative and qualitative changes in professional preparation programs. Furthermore, the legislation mandates that each state must have a comprehensive system of personnel development that: 1) includes both preservice and inservice training, 2) is conducted on an interdisciplinary basis when appropriate, and 3) addresses the needs of a variety of personnel, including public and private providers, primary referral sources, parents, paraprofessionals, and persons who will serve as case managers. Finally, states must ensure that personnel working in early intervention programs are "appropriately and adequately prepared and trained." Thus personnel preparation becomes a very real policy issue.

This chapter provides an overview of questions raised by the legislation in regard to personnel preparation. In doing so, four topics are addressed. First, I attempt to define what is unique about working with handicapped infants and preschoolers and the implications of that uniqueness for personnel preparation. Why should policy makers consider specialized preparation, and how essential is it? Second, I discuss how issues regarding personnel preparation may vary across disciplines likely to be involved in early intervention. This discussion is based on the fact that the provision of appropriate services for handicapped infants, preschoolers, and their families is not the domain of a specific profession; rather it is the ecological context within which professionals from a variety of disciplines converge to meet complex educational, medical, psychological, and social needs. This context requires professionals who can apply their discipline's principles and procedures with very young children and who also can work effectively with other professionals to provide coordinated and integrated services. Third, assuming the need for specialized preparation, I address the kinds of skills that need to be taught for successful professional practice in early intervention. Fourth, I discuss the need for inservice training and briefly review the research on effective inservice practices. This discussion is based on the assumption that preservice training most likely will be insufficient to prepare professionals for all aspects of clinical practice. Furthermore, since knowledge is rapidly changing with respect to working with young handicapped children and their families, policy makers will need to consider alternatives for ensuring that professionals are aware of and implement currently accepted best practices in early intervention.

WHAT IS UNIQUE ABOUT WORKING WITH YOUNG CHILDREN?

It is not uncommon to encounter the widely held belief that it requires very little formal training to care for young children. Warmth, patience, and a love of children are seen as the essential characteristics by those evaluating an individual's suitability for child care. Even when it is recognized that some form of training is important to work with handicapped youngsters, an assumption often is made that anyone —whether teacher, therapist, or nurse—who has demonstrated competence in working with older children has the basic skills necessary to work with handicapped infants and preschoolers. Any additional skills needed may be obtained through on-the-job experiences.

Countering those perceptions are emerging trends toward increasing differentiation of the roles and training of preschool (Mallory, 1983) and infant (Bailey, Farel, O'Donnell, Simeonsson, & Miller, 1986; Geik, Gilkerson, & Sponseller, 1982) specialists, in addition to neonatal caregivers (Sweet, 1981).

In a survey of special education programs with an early childhood focus, Bricker and Slentz (in press) found that 89% of the respondents felt that working with infants required different skills from those required to work with preschoolers, a fact that was felt to be important by respondents in designing preservice training programs. The importance of this differentiation is reflected in the recent funding by the U.S. Department of Education of a research institute devoted to the study of materials and procedures used to prepare individuals from multiple disciplines to work with handicapped infants, toddlers, and their families. These trends, coupled with the fact that states increasingly are establishing separate teaching certificates in early childhood special education (Stile, Abernathy, Pettibone, & Wachtel, 1984), point to a growing awareness that the preparation of professionals to work in early intervention and preschool programs must address the unique needs of very young children.

What is it about the infant and preschoool period that calls for specialized personnel preparation? Several factors contributing to this need are summarized in Table 1, in which various aspects of intervention are contrasted across the infancy, preschool, and elementary-age periods. They center around three broad factors: characteristics of the children, characteristics of the intervention context, and the role of families.

Characteristics of the Children

Most observers will agree that infants and preschoolers are different from older children. Three dimensions of early developmental periods, however, create unique intervention demands: population parameters, goals for intervention, and behavioral characteristics of young children.

Population Parameters Most areas of special education teacher training and certification are categorical in their orientation, focusing on groups of children with specific disabilities such as mental retardation, emotional disturbance, learning disabilities, hearing impairments, visuals impairments, severe/multiple handicaps, or chronic illness. Training programs typically focus on disability-specific aspects of interventions, with age being a secondary consideration. In contrast, training for early intervention is specifically age-focused. The implicit assumption is that in the infant and preschool period, age is a more important factor in the provision of needed clinical skills and services than is the child's specific disability. Although not empirically verified, this assumption is rein-

Table 1. A comparison of interventions with infants, preschoolers, and elementary-age children with special needs

Domain	Infants and toddlers (0–36 months)	Preschoolers (36–60 months)	Elementary (5–12 years)
I. Characteristics of children			
Population parameters	Noncategorical; developmentally delayed, conditions that typically result in delay, at risk of substantial delay; results in wide range of ability levels and types of handicaps	Noncategorical; wide range of ability levels and handicaps (some states, however, will choose categorical descriptions)	Categorical; more restricted range of ability levels and disability types; formal eligibility criteria
Goals for intervention	Behavior and motor organization, differentiated responses to environmental cues, cause and effect, early communication and social skills, attachment	Cognitive, self-help, social, fine motor, communication, behavior, toy play, gross motor	Reading, spelling, mathematics, appropriate social behavior
Schedule regularity	Low—almost entirely determined by infant	Moderate—some adult determination of schedules, but requires flexibility depending on children's needs and interest	High—preset routine and time allocation for tasks; very little in the way of child-initiated activities
Endurance	Short—interactions typically last less than 2–3 minutes	Moderate—interactions may last 5–15 minutes	Long—interactions may last 30 minutes to 2 hours
Motivation	Must come from inherent appeal of material or activity; based on infant's interest	Begin to follow adult expectations, but high-interest toys and activities are critical	Based on adult expectations for compliance; reliance on self-regulation and response to rules

(continued)

101

Table 1. (continued)

Domain	Infants and toddlers (0–36 months)	Preschoolers (36–60 months)	Elementary (5–12 years)
II. The intervention context			
Context of teaching	Parent-child interactions; feeding, bathing, diapering, and dressing routines; object play	Object play, peer interactions, adult-child interactions, routines	Classroom instruction, written materials
Sites for intervention/services	Homes, day care centers, family day care homes, specialized developmental centers, developmental evaluation centers, hospital settings (NICU, pediatrics ward)	Specialized developmental center/classrooms, day care centers, homes, developmental evaluation centers, hospital settings	Elementary schools (regular classroom, resource room, self-contained classroom)
Responsible agencies	Mental health centers, hospital, public health services, private day care, specialized nonprofit agencies, public school	Public school, mental health, Head Start, day care	Public school
Team functioning	Often involves multiple professionals from multiple agencies; considerable role overlap, requiring extensive communication and coordination	Moderate blending of roles, but work in isolation is possible	Differentiated and specific roles; isolation likely
III. Family role			
Mandated family role	Essential and family-focused—IFSP requires documentation of family needs and strengths, a statement of family goals, and the provision of family services, including case management	Very important—IEP provisions pertain, all parents' rights protected, and parent training encouraged when necessary	Important—IEP provisions pertain, all parents' rights protected

forced by federal guidelines as well as by the way in which early intervention programs are organized.

With respect to federal specifications, schools serving handicapped children older than 5 years must report children according to predetermined categorical labels (e.g., mildly retarded, learning disabled). PL 99-457 does not require states to report children ages 3–5 by disability labels, thus allowing for noncategorical approaches to child identification. (Specific definitions for eligibility, however, are required and are to be determined individually by each state.) For states choosing to serve handicapped infants and toddlers, PL 99-457 requires services both for children with documented developmental delays (the specific degree to be determined by each state) and for those who may not presently be delayed but who have a condition that typically results in a delay (e.g., Down syndrome). States also may elect, at their discretion, to serve children who are at risk for substantial delay (e.g., offspring of adolescent, low-income parents, low birth weight babies, or children at risk for abuse or neglect).

The noncategorical approach is generally reflective of the focus of early intervention services. Although some programs are specialized for young children with sensory or motor impairments, the vast majority of early intervention programs are noncategorical in nature and include children with varying handicaps functioning at different levels of development. An important implication for training programs is the need to prepare professionals to work with children with diverse disabilities.

Goals for Intervention   Teachers of elementary-age children typically will focus on the basics of reading, spelling, and mathematics, with additional instruction in science and social studies. For handicapped youngsters, self-care skills and functional daily living skills are likely to be important instructional goals, and the development of appropriate social behavior is encouraged. In contrast, the focus of infant and preschool intervention is on enhancing the *developmental prerequisites* to academic, social, and daily living skills. Generally these prerequisites fall into several broad developmental domains: cognitive, self-help, social, motor (fine and gross), and communication (receptive and expressive). Toy play, independent use of the environment, and behavioral regulation according to rules also are important intervention goals. Intervention with neonates and infants will address goals of organization of behavior states, motor control, differentiated responses to environmental cues, contingency awareness (the learning of cause and effect relationships), and the roots of social competence and social reciprocity. Thus early childhood professionals must be knowledgeable about different developmental domains and stages, must be able to use assessment tools relevant to those domains, and must be aware of treatment strategies likely to promote corresponding skills.

In addition to addressing different intervention goals, infant and preschool intervention is unique in that focus is placed on the acceleration of behaviors (e.g., walking, communicating, toy play) that normally emerge, without direct instruction, as a result of physical maturation and incidental learning. In contrast, the skills taught in elementary education (e.g., reading, math, spelling) are much less likely to be acquired without direct instruction. Given that acceleration goals may require a different approach to intervention than instructional goals, training programs must prepare professionals to make that differentiation and modify learning environments accordingly.

Another characteristic differentiating early intervention from school-age programs is the primary goal of *prevention* of later impairments. While teachers and therapists working with school-age children typically address existing delays or disabilities, early childhood professionals may work with children whose deficits are minimal or who are at risk only for future problems. For example, physical therapy will be provided for infants who have cerebral palsy in order to prevent or reduce the future likelihood of contractures or reduced range of motion. Likewise, special educators will work with Down syndrome infants who display no current significant delays in order to minimize later delays in cognitive, communication, motor, or social skills. A preventive orientation to intervention differs from an ameliorative or corrective orientation in that it is a more nebulous context, since the specific instructional strategies or target skills necessary to prevent deficits are not well-known.

Behavioral Characteristics Elementary school-age children are able to follow a schedule, can work for extended periods of time at a single task, and generally respond to teacher-directed activities. Elementary school teachers have a high degree of regularity in the schedules they follow. Children arrive and depart at specified times, a preset routine exists, and precise amounts of time are allocated for various instructional slots. An important skill for professionals at this age level is to be able to establish such a schedule, follow it consistently, and keep children moving in accordance with the schedule. At the preschool level there is some adult determination of schedules, but a considerable amount of flexibility is needed since young children's interests are likely to vary. For infants and neonates, the schedule is much more likely to vary according to the child's responsiveness and interest. It would be unrealistic, for example, to have a rigid schedule for children under 12 months of age. Thus, professionals preparing to work in early childhood programs must learn to be extremely flexible and to "read" children's behavior in order to capture optimal opportunities for intervention.

In a similar vein, scheduling must be more flexible at the early childhool level because of young children's inability to engage in tasks for extended periods of time. Whereas elementary-age children are expected to work 30–120 minutes at a time on assigned tasks, preschoolers are more likely to work and play at 5- to 15-minute activities and infants for even briefer periods, with interactions with people and objects lasting anywhere from 3 minutes down to a few seconds. Early interventionists, thus, must be flexible and able to plan brief, but effective, interactions with children.

Finally, early intervention professionals must be able to provide high-interest toys and materials, since young children's motivation for engaging in activities most frequently is based on their interest elicited by the inherent appeal of a material or activity. Although preschoolers begin to respond to adult expectations, high-interest toys and materials are essential.

The Intervention Context

Contextual aspects of early intervention also create unique professional demands and thus require professional training programs. These aspects include the sites for intervention services, responsible agencies, and interactions with professionals from multiple disciplines (team functioning).

The Intervention Site Services for handicapped children in the elementary years almost always occur in school classrooms. The sites for early intervention services are more diverse and thus require a broader range of skills by the interventionist. Professionals may work in specialized developmental centers or classrooms, regular day care centers, homes, developmental evaluation centers, family day homes, or hospital settings such as the Neonatal Intensive Care Unit (NICU) or a pediatric ward. In contrast to teachers, interventionists often work in environments they do not control (e.g., hospitals, regular day care programs, or homes) and their work is primarily consultative rather than instructional in nature. Early intervention professionals thus need to be familiar with the range of typical environments, be able to work within and design modifications for those environments, and communicate effectively with adults in those environments.

Responsible Agencies While the public school is the primary agency serving elementary-age children, young handicapped children must deal with multiple agencies as they seek appropriate services. Although education also is the lead agency for 3- to 5-year-old children, in reality these children may be served in Head Start programs; private day care centers; mental health programs; or private, nonprofit agencies. Infants may receive public health nursing services, or may participate in programs sponsored by public schools, health departments, or departments of human resources. Each agency has its own mission, traditions, and philosophical orientation. Early childhood professionals, more than teachers of older children, need to be aware of the unique aspects and constraints of multiple agencies, be able to integrate and coordinate services at the local and state level, know and adhere to the regulations of diverse agencies, and help families gain access to and coordinate services from various agencies, often by providing case management services.

Multiple Professionals Although multidisciplinary services are desirable for handicapped children at all ages, at the elementary level these services are likely to be isolated and specific. Early intervention often involves professionals from multiple agencies. There is a greater blending of roles and often a transdisciplinary model is required in which a primary caregiver (e.g., parent, special education teacher, day care teacher) must implement recommendations by professionals from other disciplines. Critical skills for early childhood professionals include the ability to participate effectively on multidisciplinary teams; communicate with, teach, and learn from other professionals; serve as advocates for children and families; and recognize and solve problems encountered when professionals from multiple disciplines must interact with each other.

Family Involvement

Finally, the preparation of professionals to work with handicapped infants and preschoolers is unique with respect to the importance of skills in working with families. PL 94-142 (The Education for All Handicapped Children Act of 1975) required parent involvement in the Individualized Education Program (IEP) process and afforded certain rights to parents, but did not encourage schools to address family needs. Historically, early intervention has been a more family-focused endeavor, a fact reflected in PL 99-457.

At the preschool level, the PL 94-142 regulations apply; however, the committee report accompanying the legislation encouraged the provision of parent training programs when appropriate. A more radical shift is seen in the infant/toddler component of the legislation. Instead of an Individualized Education Program, a multidisciplinary team must develop an Individualized Family Service Plan. In addition to the usual child-related components, the IFSP must include a statement of family strengths and needs, family goals and objectives, and services designed to meet family needs, including counseling if necessary. In addition, a case manager must be designated to serve as an advocate and coordinator of services.

Family support is uniquely important in early intervention because it is likely that families only recently have learned of their child's disability. Professionals assume a special responsibility in: 1) helping parents cope with and learn about their child's disability, 2) helping parents identify and secure needed services, and 3) preparing parents to be effective participants in the process of planning and providing services for their children.

Professionals in early intervention programs, thus, need expertise also with families. Essential skills include those related to working with the child in the context of the family, assessing family strengths and needs, communicating effectively with parents in order to identify goals of importance to them, providing family services, and acting as case managers.

Summary

In this section, I have argued that work with handicapped infants and preschoolers requires specialized professional training because of the unique characteristics of the children served, the complexity of the early intervention context, and the central role of families. Peterson (1987) reinforces this position by characterizing early childhood special education as a new field that, although still evolving, is unique in the following ways: 1) its blend of practices and values; 2) its cross-categorical nature; 3) an intervention focus; 4) unique service delivery approaches and curricula priorities; 5) specialized assessment, identification, and labeling procedures; 6) its multidisciplinary focus; and 7) the central involvement of families as team members.

The early childhood field may be further divided into two subcomponents—infancy and preschool—each with its own unique professional demands. This differentiation has been described by Bailey et al. (1986) and Geik et al. (1982) and documented in a study comparing the roles of personnel employed in special programs for the two age groups (McCollum, 1987). Of 23 major professional roles, significant differences between the two age groups were found in 14. Professionals working with preschoolers spent more time organizing the learning environment, planning and implementing group learning activities, collecting and analyzing data, and working with aides and volunteers. Infant specialists spent more time working with families, collaborating and coordinating with other professionals, and on record keeping/paperwork. Similar differences were found in the emphasis respondents felt should be placed on each role in preservice training programs. Although the author recognized that these findings may have reflected differences in home- versus center-based services, it is clear that in this context, infant specialists desired and needed different skills and training than did preschool teachers.

HOW DO PERSONNEL PREPARATION ISSUES VARY ACROSS DISCIPLINES?

Early intervention is, of necessity, a multidisciplinary endeavor. Historically speaking, some professionals have been more intensively involved in early intervention than others, and the roles and responsibilities embraced have varied widely, as has the extent to which various professionals have received specific training related to working with young children and their families. If any fact about early intervention is clear, however, it is that many disciplines will have significant responsibilities. What issues and implications emerge from this multidisciplinary effort?

In Table 2, 10 disciplines likely to be involved in early intervention are listed. The primary missions and major roles of each are described, and the most likely settings in which they would come into contact with handicapped infants, preschoolers, and their families are listed. An analysis of these descriptions reinforces the complexity of the intervention context, the diversity of roles that are the focus of various disciplines, and the variety of sites and settings in which professionals are likely to have contact with handicapped youngsters and their families. Some roles are very discipline-specific, for example, assessment and communication skills by the speech/language pathologist or the design of adaptive equipment by the physical therapist. Others, such as working with families, functioning on an interdisciplinary team, consulting with other professionals, program evaluation, and case management may be embraced by multiple disciplines and provide fruitful context for interdisciplinary training.

It must be recognized that each discipline has its own formal education sequence, licensure or certification requirements, and professional organizations. Very few disciplines specifically focus on the preparation of personnel to work with young children with handicaps and their families.

Given the current status of professional education, at least four levels of change in existing preservice disciplinary programs may be needed. First, within each discipline there is a need to extend the principles and

Table 2. Descriptions of early intervention professions

Discipline	Primary mission	Major roles	Most likely infant contacts*	Most likely preschool contacts*
Special education	To ensure that environments for handicapped infants and preschoolers: 1) facilitate children's development of social, motor, communication, self-help, cognitive, and behavioral skills; and 2) enhance children's self-concept, sense of competence and control, and independence	1. Assess children's developmental status 2. Plan educational interventions 3. Provide educational services 4. Coordinate interdisciplinary services 5. Implement consultants' recommendations 6. Assess family needs 7. Plan and implement family support services or family training 8. Coordinate services from multiple agencies 9. Evaluate program effectiveness 10. Advocate for children and families	1. Home-based infant program 2. Combination home-based/center-based infant program 3. Center-based infant program 4. Developmental evaluation center 5. NICU or other hospital environment	1. Center-based preschool program 2. Combination home-based/center-based preschool program 3. Developmental evaluation center 4. Hospital pediatrics unit
Psychology	To derive a comprehensive picture of child and family functioning, and to identify, implement, and/or evaluate psychological interventions	1. Assess psychological/behavioral characteristics of children and/or families 2. Identify psychological needs and resources 3. Plan and provide psychological/developmental interventions	1. Developmental evaluation center 2. Home-based or center-based infant program 3. Private practice 4. Medical setting	1. Developmental evaluation center 2. School psychology service 3. Pediatric clinic 4. Private practice

(continued)

Table 2. *(continued)*

Discipline	Primary mission	Major roles	Most likely infant contacts*	Most likely preschool contacts*
		4. Coordinate interdisciplinary efforts 5. Consult with families or other professionals 6. Serve as case manager 7. Design and implement evaluations of service effectiveness		
Speech/language pathology	To promote children's communication skills in the context of social interactions with peers, family members, in school, and in the community	1. Assess children's communication skills, both specifically and in the context of overall development 2. Screen children for communication problems 3. Recommend, plan, and/or implement individual or group interventions 4. Reassess children periodically 5. Coordinate assessments with families and other professionals 6. Consult with and/or train family members or other professionals 7. Evaluate intervention effectiveness 8. Refer to other programs or professionals	1. Home-based or center-based infant program 2. Developmental evaluation center 3. Hospital clinic 4. Private practice	1. Center-based preschool classroom 2. Developmental evaluation center 3. Hospital clinic 4. Private practice

Occupational therapy	To promote children's emotional, physical, and social development through the use of purposeful activity such as play and activities of daily living	1. Assess children's developmental and functional performance in play, self-care, and interacting with the physical and social environment 2. Develop and implement occupational therapy interventions to enhance sensorimotor, cognitive, communication, physical, emotional, and adaptive skills 3. Work with families to enhance caregiving and family well-being 4. Design and develop adaptive equipment and seating to promote maximum functional ability and interaction with the environment 5. Consult with other management services 6. Provide case management services 7. Provide services to prevent secondary physical or emotional problems	1. Home-based infant program 2. Center-based infant program 3. NICU or other hospital unit 4. Developmental evaluation center 5. Home health agency	1. Center-based preschool program 2. Hospital 3. Developmental evaluation center 4. Home health agency

(continued)

Table 2. *(continued)*

Discipline	Primary mission	Major roles	Most likely infant contacts*	Most likely preschool contacts*
Social work	To support the family in its social context so that it can provide the infant or preschooler an optimum environment for development	1. Assess family capacity to manage basic nurturant needs (e.g., food, shelter, protection, medical care, employment) 2. Mobilize and link families to available supports (e.g., extended family, community groups, friends, churches, public agencies, and programs), including assessing and building family strengths 3. Investigate allegations of abuse or neglect 4. Assess and provide services related to problems in family functioning (e.g., marital relations, parent–child interactions, child support) 5. Advocate for family rights and access to community services 6. Serve as case managers 7. Consult with other professionals about family issues 8. Plan and implement family services such as parent support groups, family therapy, marital counseling, or individual counseling	1. Hospital social worker 2. Local social services agency 3. Home-based or center-based infant program 4. Developmental evaluation center	1. Local social services agency 2. School social worker 3. Developmental evaluation center

Discipline	Purpose	Roles/Tasks	Settings
Nutrition/dietetics	To ensure that handicapped infants and preschoolers achieve maximum nutritional status by facilitating: 1) physical and mental growth and development; 2) enjoyment of food and eating within the social environment; 3) independence in feeding and eating; and 4) dietary treatment to compensate for metabolic disorders, nutrition-related health problems, or adverse drug-nutrient interactions	1. Assess nutritional status and quality of food intake 2. Work with caregivers to develop nutrition care plans 3. Provide caregivers with diet counseling and nutrition education 4. Assess family needs 5. Coordinate with other members of the interdisciplinary team 6. Refer families to relevant community services (e.g., food stamps, food pantry or community kitchen, WIC program) 7. Conduct regular follow-up and evaluations of services [8.] 9. Evaluate the effectiveness of family services	1. NICU or other hospital clinic 2. Public health department, infant clinic, or crippled children's clinic 3. Special Supplemental Food Program for Women, Infants, and Children (WIC) 4. Community health center 5. Developmental evaluation center 6. Home-based or center-based infant program	1. Hospital pediatric unit or outpatient clinic 2. WIC 3. Crippled children's clinic 4. Community health center 5. Developmental evaluation center 6. Day care or Head Start
Physical therapy	To maximize handicapped or at-risk infants' and preschoolers' sensorimotor development, neurobehavioral organization, and cardiopulmonary status	1. Assess children's neuromusculoskeletal status and motor skills 2. Assess children's cardiopulmonary status 3. Design and implement therapeutic interventions 4. Evaluate intervention effectiveness	1. Home-based or center-based infant program 2. Pediatric hospital or general hospital pediatric unit (inpatient and outpatient) 3. NICU	1. Center-based preschool program 2. Hospital 3. Developmental evaluation center 4. Private practice

(continued)

Table 2. *(continued)*

Discipline	Primary mission	Major roles	Most likely infant contacts*	Most likely preschool contacts*
		5. Screen for neuromusculoskeletal or cardiopulmonary dysfunction 6. Develop and monitor family recommendations 7. Participate in interdisciplinary planning 8. Consult with other professionals and family members 9. Recommend and/or fabricate adaptive equipment and mobility devices 10. Recommend/implement environmental modifications	4. Developmental evaluation center 5. Private practice	
Nursing	To diagnose and treat actual and potential human responses to illness; for handicapped infants and preschoolers, this means: 1) promoting highest health and developmental status possible, and 2) helping families cope with changes in their lives resulting from child's handicaps	1. Implement medical plans to treat underlying cause or helping parents to implement treatment plan 2. Work with parents to meet basic needs of child (e.g., health needs, daily care, feeding) 3. Recommend, plan, and/or implement interventions to improve child's developmental status 4. Enhance child's and family's abilities to cope with child's handicaps 5. Serve as case managers 6. Refer to other programs or professionals	1. NICU or other hospital environment 2. Public health nursing follow-up 3. Outpatient medical clinic 4. Center-based infant intervention or evaluation program 5. Home-based infant program	1. Out-patient medical clinic 2. Hospital 3. Public health nursing follow-up 4. Day care or other school setting 5. Center-based preschool intervention or evaluation program 6. Home-based preschool program

| Audiology | To provide and coordinate services to children with auditory handicaps, including detection of the problem and management of any existing communication handicaps | 1. Assess pure tone air conduction thresholds, speech thresholds, and predict hearing loss from acoustic reflex, reflex eliciting auditory tests, and communication handicap inventories
2. Conduct extended evaluation including air conduction, bone conduction, speech thresholds, and word/sentence recognition tests
3. Conduct behavioral evaluation for sensorineural site that includes advanced acoustic reflex tests, tests of auditory adaptation, tests of frequency discrimination, and tests of intensity discrimination
4. Conduct auditory prosthetic evaluations, including such sound field tests as aided word/sentence recognition, warble tone thresholds, narrow band noise thresholds, and comfortable and uncomfortable loudness levels while wearing an auditory prosthesis (e.g., hearing aid or assistive listening device)
5. Coordinate auditory (aural) rehabilitation, including orientation to auditory prosthesis, auditory training, and speech reading training | 1. NICU
2. Hospital speech and hearing clinics
3. Audiology practices associated with otolaryngology practices
4. University speech and hearing clinics
5. Developmental evaluation centers
6. Community speech and hearing clinics
7. Speech pathology private practices
8. Audiology private practices
9. Children's special health services clinics
10. Pediatrician referrals
11. Family practice physician referrals | 1. Audiology practices associated with otolaryngology practices
2. Pediatrician referrals
3. Developmental evaluation centers
4. Children's special health services clinics
5. Local public health departments
6. Hospital high-risk registry follow-ups
7. Hospital speech and hearing clinics
8. University speech and hearing clinics
9. Daycare hearing screening programs
10. Community speech and hearing clinics |

(continued)

115

Table 2. *(continued)*

Discipline	Primary mission	Major roles	Most likely infant contacts*	Most likely preschool contacts*
				11. Public school system referrals 12. Speech pathology private practices 13. Audiology private practices 14. Family practice physician referrals
Medicine	To assist families in the promotion of optimal health, growth, and development for their infants and young children by providing health services	1. Assess health, growth, development, and deviation 2. Diagnose and treat health problems 3. Advocate for health and well-being of child and family 4. Provide referral and consultation to other agencies 5. Coordinate and integrate services 6. Provide education and support to families	1. NICU 2. Pediatric wards 3. Private practice 4. Health clinics 5. Developmental evaluation center	1. Private practice 2. Health clinics 3. Developmental evaluation center 4. Pediatric wards

*In order of estimated likelihood.

procedures to handicapped infants and preschoolers. Second, multidisciplinary content needs to be included in preservice programs. For example, special educators need to know more about the specific skills and knowledge of related service personnel (Esterson & Bluth, 1987), whereas disciplinary therapists need to know more about learning theory, family involvement, and environmental management. Third, professionals from each discipline need to be able to view clients from a broad systems perspective and incorporate that view into a "wholistic" approach with handicapped youngsters and their families. Fourth, professionals from each discipline need to learn how to work with each other in a truly interdisciplinary team fashion in planning and implementing appropriate services.

These changes could be accomplished using a variety of models of personnel preparation. Following the traditional departmental focus, one model would require professional training programs to expand their existing training efforts to the infant and preschool period. Other models could include: 1) educationally based disciplines collaborating with other disciplines such as physical therapy or speech-language pathology to broaden the clinical skills of students; 2) combining specific clinical training programs (e.g., special education, occupational therapy) with another discipline with a more broad-based approach such as psychology, maternal and child health, nursing, or social work; or 3) developing a new interdisciplinary curriculum with courses selected from several different departments. Perhaps many different models could be used to achieve the goal of preparing effective infant and preschool specialists. At present, no one model is generally accepted or used (Bruder & McLean, 1988), and there remains a need to continue to develop, implement, and evaluate different approaches to training.

Dunn and Janata (1987) argue that certain problems necessitate an "interprofessional" approach to training:

1. those that are unusually complex
2. those that are chronic in our society
3. those that require substantial societal expense
4. those for which no single profession can provide a solution
5. those, that, despite efforts by a single profession, flow beyond and into another area of the individual's life or have affected a significant other. (p. 100)

These criteria would seem to apply to early intervention. An examination of professional development in related fields may be helpful. Casto (1987) has described an interprofessional preservice training effort of interest. This program focuses on complex problems, uses a team teaching approach, integrates students across disciplines, integrates students and practicing professionals, and uses a case study format. The program emphasizes values, ethics, and policy issues as a part of its training. A policy analysis of alternative preservice and inservice training options should consider the costs and benefits of implementing an interprofessional approach versus the more traditional departmental approach in the context of early intervention.

WHAT FRAMEWORKS COULD BE USED IN DESIGNING TRAINING PROGRAMS?

The conceptualization of professional knowledge and skills can be approached from many different perspectives, each of which bears important implications for how preservice programs are organized and evaluated. Four approaches are briefly described here.

One framework for professional knowledge and skills involves describing the *behaviors* in which effective professionals are engaged, particularly behaviors that are empirically related to student outcome. Recent studies, for example, have attempted to identify the behaviors in which effective teachers are engaged by relating observed teacher behaviors to student achievement (Bickel & Bickel, 1986). Most of these studies, however, have focused on elementary-age, nonhandicapped children; thus, their relevance to younger handicapped children is questionable (McCollum & McCartan, 1988). Carta and Greenwood (1985) described an ecobehavioral approach to relating the behavior of early childhood teachers to children's developmental progress, but effective teaching studies with young handicapped children are rare and their findings not yet complete.

In contrast to the effective teaching literature, which is data-based in its orientation, many training programs identify specific *competencies* assumed to be necessary for working with young children. These competencies, which are rarely empirically based and usually vary according to individual programs, may be broad and inclusive, or very specific. Bruder and McLean (1988) surveyed federally funded infant personnel preparation programs and found a range from 7 to 380 in the number of competencies taught by a given training program! An example of a specific and detailed approach to early childhood competencies was presented by Kinney and Blackhurst (1987) who described 34 competencies for teachers of young children with severe handicaps with respect to using media technology (e.g., adaptive switches, microcomputer, electronic mail) effectively. In contrast, Bailey et al. (1986) describe seven broad competencies addressed in their interdepartmental training program in special education and maternal and child health.

Another approach to training is to descibe the *roles* of professionals. Bricker (1986), for example, described five major roles of early interventionists:

> A conceptualizer approaches teaching from a broad conceptual base. A synthesizer seeks and coordinates input from a variety of professionals. An instructor provides information and models instructional approaches for parents and paraprofessionals. An evaluator designs and implements strategies for determining program impact. A counselor listens and provides appropriate feedback to parents. (p. 229)

As an alternative to role, competency, or behavior approaches, a broader perspective can be considered. Shulman (1986) has proposed a framework for classifying the types of knowledge teachers need, a framework that seems applicable to any clinically focused profession. As displayed in Figure 1, Shulman suggested three forms of clinical knowledge. The first is referred to as *propositional knowledge,* which occurs in three forms: principles (knowledge derived from empirical research), maxims ("the accumulated wisdom of practice," p. 11), and norms ("propositions that guide . . . not because they are true in scientific terms, or because they work in practical terms, but because they are morally or ethically right," p. 11). Propositional knowledge is essential because it provides

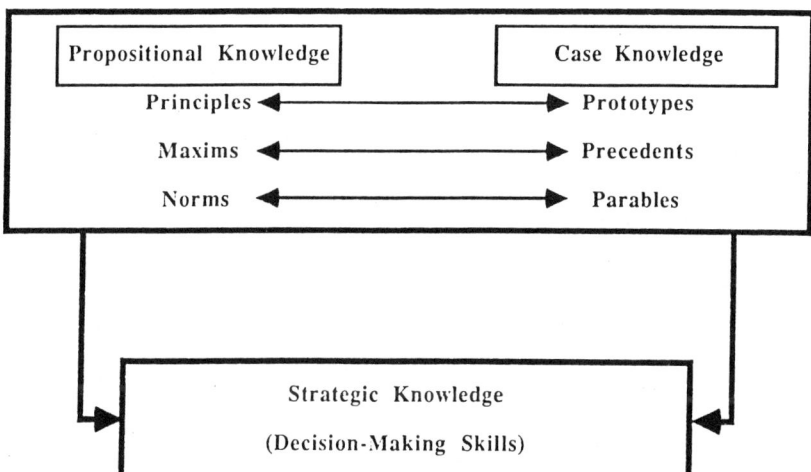

Figure 1. Framework for classifying knowledge. (Adapted from Shulman [1986].)

professionals with a wealth of information obtained from research and years of clinical practice.

The second form is *case knowledge*, the "knowledge of specific, well-documented, and richly described events" (p. 11), and is the mechanism by which professionals see how propositional knowledge is actually implemented. Shulman proposed three types of case knowledge that parallel the three forms of propositional knowledge: prototypes (case studies that exemplify theoretical prinicples), precedents (case studies demonstrating maxims), and parables (case studies depicting normative or value-based decisions).

Third is *strategic knowledge*, the knowledge required for decision-making, when the professional "confronts particular situations or problems, whether theoretical, practical, or moral, where principles collide and no simple solution is possible" (p. 13). The application of strategic knowledge probably requires propositional knowledge and case knowledge relevant to the particular situation or problem, but also requires additional skills such as the ability to generate alternative solutions to a problem, evaluate alternatives, and work collaboratively with other interested parties (e.g., parents, other professionals) to reach a mutually acceptable, yet effective solution. Strategic knowledge is necessary in any human service system because the complexity of human needs and behavior makes conflicts inevitable.

This framework is presented here to make the point that the preparation of personnel to work with handicapped infants, preschoolers, and their families cannot consist entirely of propositional knowledge—the principles, maxims, and norms embraced by the field. Although propositional knowledge is necessary, it likely is insufficient for effective clinical practice. Shulman (1986) described two weaknesses of propositional knowledge. First, the propositions embraced by a field generally are quite extensive, and as the list becomes longer, they are hard to remember. Second, propositions are useful and economical because they are "decontextualized, stripped down to their essentials, devoid of detail, emotion, or ambience. Yet to be remembered and then wisely used, it is precisely the detail and context that may be needed" (p. 11).

I suggest that a third fundamental weakness of propositions is that in fields such as early intervention, where knowledge is changing rapidly, and in which the empirically based knowledge is limited, sole emphasis on propositional knowledge could result in several problems. For example, in Table 3 I have attempted to provide descriptions and examples of some aspects of propositional knowledge in early intervention. It is clear that many of our fundamental underlying beliefs (e.g., early intervention is

Table 3. Descriptions and examples of propositional knowledge in early intervention

Propositional knowledge: The accumulated knowledge in a profession, based on research, theory, and clinical experiences

Principles — Knowledge derived from empirical research		Maxims — The accumulated wisdom of practice, never confirmed by research		Norms — The values or ideological/philosophical commitments that we wish clinicians to incorporate and employ	
Well-documented	Emerging documentation	Generally accepted	Somewhat controversial	Generally accepted	Controversial
1. The quality of a child's physical and social environment exerts a significant influence on the child's behavior as well as on the child's long-term development. 2. When handicapped children are taught skills under artificial training conditions, newly ac-	1. Interventions that build heavily on children's initiations are likely to result in greater acquisition and use of functional skills than interventions that are solely teacher directed. 2. Speech therapy is likely to be more effective when con-	1. Early intervention is effective in reducing or ameliorating the effects of handicapping conditions. 2. Individualized assessment of children's abilities is a necessary prerequisite to effective intervention. 3. When teaching children with multiple impairments, clinicians should teach to the child's strengths	1. Home-based intervention is preferable for infants, whereas center-based services are preferable for preschoolers. 2. Physical and occupational therapy services significantly affect children's long-term development and functional status.	1. Parent involvement is essential to appropriate early intervention services. 2. Early intervention is most effective when professionals work together in an interdisciplinary team.	1. Early intervention should focus on parent not professional priorities for services. 2. All handicapped infants and preschoolers should be served in the least restrictive environment, with opportunities to interact with

(continued)

Table 3. *(continued)*

Principles Knowledge derived from empirical research		Maxims The accumulated wisdom of practice, never confirmed by research		Norms The values or ideological/philosophical commitments that we wish clinicians to incorporate and employ	
Well-documented	Emerging documentation	Generally accepted	Somewhat controversial	Generally accepted	Controversial
quired skills are not likely to generalize to other contexts without planned generalization activities.	ducted during natural routines, in typical environments, and in the context of ongoing interactions with peers and adults.	rather than focusing on building the child's deficits. 4. Intervention must be developmentally based, teaching skills according to normal developmental sequences.			nonhandicapped children.

effective, individualized assessment is important, intervention must be developmentally based) are not grounded in empirical research, and some are controversial within the field. Given the lack of hard data, professionals need to be able to make informed decisions based on a combination of propositional, case, and strategic knowledge.

Furthermore, it is clear that as early intervention becomes increasingly family-focused, issues regarding conflicts between the values and priorities of professionals and those of parents likely will emerge (Bailey, 1987). Preparing professionals to deal with these conflicts cannot consist of a collection of facts, but requires the development of sophisticated communication skills and an open and responsive attitude.

Additionally, personnel preparation programs in early intervention do not have a body of well-defined and elaborated case studies. Although each of the relevant disciplines has a rich clinical history, Shulman (1986) argues that it is not merely examples of clinical practice that are needed, but rather high quality examples that "exemplify, illustrate, and bring alive theoretical propositions" (p. 12). Case studies must be grounded in theory, but, as Odom (1987) suggests, professionals must ultimately create their own personal theories of early intervention. Good case studies should help professionals differentiate the ways in which alternative theories lead to alternative practices and thus result in informed decision-making.

The case study method has been defined as the "creation of a problem situation which raises issues in enough detail for learners to suggest possible solutions" (Graham & Cline, 1980). The case study method involves providing a student with individual "cases," descriptions of potentially problematic real-world phenomena that they read, analyse, and discuss for the purpose of applying derived insights to principles in actual operation (Kreps & Lederman, 1985). The case study approach has a number of strengths as a training tool. Graham and Cline (1980) state that it: 1) lends reality to indirect experiences, 2) deals with concrete problems, 3) promotes decision-making skills, 4) broadens trainee experiences, and 5) assures multiple perspective taking. The concrete rather than abstract nature of the case method is likely to enhance its appeal both in learning and in generalization. Unfortunately, early intervention training programs do not have ready access to case studies that meet the criteria for effective training. Thus, there is a real need in the field for the development and evaluation of suitable case study materials likely to facilitate the acquisition of both case and strategic knowledge.

Finally, without a primary focus on strategic decision-making skills, professionals will be limited in their effectiveness because the complexity of human problems rarely results in "textbook" cases for which there are easy solutions. Zeichner and Liston (1987) argued that from the very first student teaching experience, teachers need to be encouraged and taught to be reflective in their approach to intervention rather than to follow routine actions. Shulman (1987) described a model of pedogogical reasoning and action involving a cycle of activities of comprehension, transformation, instruction, evaluation, and reflection. While basic comprehension (propositional knowledge) is the foundation and beginning point in this process, it is clear that it is but one of several key steps to effective clinical practice.

INSERVICE EDUCATION AND EARLY INTERVENTION

A critical issue in personnel preparation is how professionals working with handicapped infants, preschoolers, and their families can gain access to emerging information and research findings in their own and related disciplinary areas. Continued professional education is essential for at least three reasons. First, preservice training has beeen characterized as but an introduction to the world of professional practice (Schmid, Korinek, & McAdams, 1985). It is through experiences in applying preservice knowledge in real-world settings and across multiple client needs that professionals refine their skills and develop their own individualized styles of service delivery. Continuing education may be useful in teaching more advanced or more specific skills related to professional practice. Second, knowledge and research in infant intervention is developing at a rapid rate. Continuing education is important as a mechanism for professionals to keep abreast of new information and replace obsolete practices with those documented to be more effective (Evans, 1982). Third, some practicing professionals have never had specific training related to early intervention, yet are practicing it because of the shortage of qualified personnel. Thus, inservice education is necessary to ensure adequate basic training.

What Is Inservice Education?

Inservice education is the process by which practicing professionals are provided experiences designed to improve or change professional practice. Inservice education may vary according to both the purpose for and manner in which it is provided. For example, Schmid, Korinek, and McAdams (1985) reviewed more than 100 reports of inservice education and identified three common purposes: information transmission, skill acquisition, and behavior change. The manner in which inservice education is provided can vary in many ways. Cruickshank, Lorish, and Thompson (1979) describe four classes of variables in an inservice effort: presage variables (characteristics of inservice leaders and instructors), context variables (participant characteristics, professional setting characteristics, and aspects of the instructional context, including time available, group size, or materials), process variables (the actual instructional activities provided), and product variables (the various short- and long-term outcomes of inservice education). Thus, inservice is a complex, multifaceted activity.

What Does Research Suggest about Inservice Education?

Because of the obvious and recognized importance of inservice education, considerable research has addressed inservice practices. The breadth of this research across diverse fields, however, makes it difficult to synthesize, as is reflected by two recent meta-analyses that reached different conclusions about the effectiveness of various inservice practices (Showers, Joyce, & Bennett, 1987; Wade, 1985). Good empirical research is difficult to conduct because of the multiplicity of variables involved in any inservice endeavor, the variety of contexts within which new skills are expected, and variability in administrative support for the implementation of new practices. The empirical research that has been published suggests that the vast majority of inservice is not conducted in accordance with known best practices and subsequently is ineffective (Guskey, 1986). Furthermore, even when best practices are incorporated, long-term changes in professional behavior may not occur (Porter, 1986).

In the study of the effects of inservice education, various aspects of the process have been investigated. For example, some studies have focused on the initial planning process, with a particular emphasis on the role of participants in identifying inservice education needs and planning inservice education programs. Griffin (1983) concludes that while insufficient research has been conducted in this regard, it appears that inservice education efforts are more likely to be accepted positively by staff who view the training as responsive to their own needs and are involved in the planning process. Richardson-Koehler (1987) argues that when school systems or state agencies take a hierarchical approach to mandatory teacher change, the result is an atmosphere of distrust and resistance.

A second line of inquiry has focused on the role of theory and rationale in the process of inservice education. At issue is the extent to which the inservice process should justify the proposed change in professional behavior as opposed to actually teaching specific skills. Several studies have suggested that while organizational time is important at the beginning of an inservice education program, too much time spent on theory, particularly if done early in training, does not reduce participants' concerns and may, in fact, reduce the effectiveness of later skill-focused activities (Broyles & Tillman, 1985; Harmon, 1980). Guskey (1986) suggests that the traditional model of inservice that first attempts to change teacher beliefs, attitudes, or perceptions and *then* focuses on specific skills related to the proposed changes is ineffective, particularly in the case of experienced teachers. He argues that "significant change in teachers' beliefs and attitudes is likely to take place only *after* changes in student learning outcomes are evidenced" (p. 7). In other words, teacher beliefs and attitudes will change only when teachers can see that the practices taught in inservice programs actually work when applied in the intervention context, thus arguing for a reduced role of theory and rationale in the initial stages of inservice education. Joyce and Showers (1980) conclude that the presentation of theory "is not powerful enough alone to achieve much beyond the awareness level, but when combined with [other training components], it is an important component" (p. 382).

A third line of inquiry has focused on the actual nature and format of inservice education activities related to teaching specific professional skills. Again, research in this area has been described as limited and flawed due to methodological limitations of existing studies. However, components of effective inservice education appear to include clear training objectives, modeling and demonstration of specific techniques, the opportunity to practice skills under simulated conditions, structured feedback, open-ended discussion, and liberal use of varied, real-world examples (Cruickshank, 1979; Guskey, 1986; Joyce & Showers, 1980; Thompson & Cooley, 1986).

A fourth line of inquiry has focused on the extent and nature of follow-up after inservice education has occurred. Joyce and Showers (1982) state that the biggest problem confronting inservice educators is the lack of transfer of training to daily practice. They conclude that follow-up coaching is essential to the training process. However, for coaching to be effective, they believe three prerequisites to be important: 1) professional recognition that transfer is an inherently difficult process, 2) professional attainment of the highest possible level of skill during training, and 3) professional "executive control," in which there is a clear understanding of how a model or procedure works and how to adapt its implementation across varied cases. Guskey's (1986) review concludes that continued support and follow-up after initial training is critical, and should include ongoing guidance and directions to facilitate adaptations to new situations. Further components should include the availability of assistance when problems develop, coaching and feedback, and repeated opportunities to interact and share ideas in an atmosphere of collegiality and experimentation rather that one with threats and punishment. In a study of alternative approaches to training, Sparks (1986) found that workshop effectiveness was enhanced more under conditions of peer observation than trainer-provided coaching.

Throughout the empirical literature on inservice education, one theme is apparent: more and better research on the process of inservice education is desperately needed. Research must focus on the various components of inservice education, including planning, presentation, and follow-up, and must determine impact in multiple outcome domains including participant satisfaction, change in participant behavior and attitudes, and, ultimately, benefits for clients served by professionals participating in inservice education. Broyles and Tillman (1985) argued that most research has included only minimal descriptions of what actually occurs during inservice training. Research is needed that more clearly describes training components and examines the relationship between specific components and subsequent participant outcomes.

What Is the Current Status of Inservice Education?

Unfortunately, most inservice education activities today bear little resemblance to the principles and procedures that have emerged thus far in the empirical literature. Cooley and Thompson (1985–86) found that only 25 states mandate staff development programs for school districts. Although staff development activities appeared to be increasing, considerable variability was found in resources available for inservice education. In a subsequent national study of outstanding staff development programs, Thompson and Cooley (1986) found several discrepancies between what respondents felt to be best practice as compared to actual practice. For example, less than one-third felt that university coursework sufficiently met inservice needs, yet half reported that such courses were used. Teacher supervision in use of inservice concepts and skills was rated important by 86% of the respondents, yet only 29% actually provided such supervision. Ninety percent felt that follow-up discussion sessions were important, but only 33% scheduled such sessions. Reported barriers to implementing these best practices included time available for activities, financial resources, and changing teacher and administrator attitudes toward staff development.

Fuller, Noel, and Malouf (1985) question whether staff development programs initiated at the state level realistically can be expected to affect the competence of local staff. In a study of a special education staff development program in Maryland, they found that "the program was efficacious only in imparting knowledge related to procedures that ensure legal compliance (not instructional skills), and effects were strongest among administrators (not teachers)" (p. 343). They recommend that states: 1) adopt a more collaborative, "bottom-up" model, 2) engage in systematic evaluations of long-term impact of staff development programs, and 3) examine the relative emphasis in training and monitoring on rigid compliance with regulations versus the provision of high-quality service programs.

The recent passage of PL 99-457, however, makes inservice education an immediate necessity for professionals currently working with handicapped infants. Requirements for family assessment, the Individualized Family Service Plan, and case management services mean that professionals from multiple disciplines must be trained to engage in these activities. A major concern, of course, is how best to conduct their training. Traditional strategies, such as formalized coursework, state conferences, written materials, or brief workshops need to be evaluated and, when needed, replaced with more innovative and effective approaches to meet the needs and wishes of practicing professionals. Dworkin, Shonkoff, Leviton, and Levine (1979), for example, surveyed practicing pediatricians to determine their preferences for further education in developmental pediatrics, and found that part-time longitudinal clinical experiences were greatly preferred over written materials or postgraduate coursework. A complicating factor in the provision of inservice training is that some disciplines, such as education, dietetics, or medicine, require praticing professionals to participate in some form of continuing education, whereas other fields, such as occupational therapy, encourage but do not require it (McLean, 1987).

BARRIERS TO CHANGE

Despite the arguments made here and elsewhere for changes in both preservice and inservice education, significant barriers exist indicating that such changes are not likely to be easy. In a time of diminishing resources, for example, university training programs are not likely to receive significant increases in state funds to support new faculty positions or new areas of specialization. This means that many institutions of higher education wishing to expand the focus of their training to include young children and their families will have to choose one of two basic options: either the program will need to be funded by grant money, or existing faculty will need to participate in faculty development activities to ensure that they have the competencies needed to apply their disciplines' principles and procedures with young children.

Each option brings with it a set of defined limitations. Grant-funded programs are inherently tenuous in nature, often resulting in uncoordinated and uncertain training. However, they generally do provide significant financial support for students and support for faculty positions dedicated to the area of interest. Changing the skills and orientation of existing faculty has the advantage of creating an enduring change in a program and can have a positive "renewal" effect on faculty. The motivation and payoff for significant investment in a faculty development program, however, is generally low. In fact, Eash and Lane (1985) have characterized university faculty as driven by personal or professional self-interest rather than a significant committment to organizational change.

Another barrier is the inevitable fact that territoriality and boundary issues exist among disciplines. Ownership of both intervention programs and training programs will continue, despite the obvious need for interdisciplinary coordination. The integration of knowledge and skills from and within multiple disciplines constitutes perhaps the single greatest challenge to any significant changes in personnel preparation.

Barriers also may limit the development of new and expanded inservice education efforts. Despite the existing knowledge about effective inservice practices, lack of organization, funds, and follow-up likely will continue. Although resources will be needed to enhance inservice efforts, the greatest challenge will be in leadership and organization at both the state and local levels. Through a series of planned and coordinated inservice activities, followed by on-site supervision, feedback, and discussion *by colleagues,* inservice education efforts have the potential for creating significant changes in professional practice.

SUMMARY

Despite the barriers described, it is clear that the increase in services to handicapped infants, toddlers, and their families will raise policy questions and influence policy decisions with regard to the preparation of professionals from many disciplines. Issues raised in this chapter include identifying the unique skills required of early childhood specialists, the variability of personnel preparation across disciplines, addressing interdisciplinary skills and programs, and needs related to inservice education. Other critical questions include such basic ones as how to attract and keep sufficient numbers of qualified personnel and whether specific licensure or certification requirements should be imposed on professionals who work with young children.

Ultimately, state agencies, universities, and local programs will have to find a reasonable balance between the desire for well-trained, highly qualified professionals and the need for a minimum number of professionals to fill available positions. If standards and training requirements are set too high, few will enter the field and shortages will occur. However, by reducing requirements for training, the quality of services provided may be compromised. As states develop their comprehensive systems for personnel development, the complexities of these issues will need to be recognized and incorporated into the planning process.

REFERENCES

Bailey, D.B. (1987). Collaborative goal-setting with families: Resolving differences in values and priorities for services. *Topics in Early Childhood Special Education, 7*(2), 59–71.

Bailey, D.B., Farel, A.M., O'Donnell, K.J., Simeonsson, R.J., & Miller, C.A. (1986). Preparing infant interventionists: Interdepartmental training in special education and maternal and child health. *Journal of the Division for Early Childhood, 11,* 67–77.

Bickel, W.E., & Bickel, D.D. (1986). Effective schools, classrooms, and instruction: Implications for special education. *Exceptional Children, 52,* 489–500.

Bricker, D.D. (1986). *Early education of at-risk and handicapped infants, toddlers, and preschool children.* Glenview, IL: Scott, Foresman.

Bricker, D., & Slentz, K. (in press). Personnel preparation: Handicapped infants. In M.C. Wang, H.J. Walberg, & M.C. Reynolds (Eds.), *The handbook of special education research and practice (Vols. 1–3).* Elmsford, NY: Pergamon.

Broyles, I., & Tillman, M. (1985). Relationships of inservice training components and changes in teacher concerns regarding innovations. *Journal of Educational Research, 78,* 364–371.

Bruder, M.B., & McLean, M. (1988). Personnel preparation for infant interventionists: A review of federally funded projects. *Journal of the Division for Early Childhood, 12,* 299–305.

Carta, J.J., & Greenwood, C.R. (1985). Eco-behavioral assessment: A methodology for expanding the evolution of early intervention programs. *Topics in Early Childhood Special Education, 5*(2), 88–104.

Casto, R.M. (1987). Preservice courses for interprofessional practice. *Theory Into Practice, 26,* 103–109.

Cooley, V.E., & Thompson, J.C. (1985–1986). School improvement and state staff development programs: A national research summary. *Educational Research Quarterly, 10,* 2–3.

Cruickshank, D.R., Lorish, C., & Thompson, L. (1979). What we think we know about inservice education. *Journal of Teacher Education, 30,* 27–31.

Dunn, V.B., & Janata, M.M. (1987). Interprofessional assumptions and the OSU Commission. *Theory Into Practice, 26,* 99–102.

Dworkin, P.H., Shonkoff, J.P., Leviton, A., & Levine, M.D. (1979). Training in developmental pediatrics. *American Journal of Diseases of Children, 133,* 709–712.

Eash, M.J., & Lane, J.J. (1985). Evaluation of a model for faculty development: Implications for educational policy. *Educational Evaluation and Policy Analysis, 7,* 127–138.

Esterson, M.M., & Bluth, L.F. (1987). *Related services for handicapped children.* Boston: College-Hill.
Evans, J. (1982). Inservice training for the 1980s. *Journal of the Division for Early Childhood, 6,* 67–73.
Fuller, B., Noel, M.M., & Malouf, D.B. (1985). Polity and competence: Can the state change teachers' skills? *Educational Evaluation and Policy Analysis, 7,* 343–353.
Geik, I., Gilkerson, L., & Sponseller, D.B. (1982). An early intervention training model. *Journal of the Division for Early Childhood, 5,* 42–52.
Graham, P.T., & Cline, P.C. (1980). The case method: A basic teaching approach. *Theory Into Practice, 19,* 112–116.
Griffin, G.A. (1983). Implications of research for staff development programs. *The Elementary School Journal, 83,* 414–425.
Guskey, T.R. (1986). Staff development and the process of teacher change. *Educational Researcher, 15*(5), 5–12.
Harmon, P. (1980). Holistic performance analysis: It's time for an updated technology of instruction. *Educational Technology, 38,* 5–13.
Joyce, B., & Showers, B. (1980). Improving inservice training: The messages of research. *Educational Leadership, 37,* 379–385.
Joyce, B., & Showers, B. (1982). The coaching of teaching. *Educational Leadership, 40,* 4–10.
Kinney, P.G., & Blackhurst, A.E. (1987). Technology competencies for teachers of young children with severe handicaps. *Topics in Early Childhood Special Education, 7*(3), 105–115.
Kreps, G.L., & Lederman, L.C. (1985). Using the case method in organizational communication education: Developing students' insight, knowledge, and creativity through experience-based learning and systematic debriefing. *Communication Education, 34,* 358–364.
Mallory, B.L. (1983). The preparation of early childhood special educators: A model program. *Journal of the Division for Early Childhood, 7,* 32–40.
McCollum, J.A. (1987). Early interventionists in infant and early childhood programs: A comparison of preservice training needs. *Topics in Early Childhood Special Education, 7*(3), 24–35.
McCollum, J.A., & McCartan, K. (1988). Research in teacher education: Issues and future directions for early childhood special education. In S.L. Odom & M.B. Karnes (Eds.), *Early intervention for infants and children with handicaps: An empirical basis* (pp. 269–286). Baltimore: Paul H. Brookes Publishing Company.
McLean, V.P. (1987). Continuing education and maintaining professional competence. *American Journal of Occupational Therapy, 41,* 257–258.
Odom, S.L. (1987). The role of theory in the preparation of professionals in early childhood special education. *Topics in Early Childhood Special Education, 7*(3), 1–11.
Peterson, N.L. (1987). *Early intervention for handicapped and at-risk children: An introduction to early childhood special education.* Denver: Love Publishing Company.
PL 94-142, *Education for All Handicapped Children Act, 1975.*
PL 99-457, *Education of the Handicapped Act Amendments, 1986.*
Porter, A.C. (1986). From research on teaching to staff development: A difficult step. *The Elementary School Journal, 87,* 159–164.

Richardson-Koehler, V. (1987). What happens to research on the way to practice? *Theory Into Practice, 26,* 38–43.
Schmid, R., Korinek, L., & McAdams, M. (1985). Three models for the presentation of inservice education. *College Student Journal, 19,* 167–175.
Showers, B., Joyce, B., & Bennett, B. (1987). Synthesis of research on staff development: A framework for future study and a state-of-the-art analysis. *Educational Leadership, 45*(3), 77–87.
Shulman, L.S. (1986). Those who understand: Knowledge growth in teaching. *Educational Researcher, 15*(2), 4–14.
Shulman, L.S. (1987). Knowledge and teaching: Foundations of the new reform. *Harvard Educational Review, 57,* 1–22.
Sparks, G.M. (1986). The effectiveness of alternative training activities in changing teaching practices. *American Educational Research Journal, 23,* 217–225.
Stile, S.W., Abernathy, S.M., Pettibone, T.J., & Wachtel, W.J. (1984). Training and certification for early childhood special education personnel: A six-year follow-up study. *Journal of the Division for Early Childhood, 8,* 69–73.
Sweet, N. (1981). New faces and approaches in the ICN: The role of the educational specialist. In D. Gelderman, D. Taylor-Hershel, S. Prestidge, & J. Anderson (Eds.), *The health care/education relationship: Services for infants with special needs and their families* (pp. 61–82). Chapel Hill, NC: Technical Assistance Development System (TADS).
Thompson, J.C., & Cooley, V.E. (1986). A national study of outstanding staff development programs. *Educational Horizons, 64,* 94–98.
Wade, R.K. (1985). What makes a difference in inservice teacher education? A meta-analysis of research. *Educational Leadership, 43,* 48–54.
Zeichner, K.M., & Liston, D.P. (1987). Teaching student teachers to reflect. *Harvard Educational Review, 57,* 23–48.

Implications of PL 99-457 for Preparation of Preschool Personnel

7

Oliver Leon Hurley

THE FIRST COMMON SCHOOLS, THE FORERUNNERS OF THE PRESENT PUBLIC schools, were established in the seventeenth century. Teachers were hired and licensed locally; standards were low and sometimes irrelevant compared to those of today. Nevertheless, the deterioration of the quality of those schools led to the development of the first normal schools, based on the German model. Teacher certification by the state followed later and usually is thought to date from 1825. Over the next century and a half, many changes occurred; all focused on the improvement of the quality of the education being received by children and youth. States and those responsible for American education came to recognize that good educational systems require: 1) trained teachers, 2) from accredited programs, 3) that meet certain criteria of content and experiences, 4) taught by trained personnel, 5) in regular (not "normal") colleges and universities (see Haberman & Stinnet, 1973).

A significant lesson our foreparents have learned repeatedly is that quality school programming requires personnel who have been trained appropriately so that they meet some agreed-upon standards. Hiring untrained teachers and not providing them with the necessary training and supervision is an invitation to eventual widespread problems. This lesson seems to have been learned in the course of the development of every profession that now requires accreditation of training programs and licensure of its practitioners.

Those concerned about the mandates of Public Law 99-457 (The Education of the Handicapped Act Amendments of 1986) do not need to relearn this lesson. The personnel who will instruct infants, toddlers, and preschoolers with handicaps must be *appropriately* prepared. What is appropriate is subject to varied interpretations, depending on the nature of the children involved, the constellation of needs of each one, and the many agencies and professionals involved in trying to satisfy those needs.

DIFFICULTIES ARISING BECAUSE OF THE MULTIPLICITY OF AGENCIES

Historically, and necessarily, many agencies and disciplines have been involved with the preschooler, infant, and toddler. Agencies other than schools have had to take responsibility for meeting the needs of this population. Many private agencies developed because of the gap in publicly supported services. This fact alone has implications for personnel preparation. The involvement of so many agencies and professionals in the world of the handicapped preschooler demands collaboration if the letter and the spirit of the law are to be met. Collaboration is difficult (Weaver, 1979), but not impossible (Melcher & Franks, 1978). Weaver (1979, p. 24) defines collaboration as "not mere cooperation or matter of good will, but an agreed-upon distribution of power, status, and authority." She discusses the factors that make turf sharing among colleges, state departments, and local school districts so difficult: agency and individual values; preparedness to take risks; degree of resistance to taking advantage of others in the collaborative effort; training in group processes, conflict management, and negotiation; administrative structures and decision-making mechanisms; freedom of representatives to negotiate, and community expectations.

If one considers the agencies and professionals involved with children birth–5, the following can be added to the list of possible barriers to collaboration: historical relationships among agencies and/or professionals, the different foci of concern of the agencies, the foci on different primary area(s) of child development used by the different professionals, and states' traditional assignments of responsibility for child service. These factors make collaboration difficult, but not impossible, if one sees collaboration as negotiation, a political process in which the role of each constituent is worked out in terms of what it has to offer (Smith, 1974). Collaboration will need to take place at state and local levels regarding administration, supervision and case management, delivery and coordination of services, and, last but not least, the preservice and inservice preparation of personnel.

THE NEED FOR TRAINING AND THE QUESTION OF CERTIFICATION

The training of personnel would appear to be critical to the ultimate success of PL 99-457 for the same reasons usually given for the state certification of teachers [i.e., in recognition of the state's affirmative duty to prevent harm to individuals, in recognition of the complexity of teaching and to ensure that one has sufficient grasp of the skills and competencies needed to carry out the complex tasks of the teaching process, and also in recognition of the research evidence to the effect that fully certified teachers are more effective and more satisfied than those not fully certified (AACTE Task Force on Teacher Certification, 1984; Greenberg, 1983; Tingey-Michaelis, 1985)]. Pickett (1986) advocates the certification of paraprofessionals for four reasons: to guarantee quality, to provide opportunity for upward mobility, to define clearly the differentiated responsibilities, and to recognize formally the importance of paraprofessionals. All authors on these subjects see the need for appropriate training of personnel, but not all see the need for certification. Koerner (1973, p. 101), for example, states, "Had I wanted to propose an ideal solution, I would have proposed the complete abolition of state licensing." However, Greenberg (1983, p. 2) says, "The question is not, then, whether we should have teacher education or not; rather, it is a question of how we will have it and how good it can be." "How we will have it and how good it can be" will be a direct result of the necessary collaboration among the parties involved. The structure, form, and content of personnel preparation are wide open for negotiation and experimentation.

Brubaker and Nelson (1975) identify seven pitfalls in the educational change process. The one relevant here is what they call the "absolutist intolerance for ambiguity," by which they mean that things are institutionalized immediately rather than beginning as experiments. A great deal of ambiguity will need to be tolerated for some time if PL 99-457 is to have the intended impact on the lives of young handicapped children. PL 99-457 extends the mandate of PL 94-142 (The Education for All Handicapped Children Act of 1975) to 3- to 5-year-old preschoolers. There must be a state plan that treats the areas of functioning in which disabilities often exist: sensory and physical development, cognitive development, language and speech development, emotional and psychosocial development, and development of socialization skills. Special education and related services must be provided in the least restrictive environment, at no cost to the parents, in compliance with all IEP (Individualized Education Program) and due process requirements. One of the problems here is that the bulk of these services usually has been delivered to preschoolers by public and private agencies other than the schools (Collins, 1983; Enzinna & Polloway, 1982; Tingey-Michaelis, 1985)—agencies whose existence not only is independent of the schools, but relies on a sufficient number of clients needing their service; the agencies have a store of practical knowledge that most school people lack (Johnston, 1984).

Schools will need large numbers of new teachers and leadership personnel to deliver these programs. When one considers that for 3- to 5-year-olds, the service delivery system will involve many different environmental settings, including the home, it is clear that personnel must be prepared to function within many different delivery models. Such personnel include regular preschool teachers; special preschool teachers; preschool aides and paraprofessionals; home visitors who may be trained counselors, social workers, or even teachers; speech pathologists; adaptive physical education teachers; recreation specialists. The list also could include art therapists and music therapists, principals unaccustomed to having such young children in their buildings, and subject area and special education supervisory and administrative personnel. All these persons will need some degree of training or retraining.

Research evidence demonstrates clearly that those who are fully trained are more effective than those who are not. Tingey-Michaelis's (1985) meta-analysis of efficacy studies that dealt with handicapped, disadvantaged, and at-risk preschoolers, age birth to 5, yielded results in favor of certified personnel. The indirect effects of these results can be inferred from studies that surveyed state departments of education about the status of early childhood special education certification. These studies showed that, while few states certify in this area, most, if not all, are developing relevant standards (Enzinna & Polloway, 1982; Trohanis, Woodward, & Behr, 1981). Other evidence of general concern for personnel preparation in preschool education can be found in the general early childhood literature (Collins, 1983; Johnston, 1984; Lamm, McMillan, & Clark, 1983; Pickett, 1986; Verzaro, 1980).

ESSENTIAL CAPABILITIES OF PRESCHOOL EDUCATORS

While much of the literature discusses the need for training or for certification, little of it focuses on the training content. As Tingey-Michaelis (1985, p. 92) states, "Clarification of the roles of various disciplines in early intervention training, and the exact nature of the certification that should be required, are still unanswered questions." The challenge is to determine what training is needed and how much. I think that now we can talk generally about the "what." "How much" will have to wait for an answer, and the collaborative experimentation, alluded to earlier, will be very important in that regard.

There are several articles in the literature listing the competencies that preschool educators should have (Goldhammer, 1981; Haisley & Roberts, 1978; Johnston, 1984; Whitten & Westling, 1985). The competencies and clusters of competencies overlap and can all be subsumed within Lakin and Reynolds's (1982) "Ten Clusters of Capability": curriculum, teaching basic skills, class management, professional consultation and communications, teacher-parent relationships, student-student relationships, exceptional children, referral, individualized teaching, and professional values. Each of these is considered in turn.

1. Curriculum

Curriculum is used here to include a functional knowledge of child development and the milestones in the development of cognition, language, physical ability, social ability, and emotional development. One cannot identify atypical behavior in any area if one does not know what typical behavior is. Curriculum also includes a knowledge of the curricular objectives of the primary, intermediate, and secondary schools, even though the educators will be working with preschoolers and their families. This knowledge needs to be functionally useful in the development of IEPs, and in modifying objectives and methods and materials to meet individual needs. The challenge is to determine what the sine qua non of the knowledge base is, how best to transmit this to the various types of personnel in preservice training, and how best to ensure that this knowledge becomes functionally useful within the constraints of the particular professional roles of those to whom it is taught. Johnston's (1984) study of the problems of prekindergarten teachers would be instructive here.

2. Teaching Basic Skills

The first question is, "What are the basic skills for preschoolers? Which of these, then, are absolutely essential? Which would be nice to have but are not essential for the child still to function effectively?" At a minimum, these basic skills include not only those preacademic skills necessary to progress appropriately in later grades, but also those life maintenance skills necessary to function in society safely, healthily, interpersonally, and economically. The teachers and aides must know how to structure the environment so that it is compatible with each child's own ways of learning, responsive to each child as he or she searches for meaning, and diverse enough to form the background for his or her future learning. Teaching must be coordinated with curriculum, as defined above, and individuality must be valued.

The challenge here is to integrate the teaching of basic skills with the curriculum in such a way that teachers, paraprofessionals, and other professionals focus on the abilities of children and accept dealing with children's handicaps as a regular part of the job. The special teacher, however, will have a greater need for alternative approaches, techniques, and strategies, since children in self-contained units are more likely to be more seriously handicapped. How does one develop the essential teaching skills to an acceptable level of quality while providing a wider range of alternatives for the professional involved?

Personnel other than teachers have varying degrees of need for the capability to teach basic skills. Certainly, speech pathologists require a detailed knowledge of speech and language development in order to do their job as clinicians, as consultants, and as participants in staff meetings. Home visitors need some knowledge of these basic skills if they are to work with the parents effectively and to serve as parent trainers. Other personnel have their own specialized functions to fulfill, but within those functions there are probably contributions to be made to the teaching of basic skills and to curriculum. What are these contributions? What knowledge of teaching basic skills would other personnel need in order to stimulate these contributions? What knowledge of the other functions do teachers need in order to make maximum, effective use of these contributions?

3. Class Management

Class management refers to the efficient management of instructional time, the management of materials, the management of behavior, the management of instruction, the management of the classroom environment, the management of learning, and the management of content. Teachers need these skills, if children's time is not to be wasted. Preschool children with handicaps are playing "catch-up." The bottom line of the task at hand is to be sure that they are as ready as they can possibly be for the first grade they will be attending.

The challenge is how to play "catch-up" while the schools continue to move more content down to lower grades and, thereby, raise the entry behaviors required for those grades. For example, many kindergarten curricula now include many of the objectives and content that were part of the first grade curriculum 20 years ago at the beginnings of Head Start and the Handicapped Children's Early Education Program. All of the other professionals also need these management skills, if what they do with children is to achieve their objectives.

4. Professional Consultation and Communications

Professionals must be able to talk with one another, as either initiators or receivers, and share information about children, methods, and materials. They must complement one another. Furthermore, they must be able to consult productively with the professionals from various other disciplines. How does one provide the necessary interaction between preschool education personnel during inservice training and the various other professionals, so that one profession understands the job of the other, respects the skills of the other, and all talk a common language so that objective, consistent, and rational negotiation, bargaining, and cajoling can occur when there are differences of goals, values, and priorities? How do we effect training in each of the professional areas so that no one profession thinks it has all the answers (one of Brubaker & Nelson's [1975] pitfalls) and each will confer when conferring is necessary to meet the needs of the child? How is this done for preservice personnel? How is this done for inservice personnel?

5. Teacher-Parent Relationships

Parents will be much more involved in preschool programs than historically has been expected (Johnston, 1984). In fact, some programs will anticipate a high degree of involvement of the parents as home teachers, and they will require some training to avoid dissonance between the school and the home programs. Teachers and home visitors alike must understand and be senstive to the dynamics of being a parent of a child with handicaps. They must learn skills and techniques for working with parents, including skills for working with the friendly parent and skills for working with the distrustful, hostile, angry parent. They need skills in providing parents with techniques of managing behavior or managing routines, and of teaching skills to their child. They need to know when they should refer the parent to some other professional. Personnel need to learn how to respect the dreams, goals, love, guilt, intelligence, and humanity of parents of children with handicaps, and how to talk to them without being patronizing, supercilious, unctuous, arrogant, or uninformative. The challenge here is how to accomplish this within a training program for either inservice or preservice personnel. How are the needed attitudinal changes to be effected? How are changes in levels of defensiveness to be effected? How are a minimum set of skills that counselors and therapists work years to develop to be provided? What skills constitute the minimum set? How can a sufficient quantity of experiences be provided to the teacher-in-training? The same set of questions can be applied to any professional area that involves interaction with parents.

6. Student-Student Relationships

As Lakin and Reynolds (1982, p. 79) state, "When teachers have the prerequisite skill to take solid command of the social structures of their classes through effective teaching, they have a powerful additional tool with which to construct individualized learning situations." This means that teachers, and others who work with preschoolers directly, have an affirmative responsibility to assist pupils in learning how to interact productively with one another and to develop cooperation in working toward common goals, to motivate pupils to assist those with more severe disabilities, and to provide a proper balance between competitiveness and cooperativeness. Various aspects of student-student relationships were identified by prekindergarten personnel as frequent problems (e.g., not sharing and taking turns), bothersome problems (e.g., aggressive behavior, trying to feel positive about a frequently misbehaving child), and frequent and bothersome problems (e.g., hitting instead of using words) (Johnston, 1984). Where is this to be treated in the current models of personnel preparation? How is the issue of student-student relationships to be infused into the program and integrated with the curriculum and teaching of basic skills?

7. Exceptional Children

Lakin and Reynolds (1982) limit this area to knowledge of effective procedures for instructing students with various exceptionalities, including the body of practice and the literature in each area. They also included knowledge of the functions of the various specialists and of the various social and health services available. It should also include realistic, practical knowledge about the intellectual, emotional, behavioral, social, linguistic, and physical characteristics of children with exceptional conditions. In the same way that concepts are formed through experience with positive and negative instances, so a knowledge of child development and of handicapping conditions must be flavored with a proper balance of positive and negative instances, if children with educationally relevant handicaps are to be identified and appropriately instructed and children without educationally relevant handicaps are not to be mislabeled. The challenge here, of course, as it has been through the 1980s, is to decide how much and which parts of the knowledge and experience given routinely to special education teachers is needed by the regular teacher and other professionals, and vice versa.

8. Referral

This criterion continues the thought expressed in the section on exceptional children. Proper referral is a legal requirement. Failure to refer may be a violation of a person's rights. Personnel need the skills to differentiate between those who need to be referred to other persons or agencies and those who do not. Personnel need the skills of reporting systematic observations in support of their referrals. They need to view the making of appropriate referrals as a positive part of their job. A part of the task here seems to be preparing personnel to handle the paperwork efficiently and substantively, and to view it as a routine and not an imposition. There are, certainly, some attitudinal considerations here. Therefore, how, in our preservice and inservice training, are changes in attitude to be effected? How are personnel to be prepared to handle the paperwork load and do it efficiently? Instructional personnel feel the load, but so do the administrators and supervisors, who, for the most part, are the ones who lay out the paper trail. What kind of work can be done with these leadership personnel that would have a salutary effect on the paper trail?

9. Individualized Teaching

Individualized teaching is what has been targeted in all of the previous areas of capability. It means seeing each child with exceptional conditions as a unique set of abilities and disabilities, being able to assess those abilities and disabilities, formulating objectives for each child uniquely, planning instruction to achieve those objectives, modifying teaching strategies and materials necessary for instruction, keeping data on progress, and evaluating the effectiveness of all of these.

All of the professionals share in this responsibility. Teachers and aides seem to have the major share of this responsibility, but others have some responsibility to assist teachers in this area. How is a prospective preschool teacher to be taught to do all of the above effectively within a classroom of 6–30 children without negatively affecting the engaged learning time of each of the children? It is interesting to note that this was one of the areas of concern that prekindergarten teachers listed as both frequent and bothersome (Johnston, 1984).

10. Professional Values

"Teachers, in their personal commitments and professional behavior with pupils, parents, and colleagues, should exemplify the same consideration for all individuals and their educational rights as are called for in Public

Law 94-142 and in the Vocational Rehabilitation Act of 1973" (Lakin & Reynolds, 1982, p. 80). This requirement applies to all professionals equally. The personnel preparation task is to infuse these values into and throughout special education programs. A course titled: "Professional Values" will not do it.

Considering all that has been said, it is evident that preparation of personnel for preschool programming is very complex. Professionals cannot wait for the answers to some of the theoretical or philosophical questions posed; preparation of personnel right now must begin to meet the needs that the law will create. Superintendents will hire warm bodies (AACTE Task Force on Teacher Certification, 1984). We need to get a head start to ensure that those are warm bodies with adequate preparation. There already exists a body of knowledge and experience upon which we can capitalize (Bush, 1977; Coker, 1978; Collins, 1983; Howey, 1977; Johnston, 1984; Morsink, Soar, Soar, & Thomas, 1986; Quirk, 1976; Yarger & Joyce, 1977). The knowledge and experience gained through the Handicapped Children's Early Education Program projects include personnel preparation. There also are college and university training programs in many states. The law will create a demand for preschool personnel and most likely to try to fill this need will be schools, colleges, and departments of education. Existing programs will not even begin to meet the future demand. Program expansion and recruitment is needed now. However, simply tacking on a preschool component to what already exists would be a mistake, unless the existing programming were currently producing personnel with the 10 capabilities.

HOW PRESERVICE TRAINING SHOULD BE DRAWN

What should the preservice training of teachers look like? First, the regular and special education preschool teachers must be trained together, with the latter receiving more detailed training in alternatives in methodological and instructional strategies. The special education teacher must know everything that the regular classroom teacher knows and more if the preschoolers with handicaps, in the numbers now envisioned, are to be ready for the first grade. By training together, special teachers and regular teachers will learn to talk to one another and speak the same language. By training together, validity may be established for both tracks. I envision this as one program with two tracks, both tracks sharing a preponderance of the course work and experiences.

Second, special education teachers should be trained, initially, as teachers of self-contained units of children with severe levels of handicaps. It is my belief that students who have been prepared to work with children with moderate and severe levels of handicap move more smoothly, and with less complaining, into working with children with mild degrees of handicap, even when they prefer the former, provided they had the subject area skills. Conversely, those students who have been prepared to work with children with mild degrees of handicap appear to have many more problems and complaints when required to teach children with moderate or severe handicaps. Only after prospective teachers have learned to teach children with severe handicaps should they move to working with those who have mild degrees of handicap.

Third, the program should be either noncategorical or cross-categorical; to label preschoolers at the same time that the objective is to ameliorate the effects of existing handicapping conditions or to prevent developmental delays, seems to be contradictory and nonproductive. In other words, rather than focusing on labels, the program should focus on observable behaviors of children and methods of accelerating or decelerating them, as the case may be.

Fourth, this program must be field based with regular and special education teachers sharing settings and seminars, since there is such diversity among preschoolers and a very wide range of normality.

Fifth, sometime during their preparation, these teachers must be given the opportunity to meet and interact with those who are being trained for other professions. Field experiences must be planned so that various professionals in the same settings can share information and perceptions and learn each other's languages. Looking at children's abilities through the eyes of other disciplines would increase the sensitivity of all the professionals to the children's needs. Groups of students in special education, mental health, social work, physical therapy, and school psychology rarely have been gathered together to share ideas, perceptions, and points of view about children, agencies, and so forth. An implication of PL 99-457 is that this must begin now as one of the attempts to professionalize our students and create an imperative to learn all that is necessary in order to function effectively in a preschool setting. If the promise of PL 99-457 as policy is to be implemented with any degree of efficiency, the way our preschool teachers and our special educators are generally trained must change. An integrated, smoothly functioning, highly sequenced set of courses and experiences wherein most, if not all, of the capabilities may be developed is needed. This will not be achieved without collaboration among the public schools, private preschool agencies, parent organizations, community colleges, 4-year colleges, and universities (Andrew, 1981).

There is an eleventh capability that has been assumed throughout this chapter, which is that all professionals must be competent in their own professional areas; they must be theoretically competent, competent in the practices of their professions, and up-to-date.

CONCLUSION

In conclusion, Lakin and Reynolds's "Ten Capabilities" have been used to raise issues and ask questions about preparation of personnel. There is no doubt that all of the relevant disciplines need some re-tooling. The task can be as simple as "This is how schools function!" and as complex as working on attitude changes. New personnel need to be prepared; old personnel need to be updated or re-tooled. The 28 resource units developed by various authors within the "Ten Capabilities" (Lakin & Reynolds, 1982) could be a starting point for the development of training modules focused on infants, toddlers, and preschoolers. Similar modules exist within other disciplines. The wheel does not need to be reinvented, it does need to be repackaged.

Brubaker and Nelson (1975) discuss seven pitfalls in the educational change process: lack of faith; absolutist intolerance for ambiguity; imposition rather than intervention; elitism or the messianic syndrome; unclear focus on three areas of change—the person, the organization, and the culture of the organization; person-centered change; and misinterpretation of the leaders' views. In a situation in which so many agencies and disciplines are involved, the pitfalls become chasms that must be bridged carefully.

REFERENCES

AACTE Task Force on Teacher Certification. (1984). Emergency teacher certification: Summary and recommendations. *Journal of Teacher Education, 35*(2), 21–25.

Andrew, M.D. (1981). Statewide inservice without colleges and universities: New Hampshire's quiet move toward teachers' control. *Journal of Teacher Education, 23*(1), 24–28.

Brubaker, E.L., & Nelson, R.J., Jr. (1975). Pitfalls in the educational change process. *Journal of Teacher Education, 26*(1), 63–66.

Bush, R.J. (1977). We know how to train teachers: Why not do so! *Journal of Teacher Education, 28*(6), 5–9.

Coker, H. (1978). An effectiveness-directed approach to teacher evaluation and certification. *Journal of Classroom Interaction, 13*(2), 27–31.

Collins, R.C. (1983). Child care and the states: The comparative licensing study. *Young Children, 28*(5), 3–11.

Enzinna, C., & Polloway, E.A. (1982). Certification for teaching preschool handi-

capped children: A status report. *The Journal for Special Educators, 18*(4), 23–27.
Goldhammer, K. (1981). Teacher education: Reality, hope, and promise. *Journal of Teacher Education, 22*(5), 25–29.
Greenberg, J.D. (1983). The case for teacher education: Open and shut. *Journal of Teacher Education, 34*(4), 2–5.
Haberman, M., & Stinnett, T.M. (1973). *Teacher education and the new profession of teaching*. Berkeley, CA: McCutchan Publishing Corp.
Haisley, F.B., & Roberts, R.D. (1978). Individual competencies needed to implement P.L. 94-142. *Journal of Teacher Education, 29*(6), 30–33.
Howey, K.R. (1977). Preservice teacher education: Lost in the shuffle? *Journal of Teacher Education, 28*(6), 26–28.
Johnston, J.M. (1984). Problems of prekindergarten teachers: A basis for reexamining teacher education practices. *Journal of Teacher Education, 34*(2), 33–37.
Koerner, J.D. (1973). Governance of teacher education. In D.J. McCarty (Ed.), *New perspectives on teacher education* (pp. 100–111). San Francisco: Jossey-Bass.
Lakin, K.C., & Reynolds, M.C. (1982). Public Law 94-142 as an organizing principle for teacher-education curricula. In B.L. Sharp (Ed.), *Deans' grant projects: Challenge and change in teacher education* (pp. 74–85). Minneapolis: University of Minnesota, National Support Systems Project.
Lamm, L.L., McMillan, M.R., & Clark, B.H. (1983). Early childhood teacher certification: A national survey. *Journal of Teacher Education, 34*(2), 44–47.
Melcher, J., & Franks, D.J. (1978). Certification and training of teachers of young handicapped children—The Wisconsin experience. *Bureau Memorandum, 20*(1), 32–34, (Abstract).
Morsink, C.V., Soar, R.S., Soar, R.M., & Thomas, R. (1986). Research on teaching: Opening the door to special education classrooms. *Exceptional Children, 53*, 32–40.
Pickett, A.L. (1986). Certified partners: Four good reasons for certification of paraprofessionals. *American Educator, 10*(3), 31–34, 47.
Quirk, T.J. (1976). Validation issues involved in teacher certification. *College Student Journal, 10*, 346–354.
Smith, W.L. (1974). A * by any other name. *Journal of Teacher Education, 25*(1), 2.
Tingey-Michaelis, C. (1985). Early intervention: Is certification necessary? *Teacher Education and Special Education, 8*, 91–97.
Trohanis, P., Woodward, M., & Behr, S.K. (1981). Services for young exceptional children. *The Exceptional Parent, 11*(1), s13–s15, s18–s20.
Verzaro, M. (1980). Inservice programs for early childhood educators. *Journal of Teacher Education, 31*(4), 34–37.
Weaver, J.F. (1979). Collaboration: Why is sharing the turfs so difficult? *Journal of Teacher Education, 30*(1), 24–25.
Whitten, T.M., & Westling, D.L. (1985). Competencies for teachers of the severely and profoundly handicapped: A review. *Teacher Education and Special Education, 8*, 104–111.
Yarger, S.J., & Joyce, B.R. (1977). Going beyond the data: Reconstructing teacher education. *Journal of Teacher Education, 28*(6), 21–25.

Leadership and Policy Strategies for Interagency Planning
Meeting the Early Childhood Mandate

8

Brian A. McNulty

HUMAN SERVICES PROVIDERS NOW MORE THAN EVER NEED SKILLS THAT will help them manage the process of change. When these service providers are involved in interagency coordination, the need for new skills and direction becomes even more complex and problematic. This chapter presents a process for establishing joint policies as a way to coordinate services across agencies for young handicapped children and their families. It also addresses the need for providers to assume leadership roles and gives some direction as to how they might assume these roles.

SOCIETAL FACTORS AFFECTING CHANGE

We all find ourselves living in an increasingly complex and diversified society, one that offers more opportunities, but also requires more decisions and actions. State governments especially are finding this to be true. They presently are caught in a vice between local demands for increased, yet more cost-efficient, services and federal requests to assume greater responsibility concurrent with budget reductions. The rapidly changing and turbulent environment surrounding state governmental organizations demands increased responsiveness and adaptation from a system that is traditionally known for its rigidity, fragmentation, and mechanistic responses (Ferguson, 1980).

As predicted in the mid-1970s by Elliot Richardson, then Secretary of the U.S. Department of Health, Education, and Welfare, these governmental organizations are facing a crisis of both performance and control. There is a crisis of performance in that our agencies and institutions are not living up to our needs or expectations; there is a crisis of control in that the system is developing beyond the scope of executive, legislative, consumer, and public control. This is true especially in the human services sector, where rapid and massive increases in services and expenditures have created a maze of highly specialized public programs so complex and disorganized as to defy effective operation (Brewer & Kakalik, 1982).

The failure of other social institutions has exacerbated this trend, and there has been a concomitant, growing public alienation, disenfranchisement, and mistrust of government agencies and their leaders, resulting from their inability to respond adequately. As Rubens (1983, February) has noted, the government is being "progressively crippled by a syndrome of persistent political paralysis and lurching change in response only to crisis" (p. 59). One directly observable outcome is that current public leaders cannot maintain their popularity (Burghardt, 1982), and this lack of continuity of leadership is itself a factor contributing to the problem.

The extreme acceleration of change has created a sense of helplessness and confusion, overpowering the decisional capacities of these organizations and making the current political structure obsolete (Toffler, 1981). Consequently, Toffler observes that our governmental institutions are spinning from a "decisional implosion." While many potential causal factors can be postulated, the following discussion will focus on what the author perceives as two of the major contributing factors: changes in consumer demands and a lack of organizational responsiveness.

CHANGING CONSUMER DEMANDS

Given the rapid rise in expenditures for human services during the 1980s, one would expect a high degree of consumer satisfaction. However, the results of a Rand Corporation study on services to people who have disabilities (Brewer & Kakalik, 1982) clearly documented that both providers and consumers of these services found the system so complex and disorganized that it often denied access. Although a wide range of services was available, fully two-thirds of all consumers had difficulty finding them, let alone actually receiving them. As Phillip Kotler (1982) described this bureaucratic phenomenon, organizations that were originally designed to achieve a specific purpose, grow and become more complex and multipurposed, taking on more roles and responsibilities to both internal and external publics. Management, in trying to harmonize these diverse goals and interests, finds that more and more time must be devoted inward, to maintaining routines and operations. This, in turn, creates a rigid hierarchy, where personal judgment and flexibility are replaced with impersonal and often inflexible policies. "Questions of structure dominate questions of substance; means dominate ends" (p. 39). What results is an organization that, while extremely efficient in meeting the original market needs and goals, does not meet the needs of a changing market. As a result, the organization becomes unresponsive and maladapted. To the public, the organization appears more and more unresponsive to current needs. Kotler notes that this phenomenon is especially true in the case of governmental agencies facing no active competition from the private sector.

Kotler recommends that agencies develop a marketing orientation in order to develop and maintain a responsive organization. The marketing concept involves a reorientation outward, toward the consumer and away from internal and often outdated traditional policies, procedures, and products. The organization must focus on helping consumers identify and solve their real problems and on creating satisfied and healthy customers. As Kotler says, the key to the organization's long-run success is the amount of satisfaction it generates in its customers and publics. Kotler, like others, has recognized and accepted the notion that customers are intelligent and, consequently, show a preference for organizations that treat them humanely and show social responsibility.

Other writers in the field have noted a similar trend. Glazer (1983) has focused specifically on the growing discontent of the public with the capabilities of centralized government. He notes that the government is so large that it now pervades and affects many different aspects of people's lives. However, many have come to question its ability to effectively, efficiently, or equitably manage the vast array of social services it administers. In addition, the individuals who are affected by the decisions of these organizations now want to be a part of the decision-making process. The societal trends toward increased personal affluence and higher education have only heightened the demands for a greater role of the consumer in government, and in managing the services provided. Glazer (1983), Naisbitt (1982), and Toffler (1981) all find that this is true especially for the activist baby boom generation of the 1960s. Naisbitt notes that the younger, more educated, rights-conscious worker finds the notion of hierarchies and the pyramid foreign and unnatural. Glazer (1983) reiterates this, noting that the 1960s generation has been nurtured on social and personal experiences that are rooted in a distrust of bigness. The demand for greater involvement, more personal choices, and decentralization is forcing a "devolution" of our present system of government. Individuals are demanding more adaptability, responsiveness, diversity, and accountability from governmental organizations. To ensure their options, they are demanding a greater, more participatory role in government. As Naisbitt (1982) notes, this generation of individuals is better educated, and more confident about governing themselves. In the next section, we begin to see how these environmental demands are affecting organizational responsiveness.

ORGANIZATIONAL RESPONSIVENESS

It is probably fair to say that the vast majority of governmental organizations still operate under the classic pyramidal, bureaucratic model. Given this fact, it is easy to see why these organizations are experiencing difficulty in adapting to a changing and turbulent environment. Since the 1960s, it has been recognized that the major problem with the bureaucratic model is the lack of adaptability inherent in the pyramidal structure of authority. Over time, the structural elements of the organization become more differentiated and complex, while the organization itself becomes less and less adaptive.

As greater demands for adaptability, variety, and responsiveness are being made on our governmental institutions, the accelerating pace of social change is placing new and greater demands on political leaders. These demands are overpowering their decisional capacities and rendering political structures obsolete. "Our leaders . . . cannot churn out intelligent decisions as fast as events require" (Toffler, 1981, p. 407). Part of this problem is that, while problems have shifted to the state and local levels, decisional power has not. Toffler suggests that there needs to be a "rational reallocation of decision-making in a system that has overstressed centralization to the point at which new information flows are swamping the central decision makers" (p. 440). He goes on to say that "any political structure . . . can handle only so much information . . . and that the decision implosion has now pushed governments beyond this breakpoint" (p. 408). He feels that we are currently undergoing a fundamental decentralization of communication. This decentralization will result in a "decision division" by placing decisions at the levels where they belong.

Ferguson (1980) explains this transformation in terms of a major "paradigm change." The demand for increased participation, adaptability, and responsiveness necessitates a decentralization movement. She suggests that the role of government is to develop broad frameworks, not detailed, rigid structures. Toffler (1981) agrees, noting that we must:

> return to large-scale thinking, to general theory, to the putting of the pieces back together again, for it is beginning to dawn on us that our obsessive emphasis on quantified detail without context, on progressively finer and finer measurement and smaller and smaller problems, leaves us knowing more and more about less and less. (p. 310)

Toffler feels that there is a new civilization that has evolved beyond centralization, synchronization, and standardization. Consequently, individuals need and require a government that is simpler, more responsive, effective, and democratic. What is needed, Toffler suggests, are new arrangements that can accommodate and legitimize diversity, "new institutions that are sensitive to the rapidly shifting needs of changing and multiplying minorities" (p. 422). We must accept this "thrust towards diversity" and find ways to integrate disparate policies that reflect the diversity of our society. Ferguson (1980) believes that even an awareness of these multiple realities helps us to lose our "dogmatic attachment to a single point of view. A new sense of connection with others promotes social concern . . . there is a commitment to process rather than programs" (p. 192).

These noted futurists suggest that governmental organizations are faced with a major paradigm change that must integrate multiple diverse realities. Individuals are demanding greater representation and participation and, in turn, are forcing decentralization and the division of decisional levels to the state, regional, and local levels. Several levels of response to the need for more effective and responsive organizations can and should be developed.

STRATEGIC COORDINATED POLICY DEVELOPMENT

Given the concerns facing human services agencies, what can early childhood service providers do? In this section, two overarching themes are addressed; the need for and mechanisms for interagency planning and coordination, and the role of participatory decision making. The framework for addressing these issues is discussed in terms of the need for coordinated policy development.

The first level of response focuses on the critical need for more coordinated policy analysis and development, across agencies at all levels of government and aimed at specific issues that cross agency boundaries. This task should include the development of interagency goals or mission statements that define the issues, objectives, and expected outcomes of all of the participating agencies and their interactions. The development of these overarching goals or mission statements can provide a general understanding of the underlying functions and purposes of the organizations and help agencies clarify their common goals. The process forces agency personnel and consumers to think about the purposes of the organizations and, in effect, becomes a vehicle of change itself. By defining goals or missions, the statements provide a common standard for response to shared problems. These statements also can help to link agency objectives both horizontally and vertically.

We are beginning to see an emergence of these interagency policy initiatives at both the state and federal levels. For example, the recent report from the National Council on the Handicapped (1986) recommends a restructuring of disability aid programs to promote independence and self-sufficiency and to reduce the current overemphasis on income support. The report establishes clear policy priorities and makes recommendations for meeting these priorities through the reduction of existing barriers and better utilization of existing resources.

At the state level it is not uncommon to find a formalized group of human services cabinet members set up to address interagency concerns and initiatives. In addition, division directors of special education, mental health, youth corrections, health, developmental disabilities, and social services have begun to develop coordinated state policy initiatives. As an example, in Colorado, this type of group developed a document on Interagency Public Policy Principles (1987) to establish goals that affect each department and that can be addressed in a cooperative effort. In the same state, a multiagency policy document addressed transition services for disabled young adults.

Colorado's Interagency Transition Policy Document (1986) outlines a series of common policy statements, objectives, and outcomes to be addressed by all state and local providers. The adoption of these interagency policy statements was meant to provide a unified direction to all participating agencies. The policy statements purposely were kept broad based, for example, "All Colorado citizens, including youth with disabilities, will have opportunities for full participation in work and community life" (p. 3). Following these broad statements, however, is a series of more specific policy objectives to which all collaborating agencies agreed. The purpose of the objectives is to define the outcome of the process. These objectives can and should address both philosophical and programmatic issues:

> All young people with disabilities will be prepared for and offered 'real work' settings for 'real wages' with access to necessary support services . . . ; All youth with disabilities shall have access to a 'functional' lifeskills curriculum designed to prepare them to live and function in domestic, recreational, social, community, and vocational environments . . . ; All youth with disabilities will have a written individual transition plan developed by the transition team; All young people with disabilities will have access to appropriate residential options in integrated, community-based settings. (pp. 3–4)

As is evident, these kinds of statements can set clear systems objectives toward which all agencies and individuals can commit to work. It becomes the responsibility of the participating agencies to work together to remove barriers and create incentives for reaching these goals. Anyone reading the document can gain an understanding of what the outcomes are meant to be, and therefore it places performance expectations on all of the participating agencies. Unlike many of the earlier interagency efforts, which focused on "agreeing to agree," this current approach focuses on identifying and achieving common goals and missions through the adoption of joint policy statements.

While seeming somewhat commonsensical, the achievement of success in interagency initiatives has been extremely difficult. This difficulty is exacerbated when the focus of the interagency initiative is on policy development and not simply service coordination. Part of the challenge is that agency policies are controlled by both legal and political processes, and different agencies want to preserve and pursue different policies to meet the different demands of the controlling processes (Mazmanian & Sabatier, 1983). Issues such as client eligibilities, ambiguity in roles and functions, conflicting statutes and regulations, and different funding mechanisms all must be examined as outcomes of this interagency policy development process. As a result, it will require a more broad-based vision on the part of agency personnel and a variety of new management and interpersonal skills if interagency initiatives are to be successful (see McNulty, 1983; McNulty, Smith, & Soper, 1983).

Two critical components of interagency policy development are leadership and participation. Individuals must assume transformational leadership positions at all levels and work to develop more open organizations. Transformational leadership creates institutional purpose and builds on an individual's needs for meaning (Burns, 1987). The transformational leader creates a new vision of and for the organization, sells that vision, and makes it a reality, thus transforming the organization (Bennis, 1984; Tichy & Ulrich, 1984). As stated by Peters and Waterman (1982), leaders are true pathfinders. They help to define what the mission is and, in doing so, cause the goal to become a vehicle of change. In effect, they are the "social architects," in that they assist the group in defining its purposes. In turn, organizations need to be able to respond more quickly and more flexibly to new information and redirection. They also must allow for and provide for more constant intense interactions with their external environments.

Joint policy planning can achieve part of this process. This kind of planning shifts the focus of management from operations (doing) to strategy (thinking). The policy planning process also can create an opportunity for new networks of information, as it requires participation and communication about goals, strategies, and resource allocation. This will happen only through decisive leadership. The leader's role is to create a vision of the future that is realistic, credible, attractive, and better than what now exists (Bennis & Nanus, 1985; Bradford & Cohen, 1984).

Participation involves the utilization of interagency policy planning groups. These groups can provide a foundation of shared experience that can highlight common values, perceptions, and goals, and therefore facilitate communication within and between the agencies. They can provide a forum for sharing and debating divergent views about relevant environmental changes, goals, and trends (Steiner, 1979). They also may provide a broader range of perceptions and a diversity of values that can result in a more comprehensive, global picture of the changing organizational environment.

Another reason for involving a range of individuals in these groups is to reduce the resistance to change. Research has documented clearly that the recipients of change are far from passive. In order for change to be effective, those who will be affected by the proposed change must be involved in the process itself (Sarason, 1971). People do not resist changing, but they do resist being changed (Elder & Magrab, 1980). Stated more positively, people tend to support what they help to create (Huff, 1980).

Using groups in this process also is important because successful implementation of any plan depends upon the development of internal and external support groups (House, 1979; Northwest Regional Educational Laboratory, 1980). Greater representation on planning groups enhances the likelihood of diffusion and, consequently, the development of needed advocacy groups. The diversity of the group can build on existing communication networks, that, in turn, can increase interpersonal contacts, and therefore result in a larger base of group support.

There also appear to be some direct administrative benefits from group-based activities. Staff members who participate in administrative functions develop higher morale and more positive attitudes toward their administrators. A greater understanding and appreciation of administrative functions, in turn, positively affects trust, morale, and communication (Ellenburg, 1979).

Another way of looking at these groups is as networks or clans. To a greater extent than ever before, individuals are creating new information pathways across agency lines. Adapting to the turbulent environment, individuals must establish multiple information pathways, cutting across organizational and societal levels and gaining direct access to needed people, information, or resources. Although research on these issues is still in its infancy, it appears that clans (Ouchi, 1981) or networks (Cohen & Lorentz, 1977; Naisbitt, 1982) are rapidly becoming the "modus operandi" for many individuals and organizations. Networks provide a forum for individuals to tackle common problems, but from different vantage points. Members can draw freely on each other as resources. Clans function as a mini-culture and act as a resource-exchange bank (Cohen & Lorentz, 1977) where unique world views can be shared and appreciated. The greater the number of interconnecting links, the greater the variety of talents available, the more powerful the network. Networks are both integrative and synergistic. The attraction of these networks is that they are functional systems that deal with actual or potential needs. They provide a cross-disciplinary approach and a polyocular vision; they provide information in a quicker, more efficient, personal way; and they provide a framework for addressing high-level issues (Cohen & Lorentz, 1977; Naisbitt, 1982; Walker, 1979).

It has been postulated that such interactive network groups may become the dominant management style of the future. Naisbitt (1982) feels that the present pyramidal hierarchical system is foreign to the younger, more educated, rights-conscious worker. Rather than working through established channels, which slow down information and decision-making, individuals have connected diagonally across organizations, to other individuals who have similar goals, to create new networks. With successful experiences, interagency groups could develop into true networks, where the diversity in organizational bases and membership is perceived as a strength and a resource to the group. Under these conditions, these groups could address higher-level problems more effectively than any individual or any single agency (Cohen & Lorentz, 1977). The networking phenomena may affect the interagency collaborative effort in a more powerful and yet less formal way than methods currently in use. While further research certainly is needed, this type of approach may provide the flexibility and responsiveness needed in a changing environment.

These two concepts of leadership and participation should not be seen in isolation from each other. Clearly, it is through their synergistic interaction that change occurs. Similarly, by the provision of opportunities for involvement and participation, new opportunities for leadership emerge. By facilitating and encouraging the interaction of individuals and groups, we are creating new information pathways that assist in creating more open, flexible, and responsive organizations.

NEW OPPORTUNITIES AND CHALLENGES

Public Law 99-457, The Education of the Handicapped Act Amendments of 1986, has created new policy and programmatic opportunities for handicapped children ages birth to 5 years. Specifically, the statute lowers the age range specified in PL 94-142 (The Education for All Handicapped Children Act of 1975) from age 5 to age 3 and establishes a new discretionary program to serve handicapped infants and toddlers, to be phased in over a 4-year period. In addition to providing new federal appropriations for direct service to these populations, the law offers significant challenges to a complex and fragmented service delivery system. While this is true especially for the 24 states that still have no mandated services for this age group, it is also a problem for states where the existing mandate for the infant and preschool population is divided between agencies. In a study conducted by Meisels, Harbin, Modigliani, and Olson (1988), it was found that "on the average, every state listed three or four agencies as having primary responsibilities for managing birth-to-six services."

To address this problem, the statute requires the establishment of a state interagency coordinating council (ICC) composed of parents, public and private providers, a state legislator, and higher education and state agency representation appointed by the governor. While the council is required only for the infant and toddler program, it can and should be used to provide guidance for the full birth to 5 initiative. Part of this council's responsibility is to assist the lead agency in the development of a "statewide system of coordinated, comprehensive, multidisciplinary, interagency programs" through the "promotion of interagency agreements" (PL 99-457: § 676[a]).

Policy Development

Given its broad-based membership and charge, this council's first mission should be to develop an interagency policy document that describes services to young children with disabilities. This document would include the following topics:

1. Definitions: Who are the target populations and what are early intervention services? The council may choose to be either specific or more general, depending on the needs and direction of the state. It may want to adopt statewide eligibility criteria and program standards or defer to local interdisciplinary teams if an "at risk" definition is adopted.
2. Policy Statements: These statements should reflect the goals, purposes, and outcomes of intervention services, for example, "It is the policy of all human services agencies to provide for an integrated service delivery system that will support families and assist young children with disabilities to achieve maximum independence, integration, and self-sufficiency." Such statements should set the goals toward which all agencies must work. The policy should assist in defining the purpose of intervention. Is it to provide support to families, to improve school performance or school placements, to provide for social integration, and so forth, or all of these? The question to be addressed here is, "What are the purposes of early intervention services?" By defining our purposes, we also help to define what programs should look like and how to intervene more effectively (Bricker, 1987). Finally, program evaluation strategies become more evident when the purposes are well defined.
3. Policy Objectives: In order to meet goals set forth in the policy statements, the collaborating agencies need to agree to identify and achieve certain performance objectives. These objectives might state that services are to be family focused and, as such, should provide for information, support, and involvement of families. They might address the need for placements that allow for, facilitate, and maximize interaction with nonhandicapped siblings and peers, or they might address the need for flexibility in the delivery of services to meet the needs of individual children and families. They could focus on issues such as the roles and responsibilities of service providers and parents and describe how the single line of authority is to be implemented. They may define a timely evaluation, the role of private providers, personnel standards, the availability of ongoing training, and so forth. Ultimately, however, these policy objectives will provide con-

ceptual guidance to what the system should look like and how it should work. As stated earlier, they can and should address both philosophical and programmatic issues. It is also important to realize that this is a "living document" and, as such, can be added to and clarified as new issues or concerns emerge.

4. Services: This section of the document should describe how to implement the policy objectives and components of the statewide system. Again, the key is to provide conceptual guidance while not being overly prescriptive. In many cases, the actual development should be left to local communities, providers, and consumers. Five areas of services and issues should receive attention by the council:

   a. Case Finding and Management: A system must be established and implemented that ensures an active and effective public awareness campaign and Child Find services that include screening, assessment, and multidisciplinary planning. Case management should help families gain access to early intervention services, ensure the timely delivery of these services, and coordinate their provision, including those from medical and health care providers.

   b. Provisions of Direct and Support Services: The intent of the new legislation clearly identifies the family as the primary learning environment for all young children (U.S. House Committee on Education and Labor, 1986). Therefore, all providers must collaborate with parents and the family. One of the primary purposes of intervention services is to provide families with information, support, and meaningful opportunities for involvement. In addition to family services and direct intervention services to the child, policies also should be developed and implemented for the following areas: therapy services; advocacy services and procedural safeguards; transportation, medical, and respite care services; and an overall evaluation system. Finally, policies and procedures should address the utilization of existing public and private community providers.

   c. Training: Over 68% of the states reported that they lacked sufficient training programs, over 80% are now reporting shortages of trained early childhood special education teachers, and 100% are experiencing shortages of therapists (Meisels et al., 1988). Significant new initiatives must be undertaken in both preservice and inservice training. The SEA (State Educational Agencies), in conjunction with higher education, should develop a comprehensive plan for personnel development in both areas and establish and adopt standards for the certification and licensing of personnel.

d. Interagency Issues: The responsibilities for a coordinated service delivery system rest with both the state and local communities. At a minimum, the state must develop a directory of services and resources available, define contracting and reimbursement responsibilities between agencies, and establish a process for dispute resolution through formal, written interagency agreements. In addition to implementing these agreements, local providers also must ensure the coordinated delivery of services to all handicapped children and their families.

e. Transition Services: Transition services must be provided to all eligible children. A transition service can be defined as a carefully planned, outcome-oriented process, initiated by the primary service provider, who establishes and implements a written multiagency service plan for each child moving to a new program.

5. Methodology: This particular component should address document implementation and evaluation. It is highly recommended that the document be implemented initially on a pilot basis. By holding a trial run, the implementors can reduce the resistance to change, operationalize the policy concepts on a manageable level, allow for the integration of pragmatic information prior to full implementation, test the utility of the concepts, measure observable outcomes, and tinker with both the model and the system in a way that imposes minimal burden on the individuals, organizations, and systems involved. The research done at the Diffusion Research Center at Stanford University supports the need for the piloting of new approaches if they are to be successfully implemented (see Randall, 1981). (This list is not exhaustive, but gives examples of services issues that could be addressed. Many more areas need to be addressed, and the interagency coordinating council is the appropriate forum for identifying them.)

One must remember that the individuals involved in the policy making may not be sensitive to the real problems involved in the implementation of those policies. In addition, these individuals also will find that they must deal with the historical, cultural, economic, and organizational imperatives of their own organizations in the implementation process (Mazmanian & Sabatier, 1983). Initially, each individual will need to work within his or her own agency or organization to effect change. The outcome of these actions will be greatly affected by the history of change within that particular organization. Does the organization support and encourage change? Does it have a history of success regarding change? Sarason (1971) suggests that the degree of discrepancy between the "proposals made" for change and the "proposals implemented" needs to be examined. He feels that the success of any single proposal for change is "determined in part by the number of changes that have been proposed but never implemented" (p. 221). This "corporate memory," tradition, or history of success heavily affects individuals and their commitment to any proposed changes. Just as we have beliefs, attitudes, objectives, and habits that make us unique, so, too, does an organization. Over time it develops a distinctive personality of its own. The organizational culture communicates the underlying values and beliefs of an organization, and, consequently, movement toward goals and objectives is defined by a "set of beliefs about what kind of solutions tend to work well" (Ouchi, 1981, p. 41).

Leadership and Participation Issues

The creation of a useful policy document is mediated greatly by the need for leadership and productive participation, and the creation of the State Interagency Coordinating Council and subsequent working groups offers new opportunities for leadership and participation. The literature on networks has brought to our attention the fact that leadership can and does emerge from many different levels and services. It is not limited to agency executives and individuals in positions of formal authority. Given the broad-based representation that can be utilized in this initiative, multiple opportunities for leadership are present.

Since organizations are complex, diverse, and intricate entities, they often provide subtle and confusing networking phenomena that tend to be simplified and generalized by observers in order to make some of them understandable. The concept of "requisite variety" suggests that simplification is not the only way to deal with this complexity. It suggests that, instead, diversity in the networking phenomena should be matched by diversity in the inquirer, to gain a greater comprehension of the networking phenomena. Diverse experiences can be comprehended only by using diverse experiences, conceptual frameworks, and a range of inputs. Only variety can fully understand variety (Lotto, 1981). It also appears that diversity in the inquirer is enhanced by exposure to alternative or ambivalent conceptual orientations and positions.

A primary role of the leader, then, is to provide a forum where these diverse realities can be explored, to help integrate these varied realities into a realistic projection of a feasible future, and to manage the change process. A leader helps to define what previously has been implicit and articulates the common vision of the group. This common vision helps heterogeneous groups to become compatible, by keeping the discussion focused on larger issues. Focusing on goals also helps to provide motivation and more effective resolution of conflicts. As has been eloquently demonstrated by Japan in comparison, all too often our nation's companies, agencies, and organizations have lacked constancy of purpose. Consequently, there is a need for leadership in helping groups to define their purpose, their *raison d'etre*, since people feel a greater sense of security and commitment to organizations and endeavors that invest in the future (Walton, 1986).

Another major role of the leader is to manage participation in and development of the group culture. Leaders need to provide structures that value diverse perspectives from which to view and understand issues and yet achieve consensus regarding common goals and outcomes. While groups can be used effectively in the planning process to provide more broad-based information and direction, these groups must be managed appropriately, so that they can function effectively and efficiently. Situational leadership theory seems to provide us with the most assistance in understanding the interaction between the role of the leader and the function of the group.

Situational leadership theory poses a curvilinear relationship between the functions of task behavior, relationship behavior, and, in this case, group maturity. The theory attempts to provide an understanding of the relationship between an effective leadership style and the level of maturity of the group. Simply stated, the basic concept of the theory is that, as the level of maturity of the group increases in terms of accomplishing specific tasks, the leader should begin to reduce the amount of structure (task behavior) and increase socioemotional support (relationship behavior) until the group attains a moderate level of maturity. Maturity is defined as the capacity to set high but attainable goals, the willingness and ability to take responsibility, and the education and experience of the leader or group. In evaluating this maturity level, the individual leading the group must assess both his or her own and the group's technical knowledge and ability to perform the task, and the degree of self-confidence and self-respect of the participants (Hersey & Blanchard, 1977).

It would appear then, that, in the initial stages, when planning groups are being formed (and therefore maturity level is low), a more structured, systematic, task-oriented approach that allows and provides for maximum participation of the group members would prove most effective. Often it appears, however, that many groups are provided with little, if any, direction, structure, or support. Without this structure, many groups flounder, trying to understand their goals and purposes. In turn, participants rapidly grow disenchanted with the lack of outcomes and lose interest in participating in the group.

The next issue, then, is how to provide the needed structure without limiting the creative process. One of the more widely known methods is the Nominal Group Technique, developed by Andre Delbecq and Andrew Van deVen in the late 1960s (Ford & Nemiroff, 1975). The technique is used to generate, explore, and communicate ideas relevant to program planning and problem-solving situations and to assess priorities in programs requiring cooperation by two or more groups.

> The Nominal Group Technique (NGT), a variation of the brainstorming technique, has been compared with conventional interacting groups on three measures of effectiveness: (1) the number of unique ideas, (2) the total number of ideas, and (3) the quality of ideas produced. For all three measures, nominal groups have been found to be significantly superior to brainstorming groups in generating information relative to the problem. (Ford & Nemiroff, 1975, p. 160)

The Nominal Group Technique, through its structured interactive process, attempts to address the following problems:

1) Individual domination: Dominant personality types often can unduly influence the group.
2) Social pressure for conformity: Majority opinions tend to be accepted, even if their objective quality has not been assessed.
3) Status incongruities: Low-status members are overly influenced by high-status members and, as a result, are frequently acquiescent.
4) A "self-weighing" effect: An individual's feeling of self competence determines the amount of his participation.
(It should be noted that none of these first four factors is related to problem-solving ability. The "best" resource in the group—with respect to problem-solving ability—may not have the ability to influence his or her group's performance.)
5) Premature closure: Interacting groups tend to converge quickly on a decision without considering all of the available or relevant information. (Ford & Nemiroff, 1975, p. 161)

A similar and related procedure is that of "Future Forecasting." This procedure attempts to assist planners in identifying and anticipating change.

> More specifically, the use of forecasting methods and techniques can help organizations cope more effectively with forces impinging upon their environments. Because these methods are anticipatory in nature, . . . future studies enable goals to be clarified, thus overcoming some of the problems associated with a complex service delivery system. Future studies can also

deal with strategic issues, such as overcoming resistance to change. (Yates, et al., 1980, p. 2)

All this is to say, that, in the initial stages of group formation, additional attention should be focused on task processes, such as setting goals and agendas, clarifying and summarizing issues, and testing consensuses.

While obviously cursory, the point to be made here is that there is a need for leadership in terms of role, function, and structure. The leader must provide a balance between structure and vision, constantly striving to provide opportunities for full participation and interaction and also clarifying beliefs, values, attitudes, and outcomes.

The leader first must provide enough structure and direction for the groups to function effectively. However, on a deeper level, the leader must guide and manage the group in developing its own culture. This is done by helping the group to identify its assumptions, beliefs, and goals. The leader helps to create a new vision, sell that vision, and make it become a reality (Bennis, 1984; Tichy & Ulrich, 1984). It is through the management of the group's common experiences over time that the group's culture is formed. The shared resolution of internal and external problems leads the group to a shared view of the world (Schein, 1987). This shared view of the world becomes actualized in the policy planning document. It represents the best thinking and beliefs of the group on how to serve young handicapped children and their families.

Finally, although the literature is somewhat vague in identifying the components required to run an effective group, it appears that effective groups typically have some or all of the following characteristics:

1. The group leader encourages each individual to be a critical evaluator.
2. The leader and members should attempt to be impartial, especially in the early stages of deliberation.
3. Problems being addressed by the group also are assigned to outside groups, who provide their results to the group.
4. Before a consensus is reached, each member of the group should test the proposals on his or her own subordinates and report the results back to the group.
5. Outside experts should be included and encouraged to challenge the views of the group members.
6. At every meeting, someone different should be assigned to the role of "devil's advocate."
7. The group attempts to maintain contact with other working groups and to anticipate the consequences of its actions.

8. Subgroups are used to get more involvement, and then differences are addressed in the total group.
9. After consensus is reached, a follow-up meeting should be held to allow "second-thoughts" and residual doubts to be aired. (Kast & Rosenzweig, 1974)

SUMMARY

The purpose of this chapter has been to provide conceptual and pragmatic guidance to individuals responsible for, or involved in, the policy planning for young handicapped children, for example, through participation in the State Interagency Coordinating Councils required under PL 99-457. It has highlighted the need for individuals to assume leadership roles through policy planning and effective group management. Overall, what is needed now are individuals who can help articulate a better and more realistic vision of the future that motivates people to action. In doing so, they must assist the group in its actual functioning, as it is through their shared experience that a shared vision of the future will emerge. The creation of a policy planning document that describes this vision will, in and of itself, go a long way toward achieving the goals identified by the group, as it will provide a structure for identifying and reaching goals and objectives. In effect then, the document becomes a proactive control system for monitoring the success of the service system. The utilization of broad-based participation in the groups can create a much expanded network for the dissemination and implementation of their ideas and beliefs. Finally, the information provided on the need for structure and utilization of pilot programs should assist these groups in working together to identify and achieve their goals.

The State Interagency Coordinating Council can provide states with new opportunities for involvement and participation. In addition, it can foster new leadership opportunities and, if provided with appropriate leadership, can create a new and better vision of the future. Finally, through the implementation and evaluation of well-constructed policy options, it offers the hope of creating an improved service delivery system that will better meet the needs of young handicapped children and their families.

PL 99-457 has provided the early childhood community with new opportunities and challenges. While increased resources are available, new and greater expectations will tax an already fragile service system. Required services such as case management and individual family service plans, while rarely available themselves, pose an even greater challenge in that they are based on the premise of a coordinated and comprehensive service system that does not yet itself exist. However, increased pressure will be placed on program providers to meet both the spirit and the letter of the law. To meet this challege, providers will need to reorient themselves toward a more global systems view. They will need to see beyond their own disciplines and programs to meet the complex, multifaceted needs of families. We all will find ourselves stretched to meet the possibilities of a law we all had hoped for. The realization of this potential now rests with us.

REFERENCES

Bennis, W.G. (1984). Transforming power and leadership. In T.T. Sergiovanni & J.E. Corbally (Eds.), *Leadership and organizational culture* (pp. 119–138). Urbana: University of Illinois Press.

Bennis, W., & Nanus, B. (1985). *Leaders: The strategies for taking charge.* New York: Harper & Row.

Bradford, D.L., & Cohen, A.R. (1984). *Managing for excellence.* New York: John Wiley & Sons.

Brewer, G.D., & Kakalik, J.S. (1982). *Handicapped children: Strategies for improving services.* New York: McGraw-Hill.

Bricker, D. (1987). Impact of research on social policy for handicapped infants and children. *Journal of the Division for Early Childhood, 11*(2), 98–105.

Burghardt, S. (1982). *The other side of organizing.* Cambridge, MA: Schenkman Publishing Co., Inc.

Burns, J.M. (1987). *Leadership.* New York: Harper & Row.

Cohen, S.B., & Lorentz, E. (1977). Networking: Education program policy for the late seventies. *Education Development Center News, 10,* 1–4.

Education for All Handicapped Children Act of 1975, PL 94-142.

Education of the Handicapped Act Amendments of 1986, PL 99-457, 20 U.S.C. Sec. 1400, et seq.

Elder, J.O., & Magrab, P.R. (Eds.). (1980). *Coordinating services to handicapped children: A handbook for interagency collaboration.* Baltimore: Paul H. Brookes Publishing Company.

Ellenburg, F.C. (1979). Factors affecting teacher morale. In F. Griffith (Ed.), *Administrative theory in education: Text and readings* (pp. 394–401). Midland, MI: Pendell Publishing Company.

Ferguson, M. (1980). *The aquarian conspiracy: Personal and social transformation in the 1980s.* Los Angeles: J.P. Tarcher, Inc.

Ford, D.L., & Nemiroff, P.M. (1975). Applied group problem solving: The Nominal Group Technique. In *1975 Handbook for group facilitators* (pp. 276–289). La Jolla, CA: University Associates Publishers.

Glazer, B.M. (1983, Winter). Toward a self-serving society. *The Public Interest, 70,* 66–90.

Hersey, P., & Blanchard, K.H. (1977). *Management of organizational behavior: Utilizing human resources* (3rd ed.). Englewood Cliffs, NJ: Prentice-Hall.

House, E.R. (1979). The micropolitics of Innovation: Nine propositions. In F. Griffith (Ed.), *Administrative theory in education: Text and readings* (pp. 212–221). Midland, MI: Pendell.

Huff, A.S. (1980). Planning to plan. In D.L. Clark, S. McKibbin, & M. Malkas (Eds.), *New perspectives on planning in educational organizations* (pp. 34–51). San Francisco: Far West Laboratory for Educational Research and Development.

Interagency Public Policy Principles. (1987). Denver: Colorado Department of Education.

Interagency Transition Policy Document. (1986). Denver: Colorado Department of Education.

Kast, F.E., & Rosenzweig, J.E. (1974). *Organization and management: A system approach* (2nd ed.). Englewood Cliffs, NJ: Prentice-Hall.

Kotler, P. (1982). *Marketing for non-profit organizations* (2nd ed.). Englewood Cliffs, NJ: Prentice-Hall.

Lotto, L.S. (1981). Believing is seeing. In D.L. Clark, S. McKibbin, & M. Malkas, (Eds.), *Alternative perspectives for viewing educational organizations* (pp. 15–28). San Francisco: Far West Laboratory for Educational Research and Development.

Mazmanian. D.A., & Sabatier, P.A. (1983). *Implementation and public policy.* Glenview, IL: Scott, Foresman.

McNulty, B.A. (1983). Managing interagency groups. In *Perspectives on Interagency Collaboration* (pp. 49–65). Monmouth, OR: WESTAR.

McNulty, B.A., Smith, D.B., & Soper, E.W. (1983). *Effectiveness of early special education for handicapped children.* Denver: Colorado Department of Education.

Meisels, S.J., Harbin, G., Modigliani, K., & Olson, K. (1988). Formulating optimal state early childhood intervention policies. *Exceptional Children, 55*(2), 159–165.

Naisbitt, J. (1982). *Megatrends: Ten new directions transforming our lives.* New York: Warner Books.

National Council on the Handicapped. (1986). *Toward independence.* Washington, DC: U.S. Government Printing Office.

Northwest Regional Educational Laboratory (NREL). (1980). *Proceedings: Dissemination, processes seminar, collaboration—A promising strategy for improving educational practice.* Portland, OR: Author.

Ouchi, W.G. (1981). *Theory Z.* Menlo Park, CA: Addison-Wesley.

Peters, T.J., & Waterman, R.H. (1982). *In search of excellence.* New York: Warner Books.

Randall, A. (1981). Human nature: Resistance and survival. *Science Digest, 89*(11), 32.

Rubens, J. (1983, February). Retooling American democracy. *The Futurist, 17*(1), 59–64.

Sarason, S.B. (1971). *The culture of the school and the problem of change.* Newton, MA: Allyn & Bacon.

Schein, E.H. (1987). Organizational culture and leadership. In J.M. Shafritz & J.S. Ott (Eds.), *Classics of organizational theory* (pp. 381–395). Chicago: Dorsey Press.

Steiner, G.A. (1979). *Strategic planning: What every manager must know.* New York: Free Press.

Tichy, N.M., & Ulrich, D.O. (1984). The leadership challenge: A call for the transformational leader. *Sloan Management Review, 26*(1), 59–68.

Toffler, A. (1981). *The third wave.* New York: Bantam Books.

U.S. House of Representatives. Committee on Education and Labor. (1986). *Report on the Education of the Handicapped Act Amendments of 1986.* Washington, DC.

Walker, L.A. (1979). *A status report on federal interagency agreement.* Washington, DC: George Washington University, Institute for Education Leadership.

Walton, M. (1986). *The Deming management method.* New York: Dodd, Mead & Co.

Yates, J.R., Banks, S., Horton, B., Shirley, J., Fofferr, R., & Stevens, J. (1980). *Handbook for future planners.* Washington, DC: National Association of State Directors of Special Education.

FINANCING PROGRAMS FOR YOUNG CHILDREN WITH HANDICAPS

9

Harriette B. Fox,
Steve A. Freedman,
and Brian R. Klepper

IN 1986, CONGRESS PASSED PUBLIC LAW 99-457, THE EDUCATION OF THE Handicapped Act Amendments, which amended Public Law 94-142, the Education for All Handicapped Children Act of 1975 (EHA), by authorizing the development of early intervention services for children birth to 3, and the expansion of special education and related services for handicapped children 3 to 5. Key provisions of PL 99-457 called for the "identification and coordination of all available resources within the state from federal, state, local and private sources" [Title I, Part H, §676(b)9(B)], and for these monies to be used both to develop currently unavailable services and to expand existing ones.

This chapter is intended to orient educational leaders concerned with

---

It should be noted that this chapter is based in part on reports prepared by Fox Health Policy Consultants. In particular, *Medicaid Financing for Early Intervention Services* (June, 1987), *Private Health Insurance Financing for Early Intervention Services* (March, 1988), and *Private Health Insurance Coverage of Chronically Ill Children* (March, 1986) provide reviews of health care financing opportunities for children with special needs.

financing the Part H program for handicapped infants and toddlers under PL 99-457. It: 1) provides background and perspective on the financial issues attendant to programming for young children with handicaps; 2) describes financing opportunities that currently exist through families, private insurance, Medicaid, and Title V programs; and 3) offers suggestions for enhancing those financing opportunities within individual states. Some of the options cited in this chapter are available only in certain jurisdictions. Even so, they represent initiatives that can be undertaken to enhance financing opportunities for programming and that leaders might advocate for in their roles as power brokers for children's services.

BACKGROUND

In the 1970s and 1980s, the number of children surviving the perinatal period with significant impairment has grown rapidly with a corresponding rise in the need for programs that can maximize human potential and minimize the economic costs associated with such disability. Recognizing the long-term value of investing in this population, Congress has enacted laws that will provide for a range of services for special-needs infants, toddlers, and preschoolers.

A significant step in this direction was realized in 1975 with the passage of PL 94-142. The EHA called for the provision of a free, appropriate, public education for all handicapped children, independent of the severity of a child's handicapping condition, in the most normal social situation possible (i.e., in the least restrictive environment). In addition, the EHA required that schools provide "related services" at no additional cost to parents. These are ancillary services necessary to help a handicapped child benefit from special education. They are defined as "transportation, and such developmental, corrective, and other supportive services (including speech pathology and audiology, psychological services, physical and occupational therapy, recreation, and medical and counseling services, except that such medical services shall be for diagnostic and evaluation purposes only). They also include early identification and assessment of handicapping conditions in children" [§602(17)], so that children can attend school.

The opportunities for serving special needs children were broadened considerably by the passage of PL 99-457. This legislation authorized additional federal assistance to states for educational and related services for handicapped children from infancy to school age. Title I of PL 99-457 established Part H of the EHA, providing program development funding to states opting to develop early intervention services for children ages birth to 3. Title II amended Part B to expand special education and related services for 3- to-5-year-old handicapped children.

As policy, Part H is significant because it acknowledges that health care and education are functionally inseparable for the young child at risk for developmental delay. The legislation expresses a recognition of the integrity and wholeness of the developing individual, the critical role of the family in early childhood development, and the opportunity to achieve successful outcomes through early intervention techniques.

While Part B of the EHA addressed the needs of 3–5 year olds, the Part H program defines handicapped infants and toddlers as children from birth to 3 years old

> who need early intervention services because they:
>
> are experiencing developmental delays, as measured by appropriate diagnostic instruments and procedures, in one or more of the following areas: 1) cognitive development, 2) physical development, 3) language and speech development, 4) psychosocial development or 5) self-help skills; or
>
> have a diagnosed physical or mental condition that has a high probability of resulting in developmental delay. [§672(A),(B)]

Services under the Part H program may be furnished by any provider that meets state and federal standards. The law requires, however, that all early intervention services be provided under public supervision. The specification and coordination of services provided under the Part H program is to be carried out through the development of an individualized family service plan (IFSP), which is similar in concept to the individualized education program (IEP) called for by Part B. A multidisciplinary panel, including parents, is to perform an evaluation and detail the early intervention services that a child is to receive in order to improve functioning in the five developmental areas listed above. Services may extend beyond special instructions, however, to include family training, counseling, and home visits; speech and hearing therapy; occupational therapy; physical therapy; psychological services; diagnostic and evaluative medical services; and health services necessary to enable the child to benefit from other early intervention services. (The Committee report notes that this last category excludes surgical or purely medical procedures such as cleft palate surgery, shunting of hydrocephalus, or management of congenital heart ailments.) The provision of case management services also is mandatory. These services are defined in the statute as services provided to families to assist them in gaining access to early intervention services and other services identified in the individualized family service plan, to ensure timely delivery of available services, and to coordinate the provision of early intervention services with other services (e.g., medical services for other than diagnostic and evaluation purposes). Services that are not the responsibility of the Part H program, but that are part of the child's intervention program (such as medical treatment services), are to be described in the IFSP and coordinated with other interventions by the case manager.

The cost of the early intervention program will depend on each state's definition of its service population. States are given considerable latitude in the establishment of eligibility standards, with respect to: 1) how developmental delay is defined, 2) which handicapping conditions likely to result in developmental delay are included, and 3) whether environmentally at-risk children are to be served at all. As a result, estimates of the population that might be served (as well as the resulting programmatic costs) can vary widely. Early estimates based on 15 of the states that applied for EHA-H grants indicated that the number of eligible infants and toddlers approached 5% of the total U.S. population of birth to 3-year-olds (Fox & Yoshpe, 1987).

The Part H program urges development and implementation of early intervention services that will link educational, social service, and health agencies in unprecedented ways, especially in terms of programming and fiscal responsibility. Because services and the funds that support them often are located within a variety of nonassociated agencies, one lead agency is to be designated as responsible for administration and coordination of the program, with oversight by an interagency coordinating council (ICC). This arrangement undoubtedly will enhance the contact that agencies have with one another. Public health and social service providers will become more sensitive to the educational aspects of services to special needs children, and special educators will become more aware of each child's health and social service needs. The interdigitation of agencies and the coordination of required resources, however, will not be accomplished without stress.

The identification and use of appropriate public and private funds is particularly vital to the success of a state's Part H program. Financing is a significant responsibility of states participating in the program; even modest projections of service needs that are to be addressed by the Part H program underscore the importance of assured adequate funding sources. Unfortunately, federal resources currently allocated for early intervention are relatively small. In addition to planning and development activities, states are expected to use their allotments: 1) to expand on services that already are in existence, and 2) to supplement existing resources, that is, to finance services that would not otherwise have been paid from other public or private sources. Thus, the Part H program is intended as the payer of last resort for health-related services, with access to primary support funds expected through "assignment of financial responsibility to the appropriate agency" [§676(b)(9)(C)]. The law pointedly identifies Medicaid (Title XIX), Maternal and Child Health Block Grants (Title V), and private insurers as payers in early intervention programs.

Clearly, this language was designed to urge states to adapt their laws and regulations to use alternative financial resources for the Part H programming. Coordinating agencies risk becoming the principal payers if they ignore or hesitate to take advantage of alternative financial resources. The consequence of this error will be the needless shifting of an additional financial burden to the local or state taxpayer, and a compromise in the economy of the program, resulting in fewer children being served.

Schools currently do provide and pay for most services (e.g., occupational therapy, physical therapy, speech therapy, and counseling) received by 3- to 5-year-old children in special education programs under Part B of the EHA (Office of Special Education and Rehabilitative Services, 1987; Palfrey, DiPrete, Walker, Shannon, & Maroney, 1987; Palfrey, Singer, Raphael, & Walker, 1987; Walker, Palfrey, Butler, Singer, 1988; Walker, in press). While some states (e.g., California, Massachusetts, Wisconsin) have begun to develop interagency collaborative approaches to share the financial burden of special education programming, few school systems have taken full advantage of the health care financing opportunities available to them (Palfrey, DiPrete, et al., 1987). There are at least two reasons for this. First, even though the disciplines of health, social service, and education are being drawn inexorably together, it is difficult for professionals in the field of education to ascertain exactly what opportunities exist for financing. Also, historically, the health care financing community has been reticent to support "special education" services.

The Medicare Catastrophic Coverage Act (PL 100-360, 1988), though, clarifies the respective roles that Medicaid and education agencies must play in the delivery and financing of special education services. The act contains a new provision establishing that nothing in the Medicaid statute shall be construed as prohibiting or restricting, or authorizing the Secretary to prohibit or restrict, payment for covered services furnished to a handicapped infant, toddler, or child because such services are included in an individualized education program established pursuant to Part B of the Education of the Handicapped Act or in an individualized family service plan adopted pursuant to Part H of that act. The principal implication for action of this provision is that state and local administrators now have the opportunity to develop joint operating procedures with the states' Medicaid programs to ensure the appropriate financing of "related services."

The remainder of this chapter describes the private and public financing opportunities available for early intervention programming contemplated by PL 99-457. We describe the various financing possibilities that exist in federal legislation, that have come about as a result of legal precedent, or that may be available through private health insurance policies. Furthermore, this chapter provides agency leaders with effective strategies for policy changes that will benefit both the health care and educational systems, and ultimately children at risk.

FAMILY RESOURCES

Unlike the Part B program, which specifies the provision of the special education services at no cost to parents, the Part H language calls for developmental services that are provided at no cost "except where federal or state law provides for a system of payments by families, including a schedule of sliding fees" [§672(2)(B)]. It appears, therefore, that families with handicapped children may be called upon under state or federal law to contribute to the cost of services required by the child. For example, if the state determines that the family is in a position to help defer the transportation needed to and from service providers, it may require that participation.

The potential for undue burden to the family is considered by the law's requirement for a schedule of sliding fees. That is, the state cannot require a family's financial participation without reference to its ability to participate, and without a sliding fee scale that can match that ability to an appropriate contribution level.

PRIVATE INSURANCE

Private insurance represents a substantial but largely untapped funding resource for handicapped children's programming. Despite the fact that a growing number of American children lack health insurance coverage, most children are privately insured; in 1986 approximately 45.4 million or almost three-quarters of American children had private health insurance throughout the year (National Center for Health Statistics, 1987).

Insurance plans, however, vary significantly in terms of the scope of covered services and the quality of the benefit provided. The reality is that, for a significant proportion of families, health insurance coverage is marginal or inadequate. While privately insured children usually have a broad range of benefits that includes hospitalization, physician services, drugs, laboratory services, and even many therapeutic services, the utility of these benefits often is restricted by routine provisions for deductibles and copayments, as well as specific limitations on visits or dollar amounts. Expenses incurred even as the result of a child's mild illness may result in out-of-pocket charges to the parents for: 1) the insurance deductible, and 2) a large percentage of the costs of covered services. For more serious or long-term conditions, and especially for families of disabled children, these underlying mechanisms can result in a depletion of benefits and, in some cases, significant out-of-pocket expenses.

Health insurance reimbursements for publicly provided services (e.g., those delivered through special education programs) often are specifically denied. In addition, health insurance policies are regulated at the state level, and it is sometimes difficult to get legislatures to mandate appropriate benefits. Moreover, employers' self-insured plans, which are governed by federal ERISA (Employment Retirement Income Security Act, PL 93-406, 1974) laws, are exempt from regulation under state laws.

Using Private Insurance to Finance Handicapped Children's Programs

While the insurance industry has tended to cover ancillary (related) services, those same services generally have been specifically excluded from coverage when provided by the educational system. The EHA calls for a "free appropriate public education" meaning "special education and related services which . . . have been provided at *public expense*, under public supervision and direction and without charge" [§602, 20 U.S.C., 1402(16)]. Even though Part B of the act, which applies to children ages 3 and older, requires services to be provided at public expense, several states have passed legislation that requires third party insurers to pay for some medically necessary services provided during the course of the school day. Other states have established precedents that permit, but do not mandate, families to use private insurance to cover some school-provided services (Palfrey, Singer, Walker, & Butler, 1986).

Part H of the EHA, on the other hand, specifically directs states to utilize all public and private resources (including private insurance) to help defray the costs of health care related to early intervention services. However, few states as yet have developed early intervention programs that utilize private health insurance resources. Some states have programs that require the provision of services at no cost to families. Because most policies include copayment or deductible clauses, such enabling program legislation effectively bars use of private insurance for program services. In accordance with the federal statutes, appropriate changes in state laws could open new avenues of funding for early intervention programming that can significantly offset the total burden that now is borne by state and local taxpayers. Indeed, in some states public agencies have opted to pay deductibles and copayments for children who are otherwise privately insured.

Private Insurance Opportunities for the Future

While it is clear that private insurance currently is a less than ideal resource for early intervention services, it still is an option widely available for a great many children. National attention has been drawn to the issues arising out of lack of appropriate coverage for large segments of the population. Efforts are underway around the country to find viable strategies to provide insurance to the uninsured. In addition, changes in state laws can improve the availability of private insurance benefits for coverage of early intervention services. Given that good programming for handicapped children requires the broadest possible base of financial support and the fact that laws applicable to commercial health insurance are within the jurisdiction of the states, state educational leaders can have significant impact on needed insurance reform relevant to children. A further discussion of major insurance issues is presented below.

Un-Insurance At present, most people have access to private health insurance through their place of employment, but many businesses either do not offer health insurance benefits or offer insurance packages that make coverage of dependents unaffordable to employees. Consequently, large numbers of American children (approximately 15%) are without public or private coverage throughout the year (National Center for Health Statistics, 1987). When people with low incomes alone (those more likely to have children at risk of handicap or developmental disability) are considered, the percentages are considerably higher. Data from the 1980 National Medical Care Utilization and Expenditure Survey (NMCUES) indicated, for example, that while about 22% of all children were uninsured for at least some part of the year, approximately 35% of poor and near-poor children lacked coverage during the year (Butler, Winter, Singer, & Wenger, 1985). Because of their status as dependents, children are disproportionately uninsured. The development of strategies that focus on broadening the availability of comprehensive health insurance coverage to this population is vital. A recent proposal by Freedman, Klepper, Duncan, and Bell (1988) suggests using public schools (rather than employment) as the grouping mechanism for the provision of private insurance for school children and their family members.

Under-Insurance As was mentioned above, the problems attendant to under-insurance are characterized by limitations on coverage that compromise access to services. One approach to remedying the variability and inadequacy of coverage for children is to mandate benefits for health services called for under federal programs. Though such laws apply only to insured health policies sold in a state, regulatory standards can be established to ensure that uniform, minimum levels of coverage are available. One type of minimum benefits legislation for children is Florida's Child Health Assurance Act (F.S.627.6416, 627.6579), passed in 1986, which requires the provision of coverage for well-child services by all health insurance carriers doing business in the state. Covered services include a history, physical examination, *developmental assessment*, laboratory tests, immunizations, and anticipatory guidance. Covered services are exempt from cost-sharing (i.e., deductibles and other limitations do not apply), and there is no cap on covered services. The program is especially significant for children of families with little disposable income, who often forego early identification procedures because those procedures are not covered under the family's benefit package. Clearly such successful efforts to mandate coverages provide opportunities for ensuring that children at risk for handicaps are fully covered for all medically necessary diagnostic and intervention services.

MEDICAID

Medicaid is a joint federal/state program designed to provide health care financing for low-income individuals. Federal regulations for the mandatory and optional Medicaid programs are broadly drawn, and each state has extensive latitude to determine program components and eligibility criteria for participation in each program. Among the allowable Medicaid services that may be furnished to children of low-income families are many of the early intervention services required by infants and toddlers. Federal law mandates the availability of certain services, including outpatient hospital services, physicians' services, and Early and Periodic Screening, Diagnosis, and Treatment (EPSDT). It also gives states the option to cover other services such as clinic services, home health services, case management, private duty nursing, ancillary therapies, and the services of licensed practitioners such as psychologists and psychiatric social workers.

The Medicaid program provides health care financing for about half of all low-income children in the United States (House Ways and Means Committee, 1985). During 1985, there were more than 9.2 million children receiving Medicaid benefits as categorically needy. "Categorically needy" is a term applied to people in the "regular" Medicaid program. These individuals participate in one of the Medicaid cash assistance programs: Aid to Families with Dependent Children (AFDC), Supplemental Security Income (SSI), or subsidized or foster care and adoption assistance. Eligibility criteria, however, are defined at the discretion of the state legislature and consequently vary considerably from state to state. (For example, the Children's Defense Fund reported that Medicaid and AFDC state eligibility standards in 1984 varied between 16%–78% of the federal poverty level).

States may opt to offer a Medicaid "medically needy" program to individuals whose income and resources are too high for them to receive cash benefits but who are too poor to pay for medical care. (Eligibility may be based on an income of up to 133.3% of the AFDC payment level [which can vary between 35%–100% of the federal poverty level], depending on the state. States also may permit a family to qualify for assistance if it has incurred medical expenses that would adjust its income down to the medically needy income eligibility level.) In 1985, another 1.7 million children were receiving benefits as medically needy. Furthermore, in 1986 and 1987, Congress established optional poverty level eligibility categories requiring states to cover children born after September 30, 1983. Pregnant women and their infants under 1 year of age with incomes up to 185% of the federal poverty level may be covered at a state's discretion. The same is true for young children up to age 5 in families with incomes up to 100% of the federal poverty level.

It is important to emphasize the license given the states by the federal government with respect to Medicaid coverage. The federal portion of the Medicaid program covers from 50% to 83% of the states' cost-of-service provision. While provision of certain services is mandatory, each state has considerable control over the amount, duration, and scope of the services that it covers. Restrictions may be placed on the number of visits, number of days, length of time, and exact type of services for which reimbursement will be provided.

The most important source of coverage for low-income children who are at risk or handicapped is the EPSDT (Early and Periodic Screening, Diagnosis, and Treatment) program because it is designed to provide Medicaid children with health care services similar to those available to more affluent children. Since EPSDT includes screening and diagnostic services as well as treatment, it can be used flexibly to fashion programs targeted at high risk groups, such as infants and toddlers with diagnoses that have a high probability of resulting in developmental delay. Consequently, as with many other services for children required under Part H, Medicaid can be a major source of funds for early identification and intervention programming.

The requirement to provide EPSDT services is different from the requirement to offer other services in that it obligates states to inform the families of eligible children as to the availability and characteristics of the EPSDT program, assist with referral to providers, and follow-up to ensure that necessary diagnostic and treatment services are provided.

Minimum service requirements for EPSDT pertain primarily to the screening examinations, which are to be provided in accordance with a state's periodicity schedule. (A state's periodicity schedule must: 1) meet reasonable standards of medical and dental practice determined by the agency after consultation with recognized medical and dental organizations involved in child health care; 2) specify the screening services applicable at each stage of a recipient's life, beginning with a neonatal examination and extending to the age at which an individual is no longer eligible; and 3) at the agency's option, provide for screening services in addition to those specified in the periodicity schedule.) These minimum requirements must include growth and developmental assessments as well as unclothed physical examinations and appropriate vision, hearing, and laboratory tests, and also appropriate immunizations. The diagnostic and treatment services that must be provided are those available under the state plan as well as certain additional vision, hearing, and dental services.

EPSDT regulations also permit states to cover any Medicaid-allowed medical services and remedial care, even if the service is not available to Medicaid recipients generally. Thus if the state opts to extend such coverage, children enrolled in EPSDT can receive any diagnostic or treatment service found medically necessary as a result of a screening examination. Even treatments for conditions not initially identified through a scheduled screening examination may be covered, as long as the examination indicated the need for subsequent diagnosis and monitoring. States also may choose to increase the number of screening examinations over and above those described in their periodicity schedules. A state that chooses to expand coverage of diagnostic and treatment services for EPSDT children may specify limits for these additional benefits or else simply indicate in their plans that when specified criteria are met, additional services will be authorized on an individual basis (with prior authorization). Fox and Yoshpe (1987) appraised the opportunity posed by EPSDT as follows:

EPSDT's importance as a potential source of financing care for developmentally delayed infants and toddlers in states that otherwise offer insufficient early intervention services cannot be overstated. States can use the EPSDT expanded treatment option to cover services not included in their state plans or to lift restrictions on services that are available but in limited amount, duration, or scope. By expanding coverage policies under EPSDT rather than under the Medicaid program as a whole, states may offer additional benefits to the child population only. (p. 36)

The intent of Congress to invest early in the children's health needs is reflected in both the EPSDT and Part H programs of the EHA. Each program is an attempt to ensure that disabling problems will be identified and treated as early as possible. Legal precedents like *Commonwealth of Massachusetts v. Secretary of Health and Human Services*, and the language of the EHA-H identifying Medicaid specifically as a payer for early intervention services, galvanized the opportunities for using Medicaid financing to support the medical and health-related components of the early intervention and special education programs.

PROGRAMS FOR CHILDREN WITH SPECIAL HEALTH CARE NEEDS

The Maternal and Child Health (MCH) Program, authorized as Title V of the Social Security Act, has been a 50-year federal effort to "extend and improve" state health services for children and their mothers. Since 1981, states have been afforded considerable freedom to determine how federal block grant allocations and state matching funds will be distributed. The population served by the Title V program includes all women 15–44 years of age as well as children from birth to 21. Like the Part H amendments, recent amendments to the Title V regulations specify the provision of case management services as a component of states' programs for children with special health care needs.

Commensurate with congressional intent that early intervention programs be payers of last resort, Part H specifically acknowledges Title V as an important funding source. Children eligible for both programs can receive services through the early intervention but with funding drawn from block grant and state MCH resources.

IEPs AND IFSPs AS FINANCING PLANS

The Individualized Education Program (IEP) in Part B and the Individualized Family Service Plan (IFSP) in Part H are program components designed to ensure that each child in the special education or early intervention program is properly evaluated by a multidisciplinary team that includes the parents and that an appropriate plan for treatment is prescribed. Both the IEP and the IFSP are to specify all relevant services for the child and his or her family without regard to the services available from existing programs.

Once the IEP or IFSP is established, it is possible to develop a reasonable estimate of the cost of each of the services that the child and family will receive. The plans would specify service needs, outcome objectives, costs, and time frames, and could be used for both case management and the allocation of fiscal responsibility to the various public and private payers, including parents. For example, on the basis of an IFSP, a private insurance carrier could be charged for health services (e.g., physical, occupational, and speech therapy) covered in the family's policy; Medicaid could be billed for the services it provides enrolled children; and the parents, provided they had sufficient resources, could be required to finance services not covered by public or private insurance or the school system (e.g., home modifications). Periodic review of each child's plan, as called for in the EHA, will necessitate concomitant updates of the cost allocation procedure and will facilitate a progress-oriented tracking mechanism for each of the payers involved.

CONCLUSIONS

With the passage of PL 99-457, Congress has provided new tools that will expand program opportunities for children with special needs. However, the success of this effort rests on the understanding that economic and political factors underlie our abilities to ensure adequate public and private health financing. Consequently, educational leaders must commit themselves to focusing on two types of activities: 1) the optimization of funding through the coordination of existing public and private resources, and 2) advocating for health financing policy reforms that can take advantage of the opportunities provided for in state and federal legislation. Accessibility and uniformity of health insurance are particularly important for the health of children with special needs.

REFERENCES

Butler, J.A., Winter, W.D., Singer, J.D., & Wenger, M. (1985). Medical care use and expenditure among children and youth in the United States: Analysis of a national probability sample. *Pediatrics, 76*(4), 495–506.

Cohen, J. (1987). OBRA-86 Update. *American Academy of Pediatrics Child Health Financing Report. 5*(4), 3.

Commonwealth of Masschusetts v. Secretary of Health and Human Services (1987). *Federal Reporter, 816*(2), 796–805.

Devito, K.M. (1987, July–August). Medicaid funds must support "IEP" goals. *Youth Law News*, pp. 15–17.

Education for All Handicapped Children Act of 1975, PL 94-142. (August 23, 1977). 20 U.S.C. 1401 et seq: *Federal Register, 42*(163), 42474–42518.

Education of the Handicapped Act Amendments of 1986, PL 99-457. (1986).

Fox, H.B., & Neiswander, L. (1988). *Private health insurance financing for early intervention services.* Washington, DC: Fox Health Policy Consultants.

Fox, H.B. & Yoshpe, R. (1986). *Private health insurance coverage of chronically ill children.* Washington, DC: Fox Health Policy Consultants.

Fox, H.B., & Yoshpe, R. (1987). *Medicaid financing for early intervention services.* Washington, DC: Fox Health Policy Consultants.

Freedman, S.A., Klepper, B.R., Duncan, R.P., & Bell, S. (1988). Coverage of the uninsured and under-insured: A proposal for school enrollment-based family health insurance. *New England Journal of Medicine 318*(13), 843–847.

National Center for Health Statistics. (1986, July 18). Advance report of final natality statistics, 1986. *Monthly Vital Statistics Report, 35*(4).

National Center for Health Statistics. Ries, P. (1987, September 18). *Health care coverage by age, sex, race and family income: United States, 1986.* Advance Data from Vital and Health Statistics, No. 139. Department of Health and Human Services Pub. No. (PHS) 87–1250. Public Health Service, Hyattsville, MD: Department of Health and Human Services.

Office of Special Education and Rehabilitative Services. (1987). *Ninth annual report to Congress on the implementation of the Education of the Handicapped Act.* Washington, DC: Government Printing Office.

Palfrey, J.S., DiPrete, L., Walker, D.K., Shannon, K., & Maroney, E. (1987). *School children dependent on medical technology.* Washington, DC: D:ATA Institute.

Palfrey, J.S., Singer, J.D., Raphael, E.S., & Walker, D.K. (1987). *Providing therapeutic services in various educational settings: An analysis of the related services provision of P.L. 94-142 in five urban school districts.* Boston: The Children's Hospital.

Palfrey, J.S., Singer, J.D., Walker, D.K., & Butler, J.A. (1986). Health and special education: A study of new developments for handicapped children in five metropolitan communities. *Public Health Reports, 101*(4) 379–388.

U.S. Department of Health and Human Services. The National Center for Health Statistics. The National Medical Care Utilization and Expenditure Survey (NMCUES). (1980).

U.S. House of Representatives Committee on Ways and Means. (1985). *Children in poverty.* Washington, DC: U.S. Government Printing Office.

Walker, D.K., Palfrey, J.S., Butler, J.A., & Singer, J.D. (1988). Use and sources of payment for health and community services for children with impaired mobility. *Public Health Reports, 103*(4), 411–414.

Walker, D.K. (in press). Educational options for chronically-ill children. In R.E.K. Stein (Ed.), *New directions in caring for children with chronic illness.* New York: Springer-Verlag.

THE USE OF OUTCOME MEASURES IN IMPLEMENTING POLICIES FOR HANDICAPPED CHILDREN

10

Duncan MacRae, Jr.

UNTIL THE LATE 1960s, POLICYMAKERS TENDED TO ASSUME THAT WHEN they enacted a law, they knew what it would accomplish. For example, they expected parts of the Social Security Act of 1935 to provide for the security of elderly citizens and of widows with children. They did not realize that the eligible groups would grow and funds would become scarce. We now know that circumstances change and that we must continually rethink and often redesign laws that once seemed well designed. We also have come to recognize that some laws will not be implemented as they were intended. We now pay increasing attention to results and to ways to ensure that the results we expect from a policy will be achieved. Even when the causal principles embedded in a policy seem initially supported by prior research, we now recognize that, unless that research was

---

For helpful comments, I am indebted to James J. Gallagher and H. Rutherford Turnbull, III. However, they are not responsible for my conclusions.

based on a real-world intervention, it does not guarantee similar effectiveness after the policy has been enacted.

Tangible results are not, of course, the only important feature of policies. A policy may symbolize the commitment of society to a goal such as equality for handicapped children, or to a new image, for example, of the San Francisco Bay area (Krieger, 1981, p. 106), and such a symbolic statement may have value in itself. That statement also can be a way of inducing public political quiescence and a substitute for material outcomes (Edelman, 1964). When groups of advocates for persons with handicaps meet, however, no one claims that the advances of Public Law 94-142, the Education for All Handicapped Children Act of 1975, have been illusory. References to broad symbolism go hand in hand with concrete accounts of advances in child development.

Child advocates have become more concerned with designing policies so that they will be implemented—followed through and carried out effectively. The steps to be taken in this design process, however, depend on how designers define "implementation." Two major definitions of implementation often are considered: 1) carrying out the policy so as to achieve intermediate goals, such as service delivery—an "input" definition, and 2) achieving the ultimate goals, such as personal well-being, that the policy seeks—an "outcome" definition.

Implementation can be furthered not only by looking ahead, but also by using program evaluation to review past performance. This judgment as to whether a policy has been carried out properly might well lead us to a third and broader definition of implementation: 3) achieving the policy's goals while considering its costs and its side effects (Gallagher, 1981, p. 62). We might then ask: Has the policy been implemented efficiently? Have there been positive or negative side effects that need to be taken into account? Have there been human costs that could be reduced? Thus an extension of definition 2 might lead us to measure other outcomes as well.

From a detached academic viewpoint, definitions 2 and 3 might seem clearly superior to 1, as they can guide us to the furtherance of our ultimate values. From an advocate's viewpoint, however, they can be difficult to use, can divide the supporting group, and can invite criticism that might otherwise not be made. My aim in this chapter is to spell out the foundations and implications of definitions 2 and 3, while calling attention to their risks as well as their advantages.

RIGHTS, PROCEDURES, AND INPUTS CONTRASTED WITH OUTCOMES

Inputs versus Outcomes in Implementation

We are concerned here with policies as hypotheses.[1] A "policy," then, is defined as a statement that if the terms of a particular law are carried out, certain desired results will follow. A policy may then be said to have been implemented to the extent that those results occur (Pressman & Wildavsky, 1973, xiv), as in definition 2 above. With this definition of policy we may ask not only whether the terms of the law were carried out, but whether the law was well framed to further its purposes. The purposes or intent of a law may be inferred from its history, including hearings, reports, and debate (see Chapter 2, this volume). A law may then be amended to implement its purposes, as was done for Title I of the Elementary and Secondary Education Act of 1965 (Mazmanian & Sabatier, 1983, pp. 191–192).

This notion of policy as hypothesis may be applied to either inputs or outcomes, as desired consequences of the law. For policies aimed at affecting people by changing their life conditions, we speak of "inputs," by which we mean the changed conditions that are sought—for example, services delivered or desegregation, or for handicapped children, the drawing up of Individualized Education Programs (IEPs) or the provision of a less restrictive environment. These are possible results of a law, but not ultimate outcomes.[2] By "outcomes" we mean valued or disvalued characteristics of the people affected, such as learning, skills, employment, self-esteem, well-being, health, or disease.

Thus Hargrove et al. (1983) emphasize inputs in analyzing the implementation of PL 94-142. These writers go beyond schools' formal compliance with this law in mainstreaming handicapped children and providing the procedural rights of IEPs; they go on to examine the creation of the needed organizational climates in schools. They do not, however, ask

---

[1] In political science, "policy" also has been defined not in terms of hypotheses but as "what governments choose to do or not to do" (Dye, 1987, p. 2). One purpose of political scientists in defining "policy" is to study the causes of various government actions. For this purpose it may suffice to examine the things that governments do and try to explain them; the researcher may not have to ask whether a purpose was carried out well or poorly.

[2] Martin (Chapter 2, this volume) refers to "major features" of PL 94-142 that are inputs as defined here: "due process, least restrictive environment (LRE), nondiscriminatory testing, and Child Find."

about the quality of educational treatment resulting from professional judgements about children, nor about "the ultimate educational consequences for handicapped students" (p. 18).

We may need to study inputs such as organizational climates—intervening effects of organizations or groups—because they are important means to producing outcomes. Thus Dokecki and Heflinger (Chapter 4, this volume) stress the importance of strengthening the families of young children with handicapping conditions. We can monitor this strengthening, as we can other inputs, while also monitoring its effects.

We may go further, however, and consider hypotheses concerning outcomes. A number of such hypotheses are provided by the text of Part H. "Findings and Policy," of Title I of PL 99-457 (The Education of the Handicapped Act Amendments of 1986), the Title amending PL 94-142 to provide for handicapped infants and toddlers.

> Sec. 671. (a) FINDINGS—The Congress finds that there is an urgent and substantial need—
> 1) to enhance the development of handicapped infants and toddlers and to minimize their potential for developmental delay,
> 2) to reduce the educational costs to our society, including our Nation's schools, by minimizing the need for special education and related services after handicapped infants and toddlers reach school age,
> 3) to minimize the likelihood of institutionalization of handicapped individuals and maximize the potential for their independent living in society, and
> 4) to enhance the capacity of families to meet the special needs of their infants and toddlers with handicaps.
> b) POLICY—It is therefore the policy of the United States to provide financial assistance to states—
> 1) to develop and implement a statewide, comprehensive, coordinated, multidisciplinary, interagency program of early intervention services for handicapped infants and toddlers and their families,
> 2) to facilitate the coordination of payment for early intervention services from Federal, State, local, and private sources (including public and private insurance coverage), and
> 3) to enhance its capacity to provide quality early intervention services and expand and improve existing early intervention services being provided to handicapped infants, toddlers, and their families.

The word "therefore," after "POLICY," sets forth a number of hypotheses—that the various policies listed will have the effects listed under "FINDINGS." The reader who tries to link the findings above (specifying some, but not all, of the criterion values that might be used) with the policies proposed, focusing on early intervention services,[3] will recog-

---

[3] If early intervention is extended to prenatal programs that reduce the incidence of handicaps, these other programs may facilitate implementation of programs for the care and treatment of handicapped children by reducing their cost.

nize the complexity of the task, the importance of spelling out just what those policies and services are to be, and our need to know the effects of those services. As Dokecki and Heflinger (Chapter 4, this volume) note, "This telegraphic statement of the presumed theory of PL 99-457 is breathtaking. We encounter bold conjectures. . . . " The reader who has some knowledge of problems of interagency coordination also will recognize that, as they go on to say, we "are exposed to death-defying leaps over organizational chasms."

The question I shall address here concerns our efforts, not simply to set these policies in motion, but to test them repeatedly by monitoring, not just that motion, nor just their intermediate effects on inputs, but also their ultimate effects. Can we test them in this way? Should we try? What additional criterion variables might we consider monitoring? How seriously, in other words, should we take this law's complex statement of goals and policy in view of the pervasive belief among students of implementation that we cannot take for granted that these hypotheses will be fulfilled? We also ask, by implication, whether these value criteria are all that should be considered, and whether the best policies to satisfy these criteria have been formulated in full detail.

Nonteleological and Input-Based Definitions of Implementation

The criteria used to judge policy alternatives can be classified as to whether they depend on empirical knowledge of valued effects of policies—teleological criteria—or are independent of such knowledge—nonteleological criteria (MacRae & Wilde, 1979). In actuality, dependence on causal information is a matter of degree. To judge a law right or wrong in terms of its words and their meaning does not require knowledge of effects; but to judge its implementation successful in terms of setting up procedures or establishing suitable climates in schools (management objectives), we need to know something about causes and effects. To judge what children learn or how they feel, including effects in later life (program objectives), we need to know still more.

In the debates about policies for education of handicapped children, some arguments for PL 94-142 and for more recent reforms have been couched in terms that do not require any observation of ultimate outcomes. Martin (Chapter 2, this volume), for example, points out that PL 94-142 "expresses a moral commitment . . . that people with disabilities share the same constitutional rights as nondisabled people." Admission to schools in the mainstream and parental participation in the development of IEPs, if these conditions express this moral commitment, might be considered the goals of policy in this view. Hill and Madey (1982) go a step further in concluding that PL 94-142 has led to increased spending per capita for services to handicapped children (more than twice what is spent for services to nonhandicapped children), and to "more and better special educational services" (p. 21). These, however, still are not the ultimate outcomes we are discussing here.

A parallel argument for these policies is that their goals are fulfilled if certain procedures are carried out. "An 'appropriate' education under PL 94-142 is one that results from an individual planning conference, including specified participants, and is documented in an IEP, following a specified form. Thus, the legal standard is a process, not a result" (Hargrove et al., 1983, p. 13), "in the belief that a fair process will produce an acceptable result" (Turnbull & Turnbull, 1978, pp. 116–117). By this argument, we are asked to look only at inputs that result from the policy, such as least restrictive placement, and not at ultimate outcomes.

Circular Definitions versus Independent Measurement of Effects

Another way of avoiding or concealing questions of efficiency and cost is to define "handicapped" in such a way that the definition alone requires certain types of policy or excludes others. By 1960, persons with handicaps were being defined as needing separate services. This circular definition made mainstreaming logically impossible. More recently, Brewer and Kakalik (1979) have defined handicapped children as "young people from 0 to 21 years of age who are physically or mentally impaired to the degree that they need services not required by 'normal' youth" (p. 4). Kirk and Gallagher (1983) similarly state that "the exceptional child is one who deviates from the average child in ways that require changes in school practice for the child to reach full potential" (p. 28). Let us assume that "changes in school practice" means "school practices not required by 'normal' children," as in Brewer and Kakalik's phrasing. To define handicapped children in terms of services required, or exceptional children in terms of special school practices required, risks making the converse error; it logically precludes saying that any child, defined independently of treatment as physically or mentally impaired, should not be provided with special services or a different sort of school practice.

What is needed, if we are to be able to ask whether children with particular handicaps should be treated in certain ways, is to define the condition of handicap independently of the treatment, in terms of children's present capacities and their expected development under specified conditions. The proposed sort of definition would allow us to examine explicitly what the treatment, if any, should be, in view of our valuative criteria.

Professionals have, of course, reasoned from diagnosis to need in order to define specific types of handicaps, but their classifications might be clearer and more useful if this reasoning was always made explicit by the use of noncircular definitions. As Gates (1975) points out, "the eventual political identification of a need arises from the interactions of a specific service bureaucracy and a defined social group and not as the result of rational deduction" (p. 2). Clearer definitions are needed if this process is to be made more rational and less political.

Circular definitions of "handicapped" in terms of service needs also can limit the range of policies that we consider. Wang (Chapter 3, this volume) argues that "training should be emphasized as a function of special educators, school psychologists, speech clinicians, school social workers, and other specialized staff, all of whom should work to share their competencies with general education teachers and other staff members." This would not literally contradict the above definition, as services might be continued even when provided less by specialists. There is a risk, however, that a service-based definition of persons with handicaps can preserve a proliferation of specialties when they are inefficient or not needed. The same question might be raised about the multidisciplinary early intervention provided for in PL 99-457. Although multidisciplinary assessment can be a remedy for discriminatory testing (Turnbull et al., 1983, p. 498), it still can be scrutinized in terms of efficiency. The legal recognition of existing specialties may be an effective way to gain support for a proposed policy, but conceivably other professional roles would exist to permit more effective and efficient treatment of children. A redefinition of "handicapped," stripped of any explicit or implicit reference to existing service specialties, might allow us to give more consideration to possible changes in professional roles, defined in interrelation with the roles of family members.

A revised definition of this sort also might emphasize questions as to just what children should be given what treatments, as judged by measurement of benefits and costs as well as of equity and rights. It might help to cope with Wang's (Chapter 3, this volume) "Catch-22" dilemma in which a group of children make progress in a program that does not label them as handicapped, thus depriving them of the label (decertification) and the schools of their subsidy. If the children in question are identified in terms of specific characteristics such as their capacities,[4] then we can meaningfully ask whether they should be treated in special ways. Con-

---

[4] At stake here is the question of what we should do when our knowledge is uncertain. Questions of presumption and burden of proof arise more often than scientists might realize. The law deals directly with these presumptions, rather than leaving them to be governed by informal social norms.

nected with this judgment is the possibility that, for some children (e.g., aggressive children), mainstreaming may be excessively costly either to the community or to other children. This does not appear to be the same balance that would be drawn by the "least restrictive environment" principle, which allows restrictiveness only when it is necessary to further "the primary purpose of education in the public schools, namely, an appropriate education" (Turnbull et al., 1983, p. 506). This legal value criterion, incorporated in PL 94-142, does not explicitly apply to monetary or social costs to others, even though these factors are covered in an analysis of the interests affected (Turnbull et al., 1983, pp. 510–511). (Turnbull & Turnbull [1986] note that regulations concerning least-restrictive appropriate placement can take into account costs of disruption by judging that the handicapped student's needs cannot be met in that setting and that placement there is not appropriate [pp. 135–136].)

Teleological Definitions for Implementation

In a fully teleological perspective, we would judge whether policy is desirable in terms of its ultimate results. Martin (1972), for example, has stated that "Ultimately, . . . the definitive goal for both the handicapped and nonhandicapped is a productive, satisfying life as a member of society." This includes "self regard achieved through the development of competence and socialization and productive behavior achieved through employment or productivity" (p. 523). If these phrases were included in a law, we might ask whether measurement of the corresponding results would help to tell us whether the law had been well implemented or could be improved; if they were part of the official goals of a group, they might similarly guide its contributions to future policymaking.

Wang (Chapter 3, this volume) also stresses measures of effectiveness. In describing the adaptive learning environments model (ALEM) program for mildly handicapped children in New York City, she characterizes it as producing "significant achievement gains, greater than expected" in reading and mathematics. She goes on to urge that we move beyond a "service delivery mode" and examine "the relationships between the services and student learning." She points to the need to examine program effectiveness, noting that "it is not enough to implement what seem to be better services . . .; they may or may not increase and improve learning in students."

While advocating outcome measures, however, we must recognize that not all measures are equally valid indicators of the values we seek. Wang earlier notes the parallel between PL 94-142 and the Brown decision on school desegregation. Social scientists have extensively studied the effects of school desegregation on minority students' learning, but

Crain and Carsrud (1985) argue that "A good case can be made that improvement in academic test performance was at best a secondary goal of the lawyers who brought the Brown suit to court. For them, the schools were the keystone of an edifice of segregated institutions" (p. 227). Thus, outcome measures, narrowly conceived, may miss major goals of policy—even if valid measures can be obtained, which is not always the case.

EFFICIENCY AND COST-EFFECTIVENESS: INCLUDING COST AS A CRITERION

So far, we have compared perspectives that do not go to the ultimate outcomes to judge policies, with one that requires that these outcomes be examined; but even if we observe and measure outcomes, we also must ask whether they can be obtained at a cost that is not excessive, or at the lowest feasible cost. This inclusion of cost as a value criterion may be challenged by those who regard equal rights for persons with handicaps as matters of high constitutional principle; judges and lawyers who study constitutional law often are skeptical of the "balancing" of costs with benefits in such matters (Gottlieb, 1968; Tribe, 1985). Court cases concerning treatment of handicapped children by schools also have led to the conclusion that schools are required to furnish needed services "regardless of cost" (Hargrove et al., 1983, p. 8). (Turnbull et al. [1983], however, note that social policymaking typically balances competing values [p. 503].) At the same time, other advocates for persons with handicaps do consider cost. Wang is concerned with the efficiency of programs, implying that their costs matter. Senator Lowell P. Weicker (R.-CT), arguing for PL 99-457, claimed that "the savings to be derived from providing such services are far greater than the actual costs of this program" (Hook, 1986, p. 1328).

The consideration of cost can take several forms. The method most often used in this field is cost-effectiveness analysis, in which costs and effects are examined in noncomparable units of measurement. If benefits can be expressed in monetary terms, cost-benefit analysis may be used. Alternatively, one might ask whether saved costs could be used to further other policies for children with handicaps, using the effectiveness of these other policies as a measure of the value of saving costs.

From Effectiveness to Cost-Effectiveness Analysis

The transition from broad valuative principles to measurement of effectiveness and cost may be observed in the case of Medicare. When this program became law in 1964, its supporters justified it primarily in general terms similar to those that we now use in supporting policies for handicapped children. Elderly citizens were considered deserving of health care to increase their security. Since that time we have seen an escalation of costs and expenditures for health care and a concern for stabilizing or reducing costs. We also have seen a greater willingness on the part of the medical profession, faced by cost-setting in terms of diagnostic-related groups (DRGs), to encourage measurement of the effects of medical care, rather than simply of its delivery.

We may wish to look to the future of policies for handicapped children and to ask whether a similar change of emphasis could occur. If it does, advocates of these children may wish to be able to describe what has been accomplished in a statistical rather than anecdotal fashion. As they do, however, they also should consider the full range of social costs affected by policies such as PL 94-142 and PL 99-457 (a cost reduction was promised in the "Findings") and the reduced costs in time expended by parents.

Arguments about the cost-effectiveness of policies for handicapped children will be harder to support than arguments based on legal or moral principles, which require fewer data. However, when we compare public expenditures in various policy areas, such as education and national defense, the standard of cost-effectiveness can be brought to bear on policies in competing areas as well. Policy analysts prefer to ask these questions in all policy areas when possible and to substitute detailed observation for broad rhetorical appeals. There is thus a possible difference between the analyst's perspective and the advocate's as to where the burden of proof lies, especially when a policy or program is vulnerable to political attack and data are inadequate.

Screening

Although questions of morality and rights are involved in policies for handicapped children, we also can gain a useful perspective by looking at these policies from the viewpoint of efficiency alone. In this perspective, the analysis of screening by decision trees (MacRae & Wilde, 1979, Chapter 4) seems relevant. In principle, any student in a school may be categorized and assigned to a particular instructional treatment in terms of expected benefits and costs to society. The questions that arise then are: How many and what kind of categories should be established? What are the costs of screening? How are these costs related to the reliability or validity of the results of screening? What different treatments should be assigned in view of the classifications made in screening and the expected results from treating children with a particular handicap in a particular way? One then could add to these value criteria measures of equity effects. If categorization creates stigma, with resulting absolute or differential social costs, these costs can be subtracted from the net benefits that might otherwise have been obtained, and policies can be designed to reduce these costs (Gallagher, 1972).

Classification is done extensively in schools, but, in Wang's (Chapter 3, this volume) judgment, the classification of handicapped children has been inefficient. Reynolds, Wang, and Walberg (1987) point out that existing categories for mildly handicapped children are inconsistently applied, incomplete in coverage, and perhaps replaceable by "a general education system that is more inclusive and that better serves all students" (p. 384). One principle of screening tells us that if a classification of children into categories makes no difference in the effects of treatment, this classification is not worth its cost. This argument was brought to bear in favor of mainstreaming.

The logic of IEPs seems to run counter to this approach. The word "individualized" seems to suggest that there must be as many categories as there are students (the main implication of this term is, of course, the establishment of due process rights for parents and children); but in practice diagnostic categories are limited in number. The guarantee of equal treatment need not imply that all children receive the same expensive mutli-specialty diagnosis that is appropriate for those who have received an initial test and have been found to have greater prospects of benefiting from further diagnosis.

MONITORING IMPLEMENTATION AND THE USE OF INFORMATION

Judging policy implementation in terms of consequences requires measuring them (MacRae, 1985). Such measurement, or, in general terms, the use of information, is nevertheless more convenient and more useful at some stages of the policy formation process than at others.

Phases of Policymaking and Uses of Information

In the early stages of policy development, both carefully designed experiments and "bold conjectures" (Chapter 4, Dokecki & Heflinger, this volume) are most often seen when academic specialists join with advocacy groups in support of policies for children. Less frequent, until the era of social experiments of the 1960s and 1970s, have been real-life experiments to examine the effects of a policy implemented outside the "laboratory school."

The period immediately following enactment of a policy often is the time of its greatest vulnerability to evaluative information. The start-up period can involve initial inefficiencies, a need to revise procedures, and inadequate personnel training. High expectations may coexist with incomplete implementation and inadequate information. At this period, evaluation research usually is not welcomed and perhaps should not be, unless it is clearly understood as formative, seeking out the best local versions of a program so as to propagate their examples. Leaders in the movement for PL 94-142 wished at this stage to avoid the complications that Head Start encountered and therefore sought to limit research to inputs and compliance.

In this early period after enactment, opponents of a policy may favor summative evaluation, and proponents, formative evaluation. If we look to possibilities of formative evaluation, we can consider not only selection of the best examples, but also Cooley and Bickel's (1986) proposal of "monitoring and tailoring" school programs with the aid of local information systems. Here, outcome information can be used, but primarily by local service delivery organizations, rather than by hostile outside groups. Of course, eventually outsiders have a right to know what a program is accomplishing, and proponents of the purposes of a policy need this information in order to implement it effectively. Thus, the information systems that are to be set up in the states to aid implementation of PL 99-457 (Chapter 1, this volume) should provide for outcome measures that permit incremental program improvement of the sort that Cooley and Bickel propose. Monitoring also should cover intermediate outcomes, such as family capacity to meet their children's needs (Chapter 4, Dokecki & Heflinger, this volume).

Monitoring Outcomes

Suppose we took literally the "Findings" of Title 1, Part H, of PL 99-457. We should then measure the following outcome variables:

1. Development of handicapped infants and toddlers
2. Developmental delay
3. Cost of special education and related services after handicapped infants and toddlers reach school age
4. The extent to which these children later lived independently in society
5. The capacities of families to meet the special needs of their infants and toddlers with handicaps

As we develop the information systems that will aid implementation, we face the challenge of measuring these variables and using these measures to improve the programs. Our present educational systems for nonhandicapped children rarely monitor outcomes in such a way as to permit assessment of program effects. Outcome measurement is seen as difficult, costly, delayed for years with respect to long-term outcomes, and potentially embarrassing if opponents of a program use it to argue that high expectations have not been met. In addition, measuring the condition of a child after a policy treatment is not the same as measuring *results* of this treatment (MacRae & Lanier, 1988).

Monitoring might nevertheless be aided by two types of information: 1) data on broad national samples analogous to those of the National Assessment of Educational Progress (though more costly to obtain for infants and toddlers who are not yet in school), and 2) local information systems analogous to those of Cooley and Bickel (1986). A promising "accounting plan" has been developed by Rossi (1987) for tracking the progress of special education students through and beyond school in an area of California. If these approaches can be tried experimentally, and if the measurements can be used for program improvement, they may further our ultimate policy goals in an empirically verifiable way.

Information Sources for Implementation

Not only statistical information, but consultation among implementors, can help in implementing programs. Professionals and administrators need to exchange their experiences and to benefit from what others have learned. This sort of exchange is especially necessary when a wide range of professionals is involved (Chapter 7, Hurley, this volume).

Successful implementation requires a clear vision of the final stages of service delivery. Desired outcomes are unlikely to be attained if service personnel are ill-trained, if various specialists fail to understand one another or to work as a team with child and family, or if resources are inadequate for the tasks undertaken. To look ahead to these problems, and trace them back to their sources and remedies in program design, has been called "backward mapping" (Elmore, 1982).

A special opportunity for backward mapping may exist in our federal system if the states and localities are not all exactly synchronized, as PL 99-457 seems to imply that they will be. Those local programs that get an earlier start can serve as examples that later programs can imitate or modify. Thus, the development of an informal, nonstatistical, national exchange of information may be one of the most beneficial steps that can be taken to put programs in place—a prerequisite for the further task of monitoring their outcomes.

SUMMARY

The first task in implementing policies for handicapped children is to distinguish clearly between various definitions of "implementation." A case can be made for measuring the ultimate valued outcomes of the policies, as well as costs and side effects. This approach will require extensive statistics of high quality. It can conceivably lead to improvement of the programs and wider public support for them among persons outside the advocacy group. However, such statistics can show failures as well as successes. In the early phases of a program, a more formative approach to evaluation research may be desirable; but, eventually, both advocates and the public need to know the overall balance of what has been accomplished. In addition to these statistics, nonstatistical information on implementation can be provided by national networks of involved professionals.

REFERENCES

Brewer, G.D., & Kakalik, J.S. (1979). *Handicapped children: Strategies for improving services.* New York: McGraw-Hill.

Cooley, W.W., & Bickel, W.E. (1986). *Decision-oriented educational research.* Boston: Kluwer-Nijhoff.

Crain, R.L., & Carsrud, K.B. (1985). The role of the social sciences in school desegregation policy. In R.L. Shotland & M.M. Mark (Eds.), *Social science and social policy* (pp. 219–236). Beverly Hills: Sage Publications.

Dye, T.R. (1987). *Understanding public policy* (6th ed.). Englewood Cliffs, NJ: Prentice-Hall.

Edelman, M. (1964). *The symbolic uses of politics.* Urbana: University of Illinois Press.

Elmore, R.F. (1982). Backward mapping: Implementation research and policy decisions. In W. Williams and R.F. Elmore, J.S. Hall, R. Jung, M. Kirst, S.A. MacManus, B.J. Narver, R.P. Nathan, R.K. Yin (Eds.), *Studying implementation* (pp. 18–35). Chatham, NJ: Chatham House.

Gallagher, J.J. (1972). The special education contract for mildly handicapped children. *Exceptional Children, 38*(7), 527–535.

Gallagher, J.J. (1981). Models for policy analysis: Child and family policy. In R. Haskins & J.J. Gallagher (Eds.), *Models for analysis of social policy* (pp. 37–77). Norwood, NJ: Ablex Publishing Co.

Gates, B.L. (1975, September). *Needs-based budgeting.* Paper presented at annual meeting of the American Political Science Association, San Francisco.

Gottlieb, G. (1968). *The logic of choice.* New York: Macmillan.

Hargrove, E.C., Graham, S.G., Ward, L.E., Abernethy, V., Cunningham, J., &

Vaughn, W. (1983). Regulation and schools: The implementation of equal education for handicapped children. *Peabody Journal of Education, 60*(4).
Hill, P.T., & Madey, D.L. (1982). *Educational policymaking through the civil justice system.* Santa Monica, CA: Rand Corporation.
Hook, J. (1986). Senate votes new assistance for preschool handicapped. *Congressional Quarterly Weekly Report, 44*(24), 1328.
Kirk, S.A., & Gallagher, J.J. (1983). *Educating exceptional children* (4th ed.). Boston: Houghton Mifflin.
Krieger, M.H. (1981). *Advice and planning.* Philadelphia: Temple University Press.
MacRae, D., Jr. (1985). *Policy indicators.* Chapel Hill: University of North Carolina Press.
MacRae, D., Jr., & Lanier, M.W. (1988). The use of student improvement scores in state and district incentive systems. In R. Haskins & D. MacRae (Eds.), *Policies for America's public schools* (pp. 213–239). Norwood, NJ: Ablex.
MacRae, D., Jr., & Wilde, J.A. (1979). *Policy analysis for public decisions.* Belmont, CA: Wadsworth.
Martin, E.W. (1972). Individualism and behaviorism as future trends in educating handicapped children. *Exceptional Children, 38*(7), 517–525.
Mazmanian, D.A., & Sabatier, P.A. (1983). *Implementation and public policy.* Glenview, IL: Scott, Foresman.
PL 94-142, *Education for All Handicapped Children Act of 1975.*
PL 99-457, *Education of the Handicapped Act Amendments of 1986.*
Pressman, J.L., & Wildavsky, A. (1973). *Implementation.* Berkeley: University of California Press.
Reynolds, M.C., Wang, M.C., & Walberg, H.J. (1987). The necessary restructuring of special and regular education. *Exceptional Children, 53*(5), 391–398.
Rossi, R.J. (1987). *Project MAP year one final report.* Palo Alto, CA: American Institutes for Research.
Tribe, L.H. (1985). *Constitutional choices.* Cambridge: Harvard University Press.
Turnbull, H.R., III, & Turnbull, A.P. (1978). *Free appropriate public education: Law and implementation.* Denver: Love Publishing Co.
Turnbull, H.R., III, & Turnbull, A.P. (1986). *Free appropriate public education: The law and children with disabilities.* Denver: Love Publishing Co.
Turnbull, H.R., III, Brotherson, M.J., Czyzewski, M.J., Esquith, D.S., Otis, A.K., Summers, J.A., Van Reusen, A.K., & DePazza-Conway, M. (1983). A policy analysis of "least restrictive" education of handicapped children. *Rutgers Law Journal, 14,* 489–540.

THE IMPLEMENTATION OF SOCIAL POLICY
A POLICY ANALYSIS CHALLENGE

11

James J. Gallagher

THE PURPOSE OF THIS CHAPTER IS TO PRESENT THE REASONS FOR THE CURrent interest in policy analysis and to describe a seven-stage model designed to analyze the effectiveness of policy implementation. The legislation used to illustrate this process is Public Law 99-457, Part H, The Education of the Handicapped Act Amendments of 1986, which proposes a major new approach to the care and education of infants and toddlers with handicapping conditions, or those who are at risk for such conditions.

The careful analysis of public policy is a relatively new phenomenon in the United States. It seems to be part of a larger movement to systematize the design and execution of programs whose goals are the solving or the amelioration of significant social problems in our society (Haskins & Gallagher, 1981; MacRae & Wilde, 1979; Nagel, 1983; Wildavsky, 1979).

There has been growing concern about the viability of programs that had been established with much fanfare. The period from the early 1960s through the 1980s has marked the span of the Great Society initiated by President Lyndon Johnson, when many ambitious programs were launched to defeat poverty, illiteracy, injustice, crime, disease, and other social problems. Those Great Society programs left a legacy of public concern for people living with these problems. Many of the programs have survived that era but also have left a legacy of cynicism, for clearly not all of the projects were worthy, much money was wasted, and we often seem to have no clear idea of where to go next in our quest (see Steiner, 1981). This experience has led us to want some way of weighing, in advance, the possible effects of policy proposals and also to want methods to analyze the ways in which policies were executed (Brewer & deLeon, 1983; Mazmanian & Sabatier, 1983).

Each piece of public policy in the "child and family" arena, whether it be legislation or administrative regulations, or judicial pronouncements, really represents a hypothesis about human behaviors or about human organizations (see Chapter 10, this volume). For example, a program to rehabilitate juvenile delinquents through counseling is based upon the hypothesis that counseling can modify constructively the behavior of these delinquents. A policy designed to provide special education for handicapped children is based upon the assumption that such education will improve the opportunities for those handicapped citizens to adapt in the society more effectively.

TWO MAJOR STRATEGIES USED BY DECISION MAKERS IN THE PAST

As is true in the more traditional fields of science, even reasonable hypotheses are not always correct, so how does one assure oneself, as a decision maker, that one is taking the most probable route to success? A wrong decision can cost the public a pretty penny, to say nothing of the reputation of the decision maker who has been demonstrably wrong, so it is important for the public decision maker to be sure of his or her position.

Also, most of these social problems, such as poverty and issues concerning senior citizens or education, are of long standing. Their solution will require major societal investments over a considerable amount of time if there is any hope that they will be brought under control. Thus, a major policy mistake can be an economic, societal, and political disaster of considerable proportions.

Where does the public decision maker go to get help? In the past when technical information was needed from professionals (e.g., How do you prevent mental retardation?) two major strategies have been used to provide decision-makers with valid information in order to improve the decision-making. The first of these strategies can be referred to as the employment of a *professional guru* (Gallagher, 1981a). This would be a person with impressive professional credentials in his or her own particular field who is called upon to give advice on policy matters in the relevant professional domain.

This approach has resulted in the establishment of a cadre of professionals in fields such as health, education, social welfare, and so forth who have established for themselves this role of consultant. They testify before commissions, or legislative bodies, or consult on a regular basis with legislative aides or state and federal agencies. The witness lists identifying those who testify before congressional committees contain many familiar names, year after year, as the same group of experts gives their views on what proper actions should be taken on the policy problems of the moment.

The second major device to aid decision makers has been the establishment of special study committees or commissions composed of some of the most distinguished contributors to the professional field in question. In determining the membership of such commissions, due consideration is given to political factors of geography, race, and sex, as well as to ensuring representation of any raging controversies in the field. These commissions are charged with the responsibility to identify the problems in a given field, such as higher education, or health costs, or welfare, and to deliver their considered opinion on what the problem is, and what should be done about it.

Each of these strategies, employing the gurus and establishing the commissions, continues to serve useful purposes. Government officials need trusted advisors, and the commission reports highlight significant public issues. Nevertheless, both approaches have major weaknesses that have made them less useful as we become more and more committed to the need for public action on these social problems. The professional guru has the problem of being only one person with his or her own personal biases and may be giving idiosyncratic advice that would not even be supported by other members of his or her profession. The guru also shares a fundamental problem with the commission member in that, while they both may know the nature of the problem (e.g., learning disabilities), their recommended solutions may be limited by their own lack of understanding of the institutions that will be affected by their recommendations, or their understanding of how those institutions (e.g., the public schools) will react to the prospective policy shifts.

For example, many scholars have been eloquent on the need for educational reform (see Coleman & Selby 1983; Gardner, 1983), but their solutions often totally ignore the bureaucratic environment, that is, the public schools, in which the reforms must be implemented. The presence of teacher unions, the desire for autonomy by school systems, the dislike of policies being handed down from on high, all may represent barriers to policy implementation (Gallagher, 1984).

The commission strategy also may have trouble in plotting a feasible course of action to deal with the problem. Gallagher (1987) pointed out that social scientists usually have mastered one of the four areas necessary to influence public policy. This one area is the *knowledge base*, expertise in the topic at issue, whether it be young children, the family, or poverty.

The three areas not mastered by the typical social scientist are the understanding of *alternative strategies, public decision mechanisms,* and *media and communications.* While understanding the nature of the problem, they may well have an incomplete comprehension of the social institutions or systems that they propose to change. Their recommended strategies may come from their own professional disciplines rather than from the full array of policy options that should be examined because the problem almost certainly cuts across many professional disciplines. This often will result in an uncertain or unrealistic set of recommendations or alternatives that will erode the decision maker's confidence in the value of the expert.

If one wishes to modify existing legislation or regulations, then one should know how public decision making or program implementation takes place. Even sophisticated scientists often have only a vague notion of how, for example, Congress or school boards reach their decisions, and thus, scientists are unable to have the maximum influence upon them, even with valid information to deliver.

Finally, most scientists have not shown sufficient understanding of the role of the media as a communication bridge between public decision makers and professionals. Gallagher points out that if the professional wants to get a message across to the decision maker, the most promising vehicles are the popular media.

These serious strategy shortcomings make an argument for more direct and extensive training on policy development and implementation for those social scientists who wish to enter the public arena.

One particular stumbling block is the cost of the proposed "solution," which few gurus or commissions are prepared to assess. If there is anything that would ring the death knell for a promising policy, it is the failure to take into account the cost, and how that cost might be met. As we become increasingly conscious of deficit financing, cost becomes not only the last question asked, but the first as well.

It is the manifest failure of the guru and commission strategies, plus the increasing fiscal and political costs of a wrong judgment, that have led decision makers and academicians to turn to the new field of policy analysis as one possible way of helping them to design viable policies (MacRae & Wilde, 1979).

THE CHANGING ROLE OF GOVERNMENT

There has been an insufficient appreciation of the fundamental change in the role of government from the late 1930s through the 1980s. While politicians will occasionally invoke the name of Thomas Jefferson in intoning the famous phrase, "That government governs best, which governs least," it is now clear that the government at local, state, and federal levels is seen as a potential tool for solving social problems.

There are few persons who do not accept the responsibility of government to cope in some fashion with the reality of poverty or the plight of young and elderly people, or family dissolution in our society. The question asked across the political spectrum is *how* to combat the problem, not whether government should be involved. But the United States government was not designed to be an activist government. It was designed to protect us from activists, to make sure that power is not used to harm the people. Democracy, by dividing power into many different hands, effectively protects us from ugly surprises and over-ambitious men and women.

However, if government is to be used as a tool for solving social problems, there must be a concentration of power and a public consensus on what needs to be done. This consensus must be followed by action in a systematic way over a long period of time. Careful policy analysis may be one tool used to reach the consensus and to plot out subsequent courses of action.

Scarce resources are another reason for moving in the direction of a more extensive use of policy analysis. Sarason, Carroll, Maton, Cohen, and Lorentz (1977) once commented: "We have never known of a human service agency of any kind that asserted that it had the resources to accomplish its goals" (p. 19). The reason for this failure, they assert, is that the definition of the solution automatically places the solution out of reach. If physicians are necessary to the delivery of health care, or teachers with master's degrees are necessary to the education of handicapped children, then we have made certain that the goal of full service will never be reached because there never will be sufficient numbers of physicians or specially trained teachers, nor sufficient training facilities for them, to enable the society to reach the goal of full service.

Gallagher (1975) pointed out that the most popular educational model for helping emotionally disturbed and learning disabled children, the small special class, if extended to the entire group of children with special needs, would require tripling our training resources and, even then, it would take several hundred years to fully implement these models. It is necessary, sometimes, to do such policy analyses in order to see the impossibility of some options to meet the needs that are projected.

There are two types of policy analysis designed to meet two separate issues (Gallagher, 1981a). The first is designed to consider the policy options that might be available to cope with a specific problem. For example, to meet the problem of poverty in the inner city one could project options such as a jobs program, the support of early education programs, an attempt to help parents with their parenting techniques, nutritional supplements, urban renewal, and so forth. Policy analysis would attempt, by systematically displaying and examining each of the options, to help the decision maker decide which of these options, or which combination of options, might hold the greatest promise of success.

A second type of analysis may be done after policy has been established, to determine how successfully a given policy has been in meeting the problem. Hargrove (1975) once referred to implementation research as dealing with "wicked problems." He said, "These are problems which are ill formulated, in which the information is confusing, there are many clients and decision makers with conflicting values, and solutions have larger ramifications for the shape of the whole system" (p. 109). Nevertheless, these implementation analyses have been made necessary by the recognition that many seemingly good ideas in public policy have failed to achieve the goals set for them (Steiner, 1981; Weiss, 1975).

It may be that the original policy was wrongheaded, or not feasible, or poorly implemented. As we survey the wreckage of some social policies it is important that we know just what went wrong, or why things are going right in the cases when success has crowned our efforts.

The policy of sterilization of mentally retarded men and women, marked by Supreme Court Justice Oliver Wendell Holmes's ringing phrase, "Three generations of imbeciles are enough," was based on an incorrect view of genetics (see *Buck v. Bell*, 274 U.S. 200, 207 [1927]). Thus, the policy itself can be misguided.

Occasionally, we try to decree events that are beyond our power to control or influence. Like the king in *Camelot* who decreed, "The rain will never fall until after sundown, at noon the morning fog will disappear," we may decree a balanced budget, without establishing the mechanism or the necessary actions to create it.

Finally, we have to consider that the policy may be valid and within our reach but still fail because of a disjunction between the policy makers and the policy implementors (Chapter 4, this volume). As has been pointed out many times, criminal law is made by lawyers, but implemented by policemen, who may have very different views about how things should be done. Similarly, many of the recent educational reform ideas (Adler, 1984; Coleman & Selby, 1983; Gardner, 1983) have been developed by theoreticians or politicians but must be implemented by principals and classroom teachers. Sometimes there is much lost between the policy initiator and the final actor, the "street level bureaucrat" who must carry out the general policy ideas in specific cases.

POLICY IMPLEMENTATION ANALYSIS

It is the proposed implementation analysis of the legislation PL 99-457, The Education of the Handicapped Act Amendments of 1986, that will form the basis for the remainder of this chapter.

One approach to the analysis of policy implementation has been presented in the model designed by Gallagher (1981a). This model (Table 1) provides several steps that, when completed, can yield a portrait of a policy in the process of being enacted. The legislative provisions of Part H of

Table 1. Model of policy implementation analysis

Analyses steps	Analyses activities
1. Problem statement	A review of the social problem that generated the current policy
2. Policy description	A brief history, statement of goals, the anticipated beneficiaries, and the means of policy execution are noted
3. Value base for policy	A statement of the key social values that underlie the policy
4. Application of policy	The development of regulations and other measures designed to implement that policy
5. Program objectives achieved	The collection of data to indicate whether basic program objectives have been achieved
6. Barriers to implementation	Information or evidence relating to institutional, psychological, sociological, economic, political and geographic barriers inhibiting policy implementation
7. Recommendations for action	Should there be a few changes, major changes, or a search for a completely new strategy entertained?

Adapted from Haskins and Gallagher (1981).

PL 99-457 will be used to provide an illustration of how such implementation analysis steps can be taken.

1. Statement of the Problem

The first step in the implementation analysis is to review the nature of the social problem that caused the particular policy to be enacted in the first place. Many young children with handicapping conditions, or who were at risk for such handicaps, had been receiving partial or no services to meet their problems during the critical period from birth to 3 years of age. There was no vehicle to provide such children with coordinated services or care, and their families were forced to travel from one service deliverer or agency to another seeking help for their children. In many instances, the services that were provided focused exclusively upon the child and provided little assistance to the other family members who might also be in need of counseling, education, and so forth (Turnbull & Turnbull, 1986)

The prevailing professional wisdom supported the concept that the earlier in the child's life that intervention was done, the more effective the treatment, and the less energy needed to make changes at a later date (see Gallagher & Ramey, 1987). There has been continued professional and parental pressure to provide a means for coordinated and comprehensive services to be delivered to the child with handicaps and his or her family at the earliest possible time in infantile development (see Jordan, Gallagher, Hutinger, & Karnes, 1988). This gap in comprehensive services from birth to 3 has been noted for some years, and Part H of PL 99-457 was designed to close it (Chapter 1, this volume).

2. History of the Present Policy

The next stage in the analysis is to provide a brief history of the policy up to the present time. The current legislation (PL 99-457) proposes aid to states to enable them to plan and develop programs to provide services to infants and toddlers who have handicapping conditions and to their families, as appropriate. It is the latest of a long series of federal legislative initiatives to aid children with handicapping conditions, beginning in the 1960s (Chapter 2, this volume).

This federal legislative program started with some modest support to enable teachers to obtain special training to provide a better educational experience for handicapped children. A small amount of research money to be spent on the study of mental retardation also was provided in separate legislation. Over a 30-year period the federal program of legislation for handicapped children has blossomed into a billion dollar enterprise supporting research, development, dissemination, personnel preparation, and demonstration, in addition to providing substantial financial aid to the states. Prior to the federal effort, many states had provided even more extensive financial support for local programs to educate exceptional children (Kirk & Gallagher, 1986), and they continue to do so.

Legislation passed in the 1970s (PL 94-142, The Education for All Handicapped Children Act of 1975) provided assurances of special educational assistance from age 5 through 21, and in many cases from 3 through 21. There was an obvious gap in federal support between birth and 3. Therefore, Part H of PL 99-457 was designed to encourage states to provide coordinated services for young children with handicapping conditions and also coordinated services for the entire family.

This gap was not so much a legislative oversight as it was the recognition of a series of political problems that made it impossible, at the time of passage of PL 94-142, to include the infants and toddlers in that legislation. For one thing, many educators were not anxious to take on the additional responsibility of this age group, since few educators had any training or experience with infants and toddlers. Also, in the states, there often was a jurisdictional dispute about whether the agency administering health, or education, or social services should be responsible for infants and toddlers with handicapping conditions. The matter was settled for the time being in 1975 by having the youngest group of children left out of the legislation.

Although it has long been a professional goal to provide services for children with special needs from birth onward, the age gap was not closed legislatively until more than 10 years later in 1986. However, the lessons of the earlier legislation (PL 94-142) were that policies that require major changes or the modification of procedures on the part of the professionals who provide service (i.e., an individualized education program [IEP], due process, nondiscriminatory testing) were going to cause serious implementation problems in the states and local communities.

3. Value Base for Policy

All policies have a value base, either explicit or implicit, and a policy analysis needs to recognize this base in order to understand its public acceptance. Policy that is designed to reallocate our resources in a particular direction for a special subgroup of our population, that is, persons with handicaps, is sure to have some powerful value motivations behind it (Moroney, 1981). In this case, the values for providing help for infants and toddlers with handicaps are rather straightforward. They are, simply stated: "Every child should have a right to develop to the limits of his/her potential," "Families should not have to bear unreasonable burdens not of their own making," and "We need to reduce the potential dependency of these children so as to keep future fiscal commitments to this group to a reasonable level."

These value statements differ considerably from each other and have the potential for attracting different individuals and groups, each for their own value reasons. The fundamental value that we should help those less fortunate than ourselves has been noted in many policy initiatives. The concept of *vertical equity*, the unequal treatment of unequals in order to make them more equal, is well established in welfare, health, and education legislation (Washington & Gallagher, 1986).

But there are contrary values, as well, that may act to inhibit or limit resource allocation for this policy. Some of these are, "We should not expend money on children who, at best, will make little contribution to the society," and, "Other societal needs are being neglected due to the large investment in programs for handicapped children." These opposing values, so far, have slowed, but not stopped, this movement to aid children with handicapping conditions.

In the execution of the new law many other value issues have emerged. For example, the Individualized Family Service Plan (IFSP) requires an analysis of family strengths and needs as a prelude to designing a family plan to help the child. But the process of discovering these family strengths and needs may well intrude on the privacy of the family, which is valued highly in American society. Resolving this issue will require both value judgments and creative administration.

4. Policy Application

The next stage should be concerned with how the policy has been implemented up to the current time. The new legislation for infants and toddlers has been in force only for approximately 16 months at this writing, and therefore there is little track record to report upon. The recognition that it will take states a substantial amount of time to gear up for this new effort is reflected in the 5-year period in the law (Chapter 1, this volume) given to the states to plan and put in place a full array of services to these children and their families.

A new policy institute, The Carolina Policy Studies Program, has been funded by the Office of Special Education Programs (OSEP) in the United States Department of Education to conduct an analysis of how well and rapidly the states implement the legislation (Part H, PL 99-457) on infants and toddlers and what factors seem to be associated with implementation success in various states. These studies will include analyses on eligibility, personnel preparation, family plans, interagency coordination, finance, and so forth. It is hoped that some further insights into the mysterious process of policy implementation will be provided.

5. Program Objectives Achieved

In this stage the collection of data relevant to the program objectives is assembled. In a policy study it is rarely possible for the analyst to collect quantitative data from the primary sources regarding program effectiveness.

The most likely procedure is for the analyst to do a review of the available literature on the effectiveness of the program. If the program has been in existence for a while (e.g., Head Start), then there will be a myriad of sources to bring together in some type of informal synthesis or review, or perhaps a meta-analysis.

Another strategy is to seek the opinions of those closest to the program, professionals and/or clients, regarding the strengths and weaknesses of the program. This can be done through survey or interview. Even though this strategy runs the risk of bias from self-interested parties, it can yield important formative evaluation data that can, in turn, lead to important program and policy modifications.

Public decision makers have been known to trust data from individual testimony or case history even more than the standard statistical data so honored in the professions. A single dramatic case can help convince public decision-makers that something of importance is happening in the program.

The degree to which program objectives have been achieved will have much to do with the type and form of the recommendations for action from this implementation analysis.

6. Barriers to Implementation

There are few policies that do not find some barriers that stand in the way of easy implementation. Success in policy implementation often depends on knowing the nature of these barriers so that an effective strategy can be devised to overcome them. There are at least six different types of barriers that can operate to inhibit implementation, and a brief description of each plus their likely impact upon PL 99-457 are provided.

Institutional Barriers Institutional barriers arise when a policy conflicts with the current operation of established social and political institutions. For example, the current law calls for interagency coordination. It is a highly appropriate provision given the nature of the cross-disciplinary problems faced by families of children with handicaps. Nevertheless, in states where there have been limited attempts at interagency coordination in the past, there have been difficulties in getting health, social services, and educational agencies to pull together. Interagency coordination is needed because the inability to fix upon a particular agency for implementation was one of the inhibiting factors in moving forward in the first place.

The identification of a lead agency by the governor of each state is a necessary requirement for implementation of PL 99-457, but how easy will it be for the other agencies to accept such a designation, especially when such leadership may mean a possible diversion of funds from those other agencies to the purposes noted in this legislation?

Parents have yearned for the presence of a single professional through whom they could channel their diverse needs and who could help them gain access to the available resources for their child. The legislative requirement for case managers would meet that parental need, but where do these case managers come from; how easy will it be for them to call upon services from different agencies; who should pay for such services?

All of the above questions are essentially questions about the operation of existing institutions. They examine the requirement to shift responsibility and resources from traditional sources and programs and the creation of predictable tensions within the bureaucracy in both state and local agencies. There certainly will be substantial institutional barriers for this legislation to overcome.

Psychological Barriers Often a proposed policy will come into conflict with deeply held personal, religious, or cultural beliefs of the presumed clients or of those who must implement the policy. In addition, there is an inevitable feeling of resentment on the part of those professionals who may feel that they, individually or as a member of their professional group, were not sufficiently consulted in the development of the policy or in the formulation of regulations that have been devised to carry out the law.

PL 99-457 carries forward a continuing effort on the part of the federal government to empower parents with sufficient authority so that they can have an important role in the plans for their own child. There are experienced professionals, though, who have neither accepted, nor had personal experience with parental questioning of their decisions or of the appropriateness of the services being provided. The attitude of professionals often is that they are the unquestioned experts.

Any time someone loses power or authority, as the professionals might appear to in this case, one can anticipate personal resentment and resistance. Therefore, this barrier, as well, can be counted upon to be a factor in the implementation process (Zigler, Kagan, & Klugman, 1983).

Sociological Barriers Some barriers emerge from the values and mores of particular subcultures in our society that run counter to the current program. One of the potential problem areas in the current legislation lies in the requirement for family involvement through an Individualized Family Service Plan. This requirement emerges from decades of clinical experience showing that the family is a key factor in the eventual adaptation of the child with handicapping conditions (Dokecki & Zaner, 1986; Gallagher & Vietze, 1986).

While some families will respond easily to the requirements of family assessment, that is, identification of strengths and needs, as a necessary condition to receiving aid for their child, other families well may be resentful, if not rebellious. Many minority families with long histories of contact with social agencies are likely to be unenthusiastic, if not downright suspicious of someone evaluating their family, particularly when the evaluator comes from a cultural background different from their own (Haskins & Adams, 1983).

How much right do the professional agencies have to invade the traditional privacy of a family in order to catalog these strengths and needs? If the family members believe that they are forced into this situation because of the implied denial of services for their child, how cooperative will they likely be? All of these are value issues of major importance that will need to be worked out in the implementation process (Moroney, 1981).

Economic Barriers The barriers to implementation include economics as one of the most visible. Past experience with many federal programs has included promises of generous future funding only to have the state and local programs disappointed by the actual appropriations when the time came. This prior experience can lead only to caution with the current legislation. Also, the federal government, in this case, is committing itself only to helping the states to plan and develop their programs!

The government often breaks its economic promises, not so much through deviousness, as through an overanxious attempt to cope with the many problems that it confronts. There is not enough money to pay for the obligations already incurred, and so, ambitious projections shrivel when faced with the fiscal reality of the present (Gallagher, 1975).

An outstanding example of that shrivelling process can be seen in PL 94-142, the Education for All Handicapped Children Act. According to the original projections in 1975, the federal government should now be paying close to 40% of the total cost of that law's implementation (Chapter 2, this volume). As it turns out, the federal contribution for the implementation of that law to date has barely exceeded 10%—reason enough for states and local communities to be cautious about any projections from the current legislation for infants and toddlers.

Another reason for state caution is that we have yet to establish how many children will need to be served and how extensive the services are likely to be for each child. So the total future bill for these efforts is shrouded in mystery. It is not just the total amount of money that is the barrier here but also the flow of the money. How will the formal interagency agreements be constructed, defining the responsibility for each agency for paying for early intervention services? There are at least 15 different potential sources of funds, each with its own bureaucratic framework, so coordination becomes a hugh challenge. The economic issues well may be the central ones in this implementation.

Political Barriers Politics played within or between professional organizations raises barriers. It is unlikely, given the proven needs of families with handicapped children, that any established group would come forward to directly challenge the law or its implementation, but that does not mean that there may not be a continued guerilla war waged against this or that element in the law that may be politically unpalatable for a particular interest group. Also, those supporting the program are likely to hear criticism that there are too many resources going to this program, noble though it may be, and to question the judgment of those asking for needed resources for this implementation. This is predictable political behavior, and, if it is not the open warfare we expect, it is at least prolonged sniping—an expected, continuing, and persistent barrier.

Geographic Barriers In the previously discussed barriers, we have focused on the human reaction to plans, but some of the most intractable of barriers in terms of proper service delivery lie in the geography within states. The delivery of services to rural areas has plagued those providing health services and educational services in many other programs and likely will do so in this program as well. The difficulty is not solely in the physical distances that must be covered but also in the absence of needed professional resources in rural areas. Such personnel resources tend to collect in centers of population and resist distribution to lightly populated areas. Mandating services often is much easier than the delivery of them!

All of these barriers noted above would be cause for caution in the expectation of easy implementation for the new early intervention program. But the presence of barriers is not necessarily reason to criticize the law itself. It is merely a reflection of the fact that when a wide-ranging law that affects thousands, if not millions, of people is implemented, the effect will not be felt by all of them equally. For some, it will be a blessing and salvation; for others, it will be a frustration and burden. No policy can count on a unanimous favorable reception.

What can be asked is that careful analyses be conducted to ensure that irrelevancies or unnecessary barriers are removed and that the path be smoothed by intelligent policy interpretation whenever possible. Finally, we can ask that the impact of the law be accurately evaluated, after sufficient time is allowed for it to get underway, so that we can assure ourselves that the original policy hypothesis that spawned this effort was, in fact, correct or mainly correct.

7. Policy Recommendations

The final step in the policy analysis is to provide recommendations for future action on the part of the responsible decision-makers. Those conducting the analyses have the responsibility for reaching one of three general conclusions. Either—

1. The policy is sound and being implemented well with only a few minor or technical corrections needed; or
2. The policy is generally sound but has some specific flaws in need of major correction with some specific changes needed, which would be noted in the analysis; or
3. The policy objectives generally are not being met and may even have proved to be unsound. There is a need for a comprehensive review of the current policy to determine alternative strategies.

In the case of PL 99-457, possibly some regions of the country are implementing policy more easily than others. Some parts of the legislation (i.e., finance or case management or professional preparation) may have special difficulties calling for revised regulations or revised legislation. It would be the purpose of policy analyses to identify these factors so that they can be dealt with by the decision makers.

SOME FINAL THOUGHTS

This chapter has outlined a strategy for systematically analyzing the implementation of a particular policy. Our growing knowledge of policy implementation problems should allow local and state administrators to anticipate and adapt to many difficult issues that will emerge as the process continues. The results of the analysis can and should be helpful in planning the next steps for those responsible for future action. It also should contribute to a growing body of knowledge on how policies in general succeed or fail. The generic problems of policy implementation across fields rarely have been discussed. The discussion typically has focused upon a particular piece of legislation or program. One long-range goal of policy analyses would be to identify generic problems and solutions so that future policies can be planned for more effectively.

REFERENCES

Adler, M. (1984). *The Paideia program.* New York: MacMillan.
Brewer, G., & deLeon, P. (1983). *The foundations of policy analysis.* Homewood, IL: The Dorsey Press.
Buck v. Bell, 274 U.S. 200, 207 (1927).
Coleman, W., Jr., & Selby, C. (1983). *Educating Americans for the 21st century.* Washington, DC: National Science Board Commission on Precollege Education in Mathematics, Science, and Technology.
Dokecki, P. & Zaner, R. (Eds.). (1986). *Ethics of dealing with persons with severe handicaps: Toward a research agenda.* Baltimore: Paul H. Brookes Publishing Co.
Gallagher, J. (1975). Why the government breaks its promises. *N.Y.U. Education Quarterly, 6,* 22–27.
Gallagher, J.J. (1981a). Models for policy analysis: Child and family policy. In R. Haskins & J.J. Gallagher (Eds.), *Models for analysis of social policy: An introduction* (pp. 37–77). Norwood, NJ: Ablex Publishing Co.
Gallagher, J.J. (1981b). Transforming research to policy in the field of language studies. In P. Mittler (Ed.), *Frontiers of knowledge in mental retardation* (Vol. 1). Baltimore: University Park Press.
Gallagher, J.J. (1984). Policy analysis and program implementation (P.L. 94–142). In J. Neisworth, S. Garwood, A. Mori, & R. Fewell (Eds.), *Topics in early childhood special education* (Vol. 4:1). Austin, TX: PRO-ED.
Gallagher, J.J. (1986). The family with a child who is handicapped: Research focus for the 1980's. In J.J. Gallagher & B.B. Weiner (Eds.), *Alternative futures in special education* (pp. 13–24). Reston, VA: The Council for Exceptional Children.
Gallagher, J.J. (1987). Public policy and the malleability of children. In J.J. Gallagher & C.T. Ramey (Eds.), *The malleability of children* (pp. 199–208). Baltimore: Paul H. Brookes Publishing Co.
Gallagher, J.J., & Vietze, P.M. (Eds.). (1986). *Families of handicapped persons: Research, Programs, and Policy Issues.* Baltimore: Paul H. Brookes Publishing Co.
Gardner, J. (Ed.). (1983). *A nation at risk: The imperative for educational reform.* Washington, DC: The National Commission on Excellence in Education.
Hargrove, E. (1975). *The missing link. The study of the implementation of social policy.* Washington, DC: The Urban Institute.
Haskins, R., & Adams, D. (Eds.). (1983). *Parent education and public policy.* Norwood, NJ: Ablex Publishing Co.
Haskins, R., & Gallagher, J.J. (Eds.). (1981). *Models for analysis of social policy: An introduction.* Norwood, NJ: Ablex Publishing Corporation.
Jordan, J., Gallagher, J., Hutinger, P., & Karnes, M. (Eds.). (1988). *Early childhood education: Birth to three.* Reston, VA: Council for Exceptional Children.
Kirk, S.A., & Gallagher, J.J. (1986). *Educating Exceptional Children* (5th ed.). Boston: Houghton-Mifflin Co.

MacRae, D., & Wilde, J. (1979). *Policy analysis for public decisions.* North Scituate, MA: Duxbury Press.

Mazmanian, D., & Sabatier, P. (1983). *Implementation and public policy.* Glenview, IL: Scott, Foresman.

Meadows, D. (1982, Summer). Whole earth models and systems. *The CoEvolution Quarterly,* 98–108.

Moroney, R. (1981). Policy analysis within a value theoretical framework. In R. Haskins & J. Gallagher (Eds.), *Models of policy analysis* (pp. 78–102). Norwood, NJ: Ablex Publishing Co.

Nagel, S. (Ed.). (1983). *Encyclopedia of policy studies.* New York: Marcel Dekker, Inc.

Sarason, S., Carroll, C., Maton, K., Cohen, S., & Lorentz, E. (1977). *Human services and resources networks.* San Francisco: Jossey-Bass.

Steiner, G. (1981). *The futility of family policy.* Washington, DC: The Brookings Institution.

Turnbull, A., & Turnbull, H. (1986). *Families, professionals and exceptionality: A special partnership.* Columbus, OH: Merrill Publishing Co.

Washington, V., & Gallagher, J.J. (1986). Family roles, preschool handicapped children, and social policy. In J.J. Gallagher & P. Vietze (Eds.), *Families of handicapped persons: Research, programs, and policy issues* (pp. 261–272). Baltimore: Paul H. Brookes Publishing Co.

Weiss, C. (1975). Evaluation research in the political context. In E. Streuning & M. Guttentag (Eds.), *Handbook of evaluation research* (pp. 3–26). Beverly Hills: Sage Publications.

Wildavsky, A. (1979). *Speaking truth to power.* Boston: Little, Brown.

Zigler, E., Kagan, L., & Klugman, E. (Eds.). (1983). *Children, families and government.* Cambridge, England: Cambridge University Press.

INDEX

Abuse, protection from, 79–80
Acceleration goals, 104
Adaptive Learning Environments Model (ALEM), 40–41
AFDC (Aid to Families with Dependent Children), 178
Agencies
  coordination between, 147–165
  see also Interagency planning
  multiplicity of, preschool personnel preparation and, 134–135
  responsible, intervention context and, 105–106
Aid to Families with Dependent Children (AFDC), 178
ALEM (Adaptive Learning Environments Model), 40–41
Alternative strategies, 202
Alternatives, choice among, 74
Appropriate education, *see* Free appropriate public education (FAPE)
Audiology, personnel preparation issues in, 115–116

Backward mapping approach, 59–81, 195
  see also Family(ies)
Barriers
  to change, in personnel preparation, 128–129
  to implementation, 39–43, 209–213
    economic, 211–212
    geographic, 212–213
    institutional, 209–210
    political, 212
    psychological, 210
    sociological, 210–211
Basic skills, teaching of, 137–138

Behavioral characteristics
  of effective professionals, training programs and, 118
  of young children, 104–105
Brown v. The Board of Education, 35, 38
Buck v. Bell, 204

Carolina Policy Studies Program, 208–209
Case finding, 158
Case knowledge, 120
Case management, 72–74, 158
Case study method, personnel preparation and, 123–124
Certification, preschool personnel and, 135–136
Change, societal factors in, 147–148
Child Find, 22
Child Health Assurance Act, in Florida, 177
Childhood Disability in the Family: Recognizing the Added Handicap, 86
Circular definitions, independent effect measurements versus, 188–190
Civil rights movement, 68–69
Clans, for interagency policy planning, 155–156
Class management, 138–139
Classification, efficiency of, screening and, 192–193
Colorado
  Interagency Public Policy Principles of, 152
  Interagency Transition Policy Document of, 152–153

217

Index

Commission strategy, in decision-making, 201, 202
Commonwealth of Massachusetts v. Secretary of Health and Human Services, 180
Communication(s)
 media and, 202
 professional, 139
 with affected constituencies, 24–25
Community, enhancement of, 67–70
Competencies, training programs and, 118
Confidentiality, 75
Consent, PL 94-142 and, 26–29
Constituencies, communication with, 24–25
Consultation, 139
 professional gurus in, 200–201
Consumer demands, changes in, 148–150
Context, parents' need for, 87–89
Coordination, interagency, 147–165
 see also Interagency planning
Cost-effectiveness, efficiency and, 191–193
Curriculum, 137

Decision-making
 parental, 89–92
 past major strategies in, 200–203
Democracy, role of government and, 203
Demographics, 47, 50
Developmental prerequisites, 103
Developmental tasks, mastering of, family capacity for, 70–72
Diagnosis, family response to, 86–87
Direct services, 158
Discrimination, 26
Divisiveness, implementation process and, 68–69

Early and Periodic Screening, Diagnosis, and Treatment (EPSDT), Medicaid and, 178–180

Early intervention
 personnel preparation for, 97–130
 see also Personnel preparation
 recommendations for, 50–52
Economic barriers, 211–212
Education for All Handicapped Children Act of 1975 (PL 94-142)
 consent and, 26–29
 implementation of, 19–20
 intent of, 20–21
 regulation development under, 21–24
 state of the art and integration mandates of, 35–36
Education of the Handicapped Act (EHA; PL 91-230), 1
 purpose of, affirmation of, 30–32
Education of the Handicapped Act Amendments of 1986 (PL 99-457)
 intent of, 20–21
 overview of, 1–17
 Title I, *see* Title I
 Title II, 2, 5–7, 9–13
 Title III, 13–14
 Title IV, 14
Efficiency, cost-effectiveness and, 191–193
EHA, *see* Education of the Handicapped Act
Eligibility criteria, differences in, 44
Emotional disturbance, 44–45
EPSDT (Early and Periodic Screening, Diagnosis, and Treatment), Medicaid and, 178–180
Exceptional children, effective procedures with, 140–141

Family(ies), 59–81
 financial resources of, 174
 implementation analysis and, 67–80
  see also Value commitment, families and
 implementation barriers and, 211
 involvement of, personnel preparation and, 106–107

liaison or linkage functions of, 72–74
strengthening, 62–67
see also Parent(s); Parental perspective
FAPE, see Free appropriate public education
Financing, see Funding
Florida, Child Health Assurance Act of, 177
Free appropriate public education (FAPE), 33
  directions for improvement in, 53–54
  grants for, 9, 13
  individual opportunities and, 78–79
  prospects for, 46–49
  see also Integration
Funding, 169–181
  background of, 170–174
  barriers related to, 211–212
  disincentives in, 39–43
  family resources and, 174
  IEPs and IFSPs and, 180–181
  Medicaid and, 177–180
  Part H, 4–5, 8–9
  private insurance and, 174–177
  special health care needs and, 180
  Title II, 7, 9, 10–12
  training programs and, 128–129
"Future Forecasting," 162–163

Geographic barriers, 212–213
Government, changing role of, 203–205
Governmental organizations, responsiveness of, 150–151
Grants, see Funding
Great Society programs, 199–200
Groups, for interagency policy planning, 154–156, 160–164
Guru strategy, in decision-making, 200–203

Handicapped Children's Early Education Assistance Act (PL 90-538), 30

"Handicapped," definitions of, 188–190
Health insurance
  Medicaid and, 177–180
  private, 174–177
Human development liaison (HDL) model, 72, 73

IEP, see Individualized education program
IEUs (intermediate educational units), grants to, 7
IFSP, see Individualized Family Service Plan
Implementation, 199–214
  backward mapping analysis of, 59–81
  see also Family(ies)
  barriers to, 39–43, 209–213
  definitions of
    nonteleological and input-based, 187–188
    teleological, 190–191
  dimensions of, 19–20
  government role and, changing, 203–205
  information sources for, 195–196
  inputs versus outcomes in, 185–187
  issues and challenges for, 14–16
  monitoring of, 29–30
  past major strategies in, 200–203
  policy analysis and, 205–213
    barriers to implementation and, 209–213
    model of, 205–206
    policy application in, 208–209
    present policy history in, 206–207
    problem statement in, 206
    program effectiveness data in, 209
    recommendations in, 213
    value base in, 207–208
  prospects for, 46–47
Individual development, 78–79
Individual rights, 79–80

Individualized education program (IEP)
  financing and, 180–181
  implementation of, monitoring of, 29–30
  requirements for, consent and, 26–27
Individualized Family Service Plan (IFSP), 71
  financing and, 180–181
  personnel preparation and, 106–107
Individualized teaching, 141
Infants, 2–5
  see also Title I
Information
  sources of, for implementation, 195–196
  uses of, policymaking phases and, 193–194
Inputs
  implementation definitions based on, 187–188
  outcomes versus, 185–187
Inservice education, 124–128
  barriers to change in, 129
  current status of, 127–128
  definition of, 124–125
  research addressing, 125–127
Institutional barriers, 209–210
Insurance
  Medicaid, 177–180
  private, 174–177
Integration
  extant practice of, 39
    research base on, 43–46
  historical perspective on, 36–38
  implementation barriers to, 39–43
  legal basis for, 34–36
  prospects for, 46–49
Integration mandate, 34
  see also Least restrictive environment
Interactive groups, for interagency policy planning, 154–156
Interagency planning, 147–165
  consumer demands and, 148–150
  new opportunities and challenges in, 156–164

  leadership and participation issues, 160–164
  policy development, 157–160
  organizational responsiveness and, 150–151
  societal factors in change and, 147–148
  strategic coordinated policy development and, 151–156
Intermediate educational units (IEUs), grants to, 7
Intrusion, into family, unwarranted, 74–75

Joint policy planning, 154

Knowledge base, 202
Knowledge, classification of, personnel preparation and, 119–123

Lead agencies, Part H, 4, 6–7
Leadership, interagency policy development and, 153–154, 160–164
Learning disabilities, 44
LEAs (local educational agencies), grants to, 7
Least restrictive environment, 33, 190
  directions for improvement in, 53–54
  divisiveness and, 69
  individual protection and, 79
Legislative history, in policy implementation analysis, 206–207
Local educational agencies, grants to, 7

Mainstreaming movement, 37–38
  see also Integration
Marketing orientation, agencies and, 149
Media, 202
Medicaid, 177–180

Medical services, PL 94-142 and, 23–24
Medicare Catastrophic Coverage Act (PL 100-360), 174
Medicine, personnel preparation issues in, 116
Methodology, interagency policy, 159
Monitoring, outcome measurement and, 194–195
Multidisciplinary services, 106
 personnel preparation and, 129

National Association of Social Workers (NASW), 72, 73
National Council on the Handicapped, 152
National Information Center for Children and Youth with Handicaps (NICHCY), 95
Nationwide improvement, directions for, 53–54
Neglect, protection from, 79–80
Networks, for interagency policy planning, 155–156
NICHCY (National Information Center for Children and Youth with Handicaps), 95
Nominal Group Technique, 162
Nursing, personnel preparation issues in, 114
Nutrition, personnel preparation issues in, 113

Occupational therapy, personnel preparation issues in, 111
Office of Special Education Programs (OSEP), 208
Organizational responsiveness, 150–151
Outcome measures, 183–196
 cost as criterion and, 191–193
 implementation definitions and
  nonteleological and input-based, 187–188
  teleological, 190–191
 independent, circular definitions versus, 188–190
 information sources and, 195–196
 inputs versus, 185–187
 monitoring and, 194–195
 policymaking phases and, 193–194

PARC v. Pennsylvania, 35
Parent(s)
 choices of, 74–75
 enablement of, 75–78
 resources for, 95–96
 teacher relationships with, 139–140
 see also Family(ies)
Parent Training and Information (PTI) projects, 94, 95–96
Parental perspective, 85–94
 decision-making and, 90–92
 information needs and, 89–90
 need for context and, 87–89
 policy implications of, 93–94
 support for parents and, 92–93
 "violence of disclosure" and, 86–87
Part H, *see* Title I
Participation, interagency policy development and, 154–156, 160–164
Personnel preparation, 97–130, 133–144
 barriers to change and, 128–129
 inservice education in, 124–128
 interagency policy development and, 158–159
 issues in, variations across disciplines of, 108–118
 training programs for, design frameworks for, 118–124
 unique aspects of work with young children and, 99–108
  characteristics of children, 100, 103–105
  family involvement, 106–107
  intervention context, 105–106
 see also Preschool personnel, preparation of
Physical therapy, personnel preparation issues in, 113–114

PL 90-538 (Handicapped Children's Early Education Assistance Act), 30
PL 91-230 (Education of the Handicapped Act), 1, 30–32
PL 94-142, see Education for All Handicapped Children Act of 1975
PL 99-457, see Education of the Handicapped Act Amendments of 1986
PL 100-360 (Medicare Catastrophic Coverage Act), 174
Policy
 as hypothesis, 185
 assumptions inherent in, 200
Policy analysis, 199
 stages in, 205–213
 types of, 204–205
 see also Implementation
Policy application, 208–209
Policy development, coordinated, strategic, 151–156, 157–160
Policy implementation, see Implementation
Policy objectives, interagency, 157–158
Policy statements, interagency, 157
Policymaking, phases of, information uses and, 193–194
Political barriers, 212
Preschool Incentive Grants, 5
Preschool personnel, preparation of, 133–144
 certification and, 135–136
 essential capabilities and, 136–142
 multiplicity of agencies and, 134–135
 preservice training and, 142–144
 training needs and, 135–136
Preschoolers, 5, 7, 9–13
Preservice training, 142–144
Prevention of later impairments, as early intervention goal, 104
Privacy Act, 75
Private insurance, 174–177
Problem statement, in policy implementation analysis, 206
Professional guru, 200–201

Professional values, 141–142
Professionals, see Personnel preparation; Service providers; Staffing
Program objectives, achievement of, 209
Propositional knowledge, 119–122
Psychological barriers, 210
Psychology, personnel preparation issues in, 109–110
PTI (Parent Training and Information) projects, 94, 95–96
Public decision-makers, past major strategies of, 200–203

Referral, 141
Regulations, development of, 21–24
Resources
 for parents, 95–96
 availability of, 76
 scarce, role of government and, 203
Role(s)
 government, changing, 203–205
 professional, 119

Screening, costs of, efficiency and, 192–193
SEAs (state educational agencies), grants to, 7
Service providers
 consultation among, 139
 parental support by, 92–93
 parents and, shared responsibility between, 76–78
 see also Personnel preparation
Services, interagency policy document and, 158–159
Situational leadership theory, 161
Social divisiveness, implementation process and, 68–69
Social work, personnel preparation issues in, 112–113
Societal factors, change and, 147–148
Sociological barriers, 210–211
Special education
 development of, as separate educational system, 36–37

personnel preparation issues in, 109
  see also Personnel preparation;
  Preschool personnel
reform in, "Catch 22" in, 39–43
Special study committees, 201
Speech/language pathology, personnel
  preparation issues in, 110
Staffing
  system-wide improvement and, 53
  see also Personnel preparation; Service providers
State educational agencies, grants to, 7
State interagency coordinating council
  (ICC), 156–164
  see also Interagency planning
State of the art mandate, 34
  see also Free appropriate public
  education
State Operated and Supported Schools
  Program, 31
Statewide system(s)
  eligibility differences among, 44
  lead agencies in, 6–7
  minimum components of, Title I, 4, 5
Stigmatization, 68
Strategic coordinated policy development, 151–156
Strategic decision-making, past
  approaches to, 200–203
Strategic knowledge, 120
Stress, parental, minimization of, 76
Student-student relationships, 140
Support services, 158
System-wide improvement, directions
  for, 53–54

Teachers
  concerns of, 27
  parental relationships with, 139–140
  see also Preschool personnel

Teleological criteria, nonteleological
  criteria versus, implementation definitions and, 187–188, 190–191
Terminology
  interagency policy document and, 157
  parental perspective and, 93–94
Title I, 2
  description of, 2–5
  funding and, 171–173
  outcome hypotheses in, 186
Title II, 2
  description of, 5, 7, 9–13
Title III, overview of, 13–14
Title IV, overview of, 14
Toddlers, 2–5
  see also Title I
Training programs, *see* Personnel
  preparation; Preschool
  personnel
Transformational leadership, interagency policy development
  and, 153–154
Transition services, 159

Under-insurance, 177
Un-insurance, 176–177

Value commitment
  families and, 63
    community enhancement and, 67–70
    individual rights and, 78–80
    parent enablement and, 75–78
    strengthening of, 70–75
  policy implementation analysis and, 207–208
  professional, 141–142
Vertical equity, 208
"Violence of disclosure," 86–87
Voluntariness, 74–75